LIQUID CRYSTALS
AND
THEIR APPLICATIONS

Edited by Thomas Kallard

optosonic press

LIQUID CRYSTALS AND THEIR APPLICATIONS

(STATE OF THE ART REVIEW No. 2)

Copyright (C) 1970 by Optosonic Press

Published by OPTOSONIC PRESS
Box 883, Ansonia Post Office
New York, N.Y. 10023

Additional copies may be procured
by addressing the publisher and
enclosing $12.00 per copy.

Library of Congress Catalog Card No. 72-109929
Standard Book Number: 87739-001-0

PRINTED IN THE UNITED STATES OF AMERICA

PREFACE

Optosonic Press takes pleasure in offering this second volume in the STATE OF THE ART REVIEW series. We direct it to the attention of all those imaginative people in the many areas of related research who are now looking into the unique properties of liquid crystals.

A glance at the volume's bibliography will disclose material from many parts of the world: Book titles, dissertations, unclassified government R & D reports, symposium papers and conference proceedings are included.

A large portion of this book's material, however, is based on relevant patent literature and, in all instances, this patent information is given in great detail. Whenever possible illustrations, charts and tables are included. This section contains much practical technological know-how -- material not usually found in the scientific journals.

The patent literature and bibliography, in combination, serve to fulfill the purpose of this volume: to put into the hands of the reader a concise and up to date compilation of otherwise hard to find and highly specialized information. Also, with such a ready source for reference, the usually high percentage of unintentionally duplicated R&D work can be reduced to a minimum.

We regard the STATE OF THE ART REVIEW series as a continuing endeavor and, as such, recognize the need for the continual updating of its contents. To fill this need supplementary volumes will be published whenever new developments in the field make them necessary. For this purpose the Editor will welcome suggestions and contributions of bibliographic and patent survey material from readers.

We hope this volume will be a useful guide to those just entering the field of liquid crystals. To the scientist and engineer experienced in applied mesomorphics, it will perhaps suggest new points of view and serve as a source of new ideas for future research.

New York, N.Y.
February, 1970

THOMAS KALLARD
for Optosonic Press

INTRODUCTION

Although scientifically liquid crystals have been known for about 80 years, the application of liquid crystals to practical problems has been a development of the last 10 years. The use of liquid crystals as engineering materials is in its infancy, and we can expect ever-increasing applications of these liquid crystal materials.

If we consider the isotropic liquid and the crystalline solid as states of matter, then the liquid crystal phases encompass at least three states which have properties which are not just intermediate between liquid and crystal but are unique, having nothing in common with either a crystal or a liquid. In fact, many of the errors which have arisen in their use and study have related to the attempt to apply without change techniques which were applicable only in the liquid or crystalline state.

At the present time, we can give only a rather limited picture of the ultimate uses of liquid crystals. Thus far, only the nematic and cholesteric phases have found widespread interest for applications, although I am sure that the smectic phases will prove equally valuable within the next several years. Liquid crystals are of interest because they order and reorient with amazingly small energies. For instance, with the cholesteric phase, a temperature change of only one degree can cause a change to the entire rainbow of visible colors; in the nematic phase, electrical power inputs of as low as one microwatt per square centimeter can drive an element from full-on to full-off. Along with this there is a very good resolution, something on the order of 1,000 lines per inch, making possible one million elements per square inch. These properties lead us to the criteria which make liquid crystals so interesting today. Thus, in places where devices or materials are needed as indicators or detectors which should use low powers and detect very low energies with good resolution, the liquid crystal is a natural.

The present applications of liquid crystals are primarily limited to devices with optical outputs and/or inputs. The use of liquid crystals as detectors for infrared microwave fields, laser far-field patterns, gas vapor and direct thermal patterns, has made enormous strides during the last five years.

Cholesteric liquid crystals have become used in large quantities for temperature measurement. At this time, ultrasonic image convertors using nematic materials are just becoming feasible. For display purposes, the nematic phase appears to be the most promising. Low power combined with low cost and moderate driving voltages appears to make the nematic phase the logical choice for seven-segment displays and indicators which depend upon ambient lighting. Because of the relative cost on driver circuitry, large area displays are quite feasible, while the high resolution makes small high-density displays quite feasible. These are only the forerunners of devices which use no optical output but make possible operations which control other than optical properties by electric and magnetic fields. Differences in viscosity and diffusivity, depending on direction, apparently can be used in mechanical devices, although studies of these devices have not begun.

At this point, I will say that we have only begun to understand and use the non-liquid, non-crystalline properties of liquid crystals.

JAMES L. FERGASON
Associate Director
Liquid Crystal Institute
Kent State University

Kent, Ohio

CONTENTS

PATENTS

" "

441,274 (British)   *Patented Jan. 13, 1936*

IMPROVEMENTS IN OR RELATING TO LIGHT VALVES.

*Barnett Levin, and Nyman Levin, assignors to Marconi's Wireless Telegraph
Company, Ltd.   Application July 13 and Aug. 3, 1934.*

This invention relates to light valves and has for its object to provide
improved light valves of great sensitivity suitable for use as electro-optical
translating devices in television, facsimile telegraph and other systems.

The present invention is based upon the fact that certain substances,
when in the nematic phase or state which is intermediate between the solid
and the liquid states, exhibit a Kerr effect very much greater than that
which they exhibit when either in the liquid or in the solid state. For
example, whereas the Kerr constant of nitro-benzine is 4×10^{-5} and nitro-
benzine is the material which is at the moment probably the most widely used
for light valves of the kind in question - the Kerr constant of ethylanisal-
amino-cinnamate is approximately 7 when the material in question is in the
nematic phase of its crystalline state.

According to this invention, a light valve of the kind utilizing the
Kerr effect, i.e. of the kind employing bi-fringent material which is
subjected to varying electric strain to produce varying light effects, is
characterized in that the bi-refringent material employed is in the nematic
phase or state. The material in question may be almost any substance which
can exist in the nematic phase and the particular compound already mentioned
is only one of many substances which are utilizable in carrying out the
invention. This particular compound is representative of a class of which
other examples are methyl-p-ethoxybenzalamino-α-methyl-cinnamate, ethyl-p-
ethoxybenzalamino-α-methyl-cinnamate, methyl-anisalamino-α-methyl-cinnamate,
and ethyl-anisalamino-α-methyl-cinnamate. These various substances differ
among themselves as to transparency, temperature of formation of the nematic
phase, and other properties and selection among them may, of course, be made
to choose that which, having regard to its general properties, is most suitable
and convenient in any particular case.

The invention may be carried into practice in various different ways.
Generally speaking the production of birefringent material in a phase or
state between the liquid and solid states presents no practical difficulties,
but in some cases means must be specially provided for maintaining the material
in the desired state in question. Various expedients may be adopted for
maintaining a bi-refringent material in the desired intermediate state between
liquid and solid. For example, where the material is one which must be
maintained at a temperature above normal atmospheric temperatures, the necessary heating may be obtained by arranging for one of the electrodes of the cell
containing the bi-refringent substance to be heated by a wire or winding
carrying a heating current, the wire or winding being fixed on an asbestos
sheet or other carrier of good heat insulation qualities and being arranged
to be controlled by a rheostat inserted in the heating current supply circuit
for the purpose of controlling or varying the temperature.

Owing to possible difficulties concerning variations in ambient temperature
it is preferable, in cases where the bi-refringent material selected is one

needing to be heated to maintain it in the desired state, to employ as the bi-refringent substance a material in which the intermediate phase or state in which the Kerr co-efficient is at or near the maximum, occurs over a relatively large temperature range. If the bi-refringent material be so chosen, it may be possible to ignore the possibility of varying ambient temperatures,for such ambient temperature changes as may be likely to occur may be between limits which are closer together than the temperature limits between which the material remains in the state in which a high Kerr co-efficient is manifested. Where it is not convenient or practical to chose a material having a relatively large temperature range over which the desired state is maintained, the whole Kerr cell may be enclosed in a lagged or heat insulated chamber and/or any thermostatic control means as known per se may be provided to ensure that a predetermined temperature of the bi-refringent material is maintained irrespective of changes in ambient temperature.

In carrying the invention into practice, the thickness of the layer or layers of birefringent material employed should be small for the reason that if thick layers be used there is the danger that different parts of the layer will not be in the same state or phase. In practice it is preferred to use very thin layers of the order of 0.05 mm. in thickness.

One form of light valve in accordance with this invention is illustrated in the accompanying figures 1 and 2 which are schematically mutually perpendicular views (not drawn to scale) of the cell. Referring to these figures, two metal foil electrodes 1,2, each about .002" thick and 5 mm. wide and separated by a space of about 0.75 mm. are cemented between glass plates 3, 4, each about 1/16th" thick. The cement is placed above and below the electrodes and round the edges of the plates and the whole cell is baked at a high temperature. The upper glass plate 3 has a small central hole 5 about 4 mm. in diameter. A small heating wire 6 is placed between two thin asbestos sheets 7, 8, and held in position under the plate 4 by asbestos strips 9, 10. A small amount of the bi-refringent substance is placed in the hole 5 and heated so that it melts and spreads in a thin layer between the two electrodes, where it remains. When it cools it solidifies in very small crystals, as the cooling will be very rapid, and remains as a thin layer. A cell as described in connection with figures 1 and 2 can be readily constructed for a maximum voltage of the order of 200 volts.

$$Fig. 1.$$

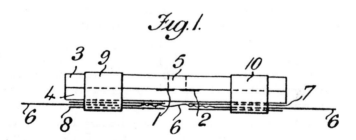

It will be realized that with a Kerr cell as illustrated in figures 1 and 2 or as so far specifically described, it will be in general impossible to secure a light valve action immediately at any time, and that in general a short time will be necessary for "starting up" in order to allow the bi-refringent material to reach the state between liquid and solid at which the maximum Kerr effect is manifested.

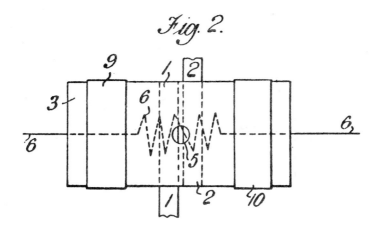

Fig. 2.

The various bi-refringent liquid crystalline substances so far specifically mentioned are organic compounds in themselves, that is to say they are
not in combination with other substances and they present two practical difficulties when employed for the purposes of this invention, namely (1) that
heating of the cell is necessary and (2) that there is some difficulty in obtaining a high degree of homogeneity. The difficulties may be avoided by employing instead of the substances already mentioned substances such as
9-bromophenanthrene-3 (or 6)sulphonic acid, the substances known under the
Registered Trade Mark "Salvarsan," m'-nitrobenzoyl-m-aminoacid and the
disodium salt of m'-nitrobenzoyl-m-aminobenzoyl-2-naphthylamino-6.8-disulphonic
acid which, when dissolved in water exist in the mesomorphic state, and at
certain concentrations are in the nematic phase of this state, the substance
in question being employed in an aqueous solution in such concentration as to
be in the nematic phase.

The concentrations at which the substances will exist in aqueous solution
in the nematic phase of the mesomorphic state will vary with the nature of the
substance. Thus, 9-bromophenanthrene-3 (or 6)-sulphonic acid requires a
concentration of 13.6 gm. in 100 ccs. of water and the disodium salt of
m-nitrobenzoyl-m-aminobenzoyl-2-naphthylamine-6.8-disulphonic acid requires
a concentration of 5 to 6 gm. in 100 ccs. of water.

Figures 3 and 4 (which are not drawn to scale) of the accompanying
drawings, are mutually perpendicular views showing schematically a form of a
cell in accordance with this invention and wherein the bi-refringent material
is such as not to require heating. The cell shown in figures 3 and 4 is made
by cementing together four pieces 11, 12, 13, 14, of glass, for example glass
sheets 2 mm. thick, the four pieces being so arranged as to surround a square
space 15 having a side of about 2 mm. The glass edges 11a, 12a constituting
one pair of opposite walls of this square space 15 are covered with metal
foil, 16, 17, for example tin foil, or are sprayed with metal for example
gold or platinum, the metal coatings forming the electrodes of the cell.
The structure thus obtained is cemented on to a glass plate 18 and the bi-
refringent material is then poured into the square space 15 which is now
closed at the bottom by the plate 18. Another glass plate 19, which is
removed in figure 3, is then placed on top to close in the bi-refringent
material. The plate 19 need be sealed only round the edges.

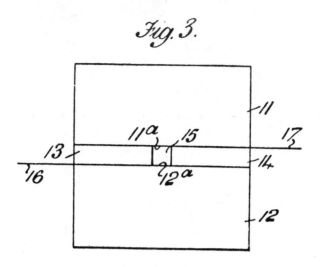

Fig. 3.

Fig. 4.

The light valve thus manufactured is a complete self-contained cell and may be used in any manner known per se in conjunction with a suitable optical optical system for electro-optical translating purposes in connection with television, facsimile telegraph or other systems.

It will be appreciated that the present invention, provides a substantial improvement as regards sensitivity when compared to known light valves utilizing the Kerr effect. With the substance ethylanisalaminocinnamate the maximum voltage to be applied to the cell is only of the order of 200 volts, though the voltage to be applied will depend upon the distance between the electrodes.

""""""""""""""""""""""""""

OPTICAL DEVICE AND METHOD AND MANUFACTURE THEREOF.

John F. Dreyer
Application March 21, 1941.

   This invention relates to a method of molecular orientation and to
products and devices having oriented molecular arrangement, and to the manufacture thereof. More particularly my invention relates to the production
of oriented light polarizing films, by depositing and orienting a film of
polarizable material upon a suitable surface.

   My present invention is based upon the discovery that certain types of
molecules which occur in known polarizable materials can be oriented by being
juxtaposed to other oriented molecules or otherwise subjected to an orienting
field.

   According to my present invention, I apply polarizable materials in solution or in a fused condition into juxtaposition to an oriented surface, or
otherwise into an orienting field, and then, by bringing the polarizable material into the nematic state, I produce a non-crystalline polarizing material
oriented in conformity to the orientation of said surface or other orienting
field; and thereafter I fix the orientation in such material by controlled
solidifcation.

   Many materials are known which are both polarizable and form nematic
liquid crystal by evaporation of solutions or by temperature change.
Numerous dyes deposited by evaporation of solutions in water or organic
solvents are examples of such materials and, when treated according to my
invention, form on an oriented surface a correspondingly oriented film.

   The molecules of the polarizable material, in the nematic state, tend
to fall spontaneously into parallelism with respect to one axis while still
retaining mobility in other respects. According to my invention the film is
subjected, during this spontaneous orientation, to a field which influences
molecules in the film so as to determine the direction of such spontaneous
orientation; and I have found that, because of this inherently assured parallelism of the molecules, only a very weak field is required to establish
complete and uniform orientation throughout the film when it enters the
nematic state; but I have found that special precautions must be taken if this
orientation is to be preserved intact in the solid film, since normally the
change from the nematic state to the solid state is attended by disappearance
of the parallelism which destroys the uniformity of polarization. I have
found that if the orientation is to be maintained, the solvent should be removed by diffusion and evaporation; not by ebullition; and conditions during
solidification must be controlled to avoid crystallization.

   The chemistry of compounds which may be brought to the nematic state has
been studied and fully discussed in the literature; see, inter alia, Vorlaender:
"Chemische Kristallographie die Fluessigkeiten," Leipzig (1924). They are
generally long chain polar molecules without heavy side chains. Among materials
which have such structure are included particularly many of the "para" substituted aromatic class.

It is also known that mixtures may show the nematic state, although the materials of which the mixture is composed do not do so when pure. Such mixtures may be used for purposes of my invention. The addition of impurities may thus be desirable to improve the range of the nematic state. Thus, for example, sodium alizarine sulfate, among others, is known to extend the nematic state. I have likewise added laurylamine to naphthol yellow S and glycerine to Basic Brown BR with improved results. Other impurities or additions are ineffective or harmful, depending upon the dichroic material being used. Especially desirable within this class of nematic materials are numerous pleochroic dyes and dye intermediates.

The materials, which I have described as "nematic materials", may be brought into the nematic state, e.g., either by cooling to the temperature range within which they exist in this state, or, in the case of solutions, by evaporating solvent therefrom. The passing into the nematic state is ordinarily indicated by a decrease in viscosity and may be observed directly by inspection in transmitted polarized light. When the nematic state is reached, in the case of polarizing materials, the nematic liquid will absorb strongly when its polarizing plane is crossed with respect to that of the polarized light; and in the case of non-polarizing materials the nematic liquid will act as a wave-plate or fractional wave-plate (depending upon its thickness) with the same characteristic effect on polarized light as other wave- or fractional wave-plates.

As the substance is brought into this nematic state its molecules should be subjected to the exterior orienting influence so that when they come into parallelism they will be directed in the decired direction. The orienting forces between the molecules then work in conjunction with the exterior orienting influence.

To produce the permanently oriented film, the molecules are set chemically or physically from the nematic state. This may be done, for example, by lowering the temperature, or by evaporating the solvent, or, in some cases by a chemical reaction which converts the liquid to a solid without disturbing the orientation of the molecules.

A solvent, if used, should be one which in the solution will readily wet without dissolving the surface on which the polarizing material is to be formed, it should not adversely affect the orienting field - particularly it should not corrode the rubbed or otherwise oriented surface nor itself form crystals nor crystallize any other ingredient of the solution under conditions of drying and should not be hygroscopic if used in an atmosphere containing moisture; it should dissolve the polarizable material in sufficient degree to disperse the molecules to produce substantial films or other bodies, and it should be sufficiently volatile to be rapidly evaporated at reasonable temperatures which will not adversely affect the various materials used. Solvents which I have used satisfactorily include methanol, water, acetone, ethyl alcohol, ethylene glycol, glycerine, acetin and mixtures of these. The choice will, of course, depend upon the particular material, bearing in mind the consideration stated herein. I general, best results have been obtained with methanol, which readily dissolves most dyes, wets most surfaces and tends to concentrate at the exposed surface of the dye solution, is highly volatile, and non-hygroscopic. The percentage of solvents used with the dye will depend primarily upon the viscosity of the resulting solution and the thickness of the film desired.

The film of the polarizing material may be applied, whether in solution or as a fused liquid, e.g., by spraying, flowing, pouring or brushing onto the surface. The film may also be applied by dipping the surface into a body of liquid and slowly removing so that the running back of the excess is essentially constant.

I have found that best results are obtained when the drying occurs in a uniform and advantageously countercurrent flow of gases, so that the vapors given off by the drying film are removed as quickly as possible from the atmosphere around the surface which is drying.

The field effect by which the orientation is secured will ordinarily be a result of an orientation of the surface on which polarizable material is deposited, but it may be created or enhanced by external means, e.g., a static electrical or magnetic field. Field magnitudes of the order of 200-10,000 gausses or more and 200-15,000 v/cm. or more may be used for orienting dipole materials (Faraday and Kerr effects), but this is unnecessarily complicated. I have found that the best results are obtained, and with extreme simplicity in manufacturing technique, by merely rubbing the surface on which the film is to be deposited before the deposition occurs, or in the case of flexible base, such as cellulosic film, by stretching. The resulting field effect may be due to Van der Waals forces, or it may be due to the physical contour of the molecules at the surface, which in turn exert an orienting field upon the molecules in the applied film. Whatever may be the explanation, I have found that strong brushing, rubbing, or stretching in one direction the supporting surface, or any other treatment which effects surface anisotropy of the support, will result in a definite orientation of the polarizable materials applied to the treated surface; and I have referred to such a surface as "oriented." The choice of material used for rubbing is not critical. Leather, silk, cotton, paper, rubber, metal, etc. may be used for this rubbing treatment. The surface to which the film is to be applied will ordinarily be thoroughly cleaned in order to get good adhesion of the polarizing film and to obtain the uniform drying and uniformity of the dried film.

The cleaning, if desired, can be done by scrubbing, advantageously with mild abrasives, e.g., rouge, chemical cleaning agents, e.g., a strong soap solution or other detergent, a strong acid, e.g., nitric acid, an alkali, e.g., tri-sodium phosphate, or an oxidizing agent, e.g., potassium bichromate plus sulfuric acid. Technically this cleaning should take place before the rubbing treatment inasmuch as the rubbing during cleaning or drying, or even the chemicals used for cleaning, might affect the orientation.

The accompanying drawing shows a view in side elevation of a lamp bulb embodying my invention with the orientation indicated diagrammatically by broken lines.

The following is an example of the practical utilization of my invention as applied, for example, to a standard headlight bulb for automobile head-lamps...

The surface of the glass is first cleaned, for example, by dipping it in a concentrated solution of 100 parts by weight of potassium bichromate and 70 parts concentrated sulfuric acid (66 degrees Baume). After ten minutes the bulb is removed from the solution and adhering chemical is washed off. The surface is then wiped dry with clean absorbent paper or cloth, rubbing in

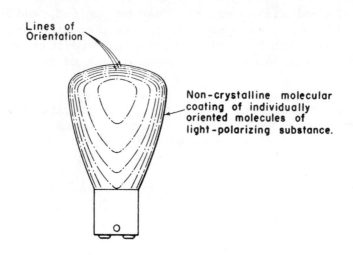

Lines of
Orientation

Non-crystalline molecular
coating of individually
oriented molecules of
light-polarizing substance.

one direction for the desired orientation. Or the surface may be dried by
evaporation if a subsequent rubbing treatment is carried out for orientation,
for example, on a clean buffing wheel, e.g., of cotton or wool cloth or felt
or of paper. The direction of rubbing, or in the case of the buffing wheel
the plane of the wheel, in this treatment will always be kept parallel to the
direction of the orientation desired in the finished polarizer. It is this
rubbing, in the present example, which produces the field for orienting the
pleochroic material which is subsequently applied.

To this rubbed surface I now apply a film of polarizable material, which
may consist, for example, of 20 parts by weight methylene blue (zinc free) dye
in 100 parts methyl alcohol.

The film may be applied by dipping the bulb into the solution and removing
it at a uniform speed of two inches per minute into an atmosphere saturated
with methyl alcohol. When the bulb is completely removed it is shifted quickly
into a current of dry air of relative humidity below 30% which flows uniformly
across its surface. The air temperature may be between 50° F. and 80° F. and
the air speed is regulated so that each point on the film dries in about 3
seconds after it comes into the dry air stream. When the coating has dried,
the bulb is dipped into a solution containing 2% concentrated sulfuric acid
and saturated with potassium bichromate. The coating is then washed gently
with water and dried in air. For further protection of the film it can be
dipped in a 5% solution of methyl methacrylate resin in toluol and again dried.
These solutions for after-treatment of the film are designed to avoid re-
dissolving the Methylene Blue and do not destroy its orientation.

This same method could, of course, be used with any glass surface as well
as for lamp bulbs.

" "

10

FLEXIBLE NONCRYSTALLINE SELF-CONTAINED POLARIZING FILMS AND METHODS OF MAKING AND USING THE SAME.

John F. Dreyer, assignor to Dreyer Laboratories.
Application May 14, 1946.

The present invention relates to the surprising discovery that polarizing dyes when uniformly oriented can be provided in film form independent of a supporting backing on which they may be formed. There are many applications where it is advantageous to apply a polarizing film to an optical surface without subjecting the latter to the treatment necessary for forming the polarizing film. In accordance with the present invention a thin transferable film is made suitable for application to various surfaces, e.g., much in the manner in which decalcomania is applied.

Fig. 1.

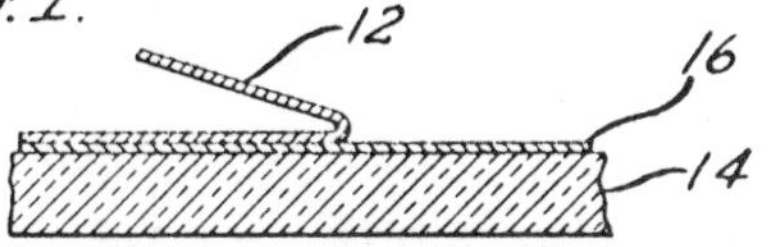

In Fig.1 is shown a film 12 embodying the present invention in process of being transferred from a glass plate 14 coated with paraffin at 16. The film shown has been made by applying a thin layer of melted paraffin to the surface of the glass 14, allowing it to solidify, rubbing along the lines of desired orientation. Advantageously a wetting agent which is compatible with the dye used is applied to the surface of the paraffin prior to the rubbing so that a very thin film of it remains adsorbed on the surface. To this prepared surface I apply a film of a water solution of a dye which can pass through the nematic state, the solution as applied being somewhat more dilute than the nematic state and carefully filtered free of any crystalline particles and being free likewise from any dissolved material which would precipitate in crystalline form before the dye is dried.

The coated glass plate with the dye film is then exposed to a gentle stream of dry air at about 85° F., whereupon the dye solution passes quickly through the nematic phase, in which it is oriented to the lines of rubbing on the base, and is dried before reorientation.

The film 12 thus formed, when fully dry may be stripped from the supporting plate 14 as shown in Fig.1, and to facilitate this, the plate is heated slightly above the fusion point of the paraffin. The film 12 when thus released may be transferred to any support on which it is to be used.

It is ordinarily desirable to increase the strength of the film, for handling, by applying to it a temporary or permanent flexible backing film 18 over the dye 12 (Fig.2). This reinforcing backing, in the example illustrated in Fig.2, is an Icryloid resin lacquer film applied in a xylol solvent vehicle.

The stripping of the film is advantageously done in the same direction as the lines of orientation, since, as with most oriented film, its strength is greatest along the direction of orientation.

After stripping from the temporary support 14, the film 12 may be applied to any article which it is desired to make polarizing. For aircraft

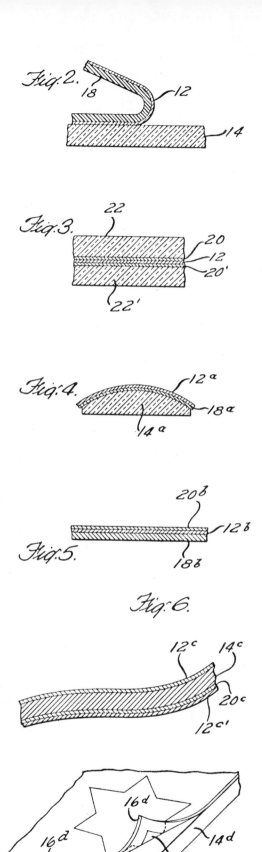

Fig.2.

Fig.3.

Fig.4.

Fig.5.

Fig.6.

Fig.7.

windows, automobile and marine wind-
shields, etc., it may be spread out on
the surface of a transparent plate, e.g.,
of glass, methyl methacrylate polymer,
etc. and covered with a second plate by
which the film is fully protected.
Advantageously this assembly is effected
in a vacuum frame. Such a "sandwich"
is shown in exaggerated cross section
in Fig.3. In this case the film formed
and transferred as described in connection with Figs. 1 and 2 is applied to
the adhesive layer 20 on the glass plate
22. The temporary backing film 18 may
then be treated to release it from film
12 and stripped therefrom, or if desired
this film may be left in place. Finally
the other plate 22' and adhesive layer
20' are applied and the assembly pressed
with heating if necessary, to form a
unitary product.

For application to lenses and other
curved surfaces the polarizing film may
be formed on a support of similar form,
e.g., as shown in Fig.4. In this case
the transfer film is intended to be applied to the back of a concave-convex
lens and therefore the reinforcing and
protective film, e.g. cellophane 18a
with its direction of stretching substantially coinciding with the direction
or orientation desired of the polarizing
film, is first applied to the support,
stretching and if necessary softening
with water or other swelling agent to
fit it eaxtly and smoothly onto the
curved surface. The surface of the
cellophane is then rubbed along the
lines of desired orientation, the dye
film 12a spread on, passed through the
nematic state and quickly dried. When
the film 18a is lifted from the support
14a it carries with it the polarizing
film 12a, which may thereupon be applied
to the surface of the lens, with or without use of a suitable adhesive, e.g.
optical pitch, Canada balsam, etc. and
with or without application of a cover
glass or second lens element to protect
its surface.

A film carrying a tacky adhesive is
shown in Fig.5. This comprises a layer
12b of oriented dye and a coating 20b

12

of a suitable tacky material, for instance a pressure-sensitive adhesive such as used in so called masking tape and transparent adhesive tape. This assembly may be formed on a backing, e.g., of flexible film 18b in the manner indicated in Fig.4, and the tacky material applied after the formation and solidification of the oriented film, or a supporting film may be used which also serves as the adhesive upon application of heat or a solvent.

The present invention may also be applied to combination of polarizing films, e.g., subtractive combinations of colored films to produce a particular spectral distribution, especially a neutral white or gray. In Fig. 6 there is shown a transparent flexible support 14c of suitable material such for instance as cellophane having on one side thereof a directly applied dye layer 12c oriented in the manner described above, and on the other side a different dye layer oriented in the same direction so as to polarize light similarly. This second dye layer is transferred as above described and applied to the cellophane without disturbing the first. It may be applied directly onto the first, or as shown onto the opposite side of the support.

In instances where differential light effects on a single medium are desirable, as in instrument dials, clock faces, advertising devices, etc., the invention lends itself to the provision thereof as is exemplified in Fig.7. A glass base 14d may have its upper surface oriented, as by brushing, and there may be applied to certain selected portions thereof a dichroic dye material in a particular desired shape or shapes 24 as in the shape of the star shown. There may thereupon be laid thereon with or without cementing, a layer 16d of transparent plastic or flexible film such for instance as cellophane to which the dye will adhere while it is being stripped from the base. The plastic film carrying with it the design of the star is shown in Fig.7 in process of being stripped, one corner of the star showing at 24.

The surface to be coated with an orientable film may be simultaneously cleaned and coated, e.g., by rubbing with a foreign substance having a cleaning action and likewise an orienting action, as, for example, paper dipped in a water solution of Lorol trimethyl ammonium hydrochloride. As indicated in Fig. 8 and 9, a supporting glass plate 14e after rubbing with Lorol to provide an anisotropic surface, is coated with a film 12e of a suitable dye, as for instance Mordant Yellow O, applied to this surface by means of a spray 26. The resulting liquid film is dried rapidly so as to pass through the nematic state and when fully oriented to solidify suddenly to facilitate the substantially complete orientation of the molecules of the dye in the oriented film. If desired, an adhesive 20e may then be applied as by spraying, and the composite film thus formed may be stripped from the base 14e as indicated in Fig.9 and used, as by being applied to the surface of lens, showcase, window, etc.

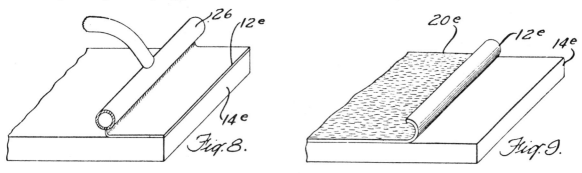

Fig.8.   Fig.9.

DICHROIC LIGHT-POLARIZING SHEET MATERIALS AND THE LIKE AND
THE FORMATION AND USE THEREOF.

John F. Dreyer, assignor to Dreyer Laboratories.
Application May 14, 1946.

I have found that dichroic dyes of different character, especially of different color, can be brought conjointly into the nematic state and thus not only give a highly satisfactory polarizing effect but also a combined color effect which is highly advantageous. By such combinations one may produce at will any desired spectral distribution whether a bright hue or a neutral gray. The substances thus combined, however, are selected for similarity of molecular form such that they readily pack in parallelism with freedom of movement parallel to and about their long axes; and thus can come conjointly into the nematic state. This is appropriately described in chemical terminology as steric similarity and the molecules as sterically similar. Extraneous material is to be avoided if of such nature as to interfere with this parallelism and freedom of movement retaining such parallelism or if of such crystalline nature as to oppose its crystal anisotropy to the anisotropy relied upon for orientation of the nematic material.

Prior to the present invention such orientation had been observed in pure solutions and fusions, but the formation of the nematic state was known to be critical and presence of impurities could prevent its occurrence, it was not expected that mixtures of dyes could be used.

It is possible, by orienting different dye molecules in optically subtractiv erelation, i.e., so that the same light rays are acted upon by both dyes within the film, to so combine dyes of different color as to produce not only a desired tinting of the light, or neutral gray with substantially no tinting, but also an increased polarizing efficiency. Where high polarizing efficiency is not required I have found also that desired color or absence of color may be obtained by films of mixed dyes in which the dye molecules are in optically additive, i.e., side-by-side, relation.

In some instances moreover a combination of dyes is more advantageous even from the standpoint of orientation than a single dye. There are some mixtures which polarize more completely than any of the individual components due to the fact that the molecules of the dichroic substances aid each other in coming into parallelism because of the complementary or other shapes or sizes of the molecules, and there are some mixtures which may be applied more readily than a single dye.

As one example, a mixture which has given excellent results with good polarization efficiency and substantially neutral color, is an aqueous solution of Resorcin Brown (Color Index No. 234) or Resorcin Brown (Color Index No.235) with Benzo Fast Blue 4GL (Color Index No. 533) in 3% solution with equal proportions of these dyes by weight. More or less of the Resorcin Brown gives more of a greenish or more of a blueish hue as desired.

The arrangement of molecules in the polarizing film including such mixtures of dyes is represented diagrammatically in Fig.3 wherein the molecules of one dye are represented by straight lines indicated for example by the reference

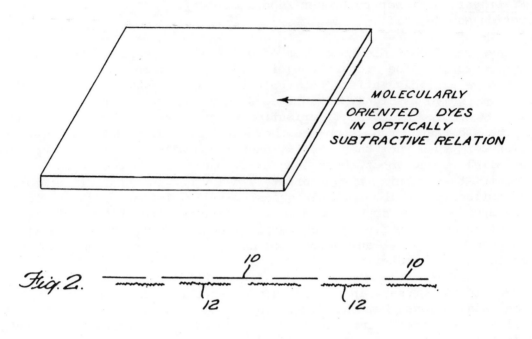

Fig. 1.

MOLECULARLY
ORIENTED DYES
IN OPTICALLY
SUBTRACTIVE RELATION

Fig. 2.

Fig. 3.

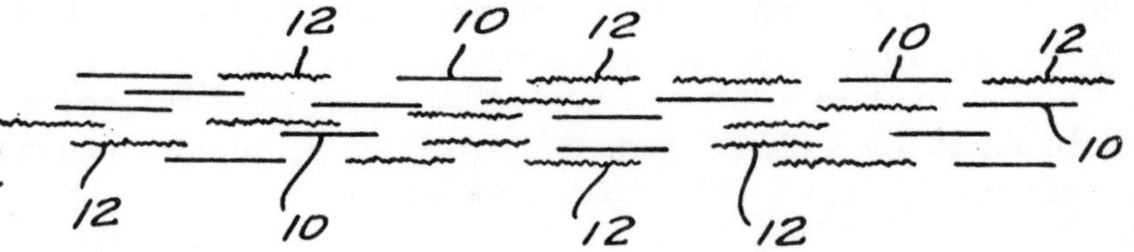

character 10 and molecules of another dye represented by waved lines indicated by the reference character 12. As indicated these molecules occur at random locations, but in any substantial area and in a substantial thickness of the film, molecules of the different dyes occur in optically subtractive relation thus giving the desired color with good polarizing efficiency.

Another highly satisfactory mixture is a 4% aqueous solution of 15 parts by weight of Benzo Fast Yellow 5GL (Color Index No. 346), 15 parts by weight of Benzo Fast Blue 4GL and 60 parts by weight of Sulfon Cyanine 5R Ex (Color Index No. 289). This also gives a gray with good polarization efficiency.

An example of a mixture with excellent orienting properties wherein a weakly orienting material is aided in effecting its orientation by a material having high orienting properties is a mixture of Resin Violet B with Methylene Blue, the latter aiding the former in its orienting properties.

The optimum in film thickness is obtained with many dyes with about 4-1/2% concentration in true solution.

Care should be taken to avoid impurities which interfere with the ability of the dyes to go into the nematic state or to retain orientation on drying.

It is important in films embodying my invention to have the several dyes in optically subtractive relation, i.e., so that the same light passes through first one dye and then another and the several dyes are not merely side by side in adjacent positions.

The present invention also contemplates the production and use of films wherein several dyes are put on as separate layers, with or without intermediate treatment to prevent any undesired solution of the first layer when the second layer is applied.

This arrangement of successive layers is indicated diagrammatically in Fig.2 wherein the molecules of one dye are represented by straight lines indicated by the reference character 10 and molecules of a different dye represented by waved lines indicated by reference character 12.

By the use of different polarizable dyes in subtractive relation, the dichroism or polarizing effect of each can be substantially enhanced, and the colors can be combined to produce a neutral gray or other desired color or colors in polarized and unpolarized light. If superposed layers of the respective dyes are used the last color applied will largely determine the appearance by reflected light and this may alter the apparent color of the film. When mixed dye films are used an additive color effect is produced in reflected light notwithstanding the subtractive effect by transmitted light.

Although I prefer ordinarily to use dyes all of which polarize light, I can also use a polarizing dye in combination with a non-polarizing dye to correct its color either in polarized or unpolarized light, and thus to give a different color in polarized light than in ordinary light; or when viewed through an analyzer to given different colors when viewed with different angular orientation.

" "

THERMAL IMAGING DEVICES UTILIZING A CHOLESTERIC LIQUID CRYSTALLINE
PHASE MATERIAL.

James L. Fergason, Thomas P. Vogl *and* Max Garbuny, *assignors to Westinghouse*
Electric Corporation.   Application March 4, 1960.

The present invention provides a device having a thermally sensitive
member of a material or materials which are capable, by reason of their
unique properties, of converting a heat pattern imposed thereon into a visible
pattern by exposure of the thermally sensitive member to visible light.

Referring to Figures 1 and 2, there is shown an enclosure 10 having a
generally rectangular cross section. The enclosure 10 has a first face 12
and a second face 14 on opposite sides thereof. The first face 12 of the
enclosure 10 is transmissive to radiation in the infrared portion of the
electromagnetic spectrum having a wavelength of about 2 microns to 15 microns.
The first face 12 may be transmissive to other than infrared radiation. A
suitable material from which the first face 12 may be made is NaCl, as is well
known in the art. The second face 14 of the enclosure 10 is transmissive at
least to visible radiation within the wavelength band of about 4200 to 7500
Angstroms. The second face may also be transmissive to radiation in other
portions of the spectrum. Many glasses are suitable materials from which
the second face 14 may be made, for example, ordinary window glass. The
enclosure 10 may have a cylindrical wall 16 for which tubular brass is one
of many suitable materials. In many instances it is desirable to operate
the device with the enclosure 10 evacuated in order to avoid temperature non-
uniformities therein. For that purpose, conventional O-ring vacuum seals 17
and 18 are employed to provide tight seals where the faces 12 and 14 and the
wall 16 join. Other suitable sealing means could, of course, be employed.
Continuous evacuation may be achieved, if desired, by providing a fitting 19
for connection to a vacuum pump (not shown). Within the enclosure 10 is
disposed a target structure 20 substantially parallel to the first and second
faces 12 and 14. The target structure 20 may conveniently be held by annular
supports 22 within the enclosure 10.

In the practice of this invention, there is no stringent requirement that
the target 20 be placed in a vacuum enclosure. This is merely an expedient to
avoid temperature variations on the target 20 due to air currents since it is
possible, and often desirable, to form a target of such high sensitivity that
even a slight air current would have a noticeable effect thereon. On the other
hand, in some applications where a less sensitive target may be employed, the
target may be exposed to the atmosphere and the enclosure 10 and transmissive
faces 12 and 14 would not be required.

As shown in Fig.2 the target structure 20 comprises three juxtaposed and
coextensive layers of material 24, 25, and 26. The inner layer 24 is a thin
support film of a material such as a polyester plastic such as polyethylene
terephthalate, sold as "Mylar", or such as aluminum oxide. The support film
has a thickness of only about .00025 inch or less. It is desirable for this
purpose to use a material which may be fabricated in a very thin sheet but which
still retains sufficient strength to support the other two layers 25 and 26.

On one side of the thin support film 24 is a layer 25 of infrared absorbing material. This material may be gold black, for example, evaporated on the thin support film 24 in an inert atmosphere such as about 1-10 millimeters of nitrogen. Nickel is also suitable as the infrared absorbing layer 25 and may be evaporated onto the support layer 24 in a vacuum. The thickness of the infrared absorbing layer 25 is not critical but should be such as to absorb a large percentage of the infrared radiation incident thereon. A thickness of the order of about one micron of gold black is usually sufficient for this purpose, as is a layer of the order of about 1-10 angstroms of evaporated nickel. The infrared absorbing layer 25 would not be necessary if it were not for the fact that most if not all of the materials suitable for use as the thermally se-sitive film 26 are substantially transparent to infrared radiation, which would result in only a negligible temperature change in the film. On the side of the thin support film 24 opposite the infrared absorbing layer 25 is a film 26 of a thermally sensitive material. Suitable materials for this film will be discussed hereinafter.

The target structure 20 is disposed within the enclosure 10 such that the infrared absorbing layer 25 faces the first face 12 of the enclosure 10 and the thermally sensitive film 26 faces the second face 14 of the enclosure. It is thereby made possible that the infrared absorbing layer 25 may be irradtiated with infrared radiation and the thermally sensitive film 26 may be irradiated with visible radiation.

External to the enclosure 10 is shown an optical system 30 disposed between the source of infrared radiation (not shown) and the first face 12 of the enclosure. The optical system 30 includes mirrors 31, 32 and 33 and apertured member 34 which comprise a concentric spherical optical system. Many other optical systems ase also suitable.

Infrared radiation from an object or scene to be viewed is directed by the optical system 30 through the first face 12 of the enclosure and focused upon the infrared absorbing layer 25 of the target structure 20. Radiation absorbed in the infrared absorbing layer 25 is converted to heat and causes a thermal image to be transmitted through the target structure. Thereby a temperature pattern is established on the thermally sensitve film 26 in accordance with the intensity of infrared radiation radiated by the objects in the scene viewed by the optical system 30. The support film 24 should be so thin as to be practically no barrier to the transmission of the temperature image from the infrared absorbing layer 25 to the thermally sensitive layer 26. Support film 24 serves primarily only as a support and its presence as an influence upon the thermal properties of the target 20 is not essential to our invention. It would often be desirable to omit the support film 24 and employ a target comprising only an infrared absorbing layer and a thermally sensitive film, if either of these layers were sufficiently strong to support the structure. The support film 24 should have a low thermal time constant, that is, the time required for it to reach a state in which it radiates as much energy as it absorbs should be short. The film 24 should also have low lateral heat conductivity to preserve resolution. These desired properties are best obtained by making the support film 24 as thin as possible in keeping with mechanical requirements.

On the side of the enclosure 10 opposite the optical system 30 is an illuminating means such as the lamp 36 directing visible radiation through a filter 37, which allows the passage of a desired portion of the spectrum, onto the second face 14 of the enclosure 10. The visible radiation is transmitted through the second face 14 and impinges upon the thermally sensitive film 26. A viewer 38 may look through the second face 14 of the enclosure 10 and view the thermally sensitive film 26 which displays a visible image corresponding to the temperature pattern imposed thereon. The viewer 38 may be human or a suitable image pickup tube or some other type of detector.

It should be noted that while it is believed most useful that the lamp 36 provide visible radiation so as to produce a visible image, the lamp 36 might be emissive in some other portion of the spectrum, such as the ultraviolet, in which case the resulting image would also be in that portion of the spectrum. Of course, it may be the case that ambient lighting provides light in the desired portion of the spectrum, in which case additional illumination by a lamp 36 would not be necessary.

The image is produced by the interaction of the light from the illuminating means 36 with the thermally sensitive film 26 upon which the temperature pattern exists. The interaction takes place in a temperature dependent manner.

The theramlly sensitive film 26 is a thin film of a material which has an optically active liquid crystalline phase and is in that phase when the device is operated. Materials having a liquid crystalline phase do not pass directly from the solid into the liquid state upon heating but have an intermediate state which is not a true solid and not a true liquid. This state may also be reached by cooling a material of this type in the liquid state. In addition, materials having a liquid crystalline phase may be caused to go into that phase by treating the material with a suitable solvent such as chloroform or petroleum ether. Once having entered the liquid crystalline phase the material will remain in that phase so long as environmental conditions are controlled within certain limits.

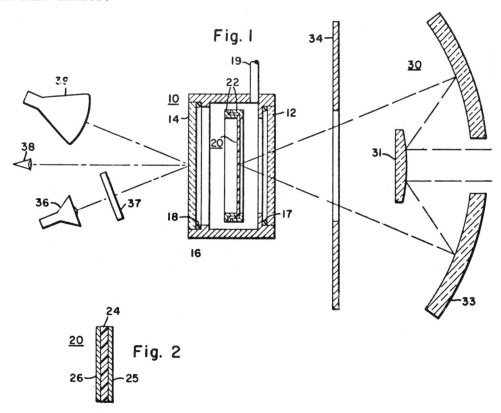

Fig. I

Fig. 2

Materials in the liquid crystalline phase are generally characterized by their having fluidity as well as birefringence. That is, while materials in this phase have some properties of liquids, they have some optical properties which are characteristic of true crystals. As used herein, the expression "materials having a liquid crystalline phase" is intended to be synonymous with "materials in the mesomorphic state." For further general information on this broad class of materials, reference should be made to the article by G.H. Brown and W.G. Shaw in CHEMICAL REVIEWS, vol. 57, No. 6, December 1957, p. 1049, entitled "The Mesomorphic State - Liquid Crystals."

It has been found that compounds having a mesomorphic state have elongated molecules, which are in some cases flattened as well, and which have one or more polar groups. By a polar group is meant a real separation of electrical charge centers. Because of the shape of the molecules, a parallel alignment to one another is favored. In the crystalline state, the molecules are arranged in this manner and are held together by attachments through the polar groups as well as by weaker Van der Waals forces. It is believed but is not essential to the successful practice of the present invention, that in going from the solid state to the liquid state, the weaker Van der Waals bonds are broken first leaving the molecules with some degree of freedom of relative movement, but retaining to a great degree the tendency for the molecules to align themselves parallel to one another.

Liquid crystalline materials have been categorized to be of three types: smectic, nematic and cholesteric. The smectic structure is characterized by the fact that the molecules are arranged in layers with their long axes approximately normal to the planes of the layers. In the nematic structure, there is no necessary layer-like arrangement, the only restriction on the arrangement of the molecules being that they preserve a nearly parallel orientation. Usually, liquid crystalline substances will show either the smectic or the nematic structure exclusively; some substances, however, can exhibit both structures, passing from one to the other upon a certain temperature change.

The arrangement of molecules in the cholesteric structure has not been definitely determined. The theory has been put forth that the cholesteric structure is a particular form of a nematic structure. The distinction of the cholesteric structure over the smectic and nematic structures is in its markedly different optical properties. Materials having the cholesteric structure are optically negative, while those having the nematic and smectic structures are optically positive. Of the three types of liquid crystalline materials only cholesteric liquid crystals have properties suitable for use in the device shown in Fig.1.

A temperature stabilization means 39 is provided to maintain the thermally sensitive film 26 at a background temperature which is uniform over the film surface and; in addition, can vary only within a restricted temperature range. This is necessary because the optical properties of the thermally sensitive film utilized in the present invention depend upon the film material being in the liquid crystalline phase. A particular material is only in the liquid crystalline phase within a definite temperature range. Therefore, it is necessary to maintain the temperature of the film in this temperature range.

Further temperature control is often desirable and may also be effected by the temperature stabilization means 39, in order to maintain the film at its most sensitive temperature range in which it is in the liquid crystalline phase. For the foregoing purposes, the temperature stabilization means 39 is shown as an incandescent heat lamp. It is obvious that other temperature stabilization means are suitable but it must be remembered that it is desirable that the film background temperature be as uniform as possible. Control of the temperature stabilization means may be made adjustable in order that the film may have an adjustable sensitivity. This would be useful, for example, to reduce sensitivity where too high a sensitivity would lead to the formation of a misleading image.

While shown in the drawing as a heat lamp, the temperature stabilization means 39 may or may not, depending on the material used for the thermally sensitive film 26, elevate the temperature of the film appreciably above ambient. Its function is to stabilize the film background temperature in the proper region so that it is thermally sensitive. Conceivably the temperature stabilization means 39 would in some cases be used to extract heat from the film 26 to maintain it at a background temperature which is below ambient. Automatic control of the heating means 39 by means of suitable feedback circuitry, which is well known in the art, is possible. Where ambient temperature is not expected to vary beyond the range in which the film 26 is in the liquid crystalline state, no temperature stabilization is required but may be used to enhance sensitivity.

Thin films of cholesteric liquid crystals exhibit a property, upon interaction with light, which may be termed selective scattering. The term scattering is used rather than reflection in order to distinguish from the effect occurring on mirror surfaces wherein light is reflected at an angle equal to the angle of incident light. A scattered light ray may leave the scattering material at an angle unrelated to the angle of incident light. A selectively scattering film, when observed with light impinging the film on the same side as that which is viewed, has an apparent color which is the complement of the color of the light transmitted by the film. That is, the light scattered from the film is within a wavelength band which, if added to the light transmitted through the material, would form white light, if white light was incident to the film.

The terms "light" and "color" as used herein have the broad connotation of referring to electromagnetic radiation generally, rather than to solely visible radiation.

Most materials do not selectively scatter light in that the light transmitted through them is not complementary to the light scattered by them but rather is within the same wavelength band. The difference in effect between selectively scattering materials and ordinary materials is believed due to the fact that in ordinary materials some light is absorbed by electron-photon interaction while in selectively scattering materials there is very little absorption. This explanation is not essential to the successful practice of our invention but may aid in understanding the operation thereof.

The phenomenon of selective scattering as exhibited by cholesteric liquid crystalline films is independent of whether the light illuminating the film is polarized or not. The color and intensity of the scattered light depends upon the temperature of the scattering material and upon the angle of incicence of illumination.

If such a film is illuminated with circularly polarized light, in addition to the property of selective scattering, it will also exhibit the property of circular dichroism. This latter effect may be defined as the differential interaction of a material upon circularly polarized light of different senses. Unpolarized light comprises right and left handed circularly polarized components of equal intensity. Upon interaction with a film of circularly dichroic material the right handed component is transmitted with a different intensity than the left handed component. The extent of the difference is a function of temperature in cholesteric liquid crystalline materials. This difference is believed to be the result of preferential scattering or absorption within the material but it is not known that this explanation has been confirmed.

Another property exhibited by cholesteric liquid crystalline material is what is commonly known as optical activity. Optical activity is observed by illuminating the material with linearly polarized light. Due to the optical activity of the material, also called optical rotatory power, the polarization vector of the light is caused to rotate. The amount of this rotation has been found to be dependent upon the temperature of the material.

Cholesteric liquid crystalline materials which are suitable for use as the thermally sensitive film 26 include derivates and compounds of cholesterol. All these compounds are characterized by having a cholesteric liquid crystalline phase. Mixtures of two or more compounds have also been used. The advantage of mixing the pure compounds is to obtain certain properties desired for a particular application; for example, to obtain high sensitivity within a particular temperature range which may be made as broad or narrow as one desires for most practical purposes.

As a particular example of a film usen in the practice of this invention a mixture was made of cholesterol crotonate and cholesterol oleate. The cholesterol oleate was prepared by a reaction of oleic acid with cholesterol in the presence of an acid catalyst. A suitable catalyst is p-toluenesulfonic acid. The cholesterol crotonate was prepared by the direct reaction of crotanyl chloride with cholesterol. A mixture of equal quantities of these compounds was then dissolved in chloroform in a concentration sufficient to form a readily flowing solution. The thermally sensitive film was formed by pouring the solution onto the support film, which in this case was polyethylene terephthalate to which the infrared absorbing layer had already been applied, and allowing the solvent to evaporate. The resulting film has a high viscosity. The particular example just described is sensitive near room temperature.

An example of another film is one of the following composition:

	Percent:
Cholesterol nonanoate	45
Cholesterol linolineate	50
Cholesterol chloride	5

This composition is sensitive over a temperature range of from about 1° to 100° C.

An alternative target structure may be formed by sandwiching the thermally sensitive film between a thin film of silicon monoxide and a thin film of aluminum oxide. On the free surface of the aluminum oxide a layer of infrared absorbing material is deposited. To make such a target, potassium bromide was first ecaporated upon a clean glass slide followed by depositing a layer of silicon monoxide in the same manner. The material from which the thermally sensitive film was to be made was then melted on the slide and a thin film of aluminum oxide was placed over it. The target was removed from the glass slide by dissolving the potassium bromide with water which allowed the target to float free. This method has been found somewhat less desirable than the previously described because of the relatively greater number and size of non-uniformities occurring in the fabricated target. Such a target, however, has been found to have a low thermal time constant and low lateral heat conductivity.

Because of the exceptional optical properties of cholesteric liquid crystalline films there are several modes of operating the device in accordance with the present invention. As before stated a film of the thermally sensitive material exhibits selective scattering of light incident to it. This light may be linearly polarized, circularly polarized or unpolarized and in addition may be either monochromatic or white light.

Referring now to Fig.3 there is shown a characteristic curve 60 resulting from the illumination of the thermally sensitive film 26 of Fig.2 with visible white light. As shwon there, the color of the scattered light is determined by the temperature of the film at the point of scattering. Visible colors will appear corresponding to the temperature of each point on the film. For example, an elemental area having a temperature of about 21° C. would appear red to a viewer while an area having a temperature of about 23° C. would appear green, as is shown at points 61 and 62, respectively, of the curve 60. The values shown in Fig.3 are merely typical, other films would be thermally sensitive in other temperature ranges.

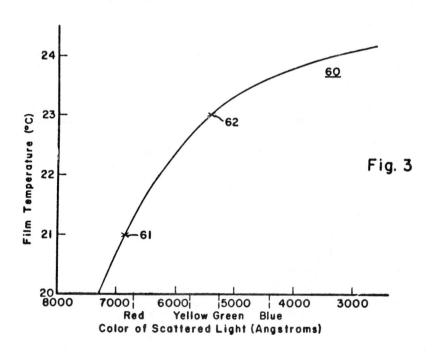

Fig. 3

If a thermal image were imposed upon the thermally sensitive film, illumination with white light would result in a color pattern because of the temperature dependent selective scattering as shown in Fig.3. For this purpose the lamp 36 would be a broad band light source whose output is substantially unfiltered before striking the film 26.

Referring now to Fig.4 there is shown a curve 70 of temperature versus intensity of scattered light for the case in which the thermally sensitive film 26 of Fig.2 is illuminated with monochromatic light. The resulting visible image is an intensity pattern. The light from an elemental area having a temperature of 22.25° C. is of markedly different intensity from that from an elemental area having a temperature of 22.5° C. as is shown at points 71 and 72, respectively, of the curve 70. For this purpose the film should be illuminated by a light of a wavelength to which it is thermally sensitive. In this case the lamp 36 may be a mercury discharge light source used with a filter 37 allowing the passage of only the 5540 A. radiation.

The curves 60 and 70 of Figs.3 and 4, respectively, closely approximate the results obtained when using a thermally sensitive film having a composition of about 30% cholesterol butyrate and about 70% cholesterol myristate made in accordance with the foregoing teachings.

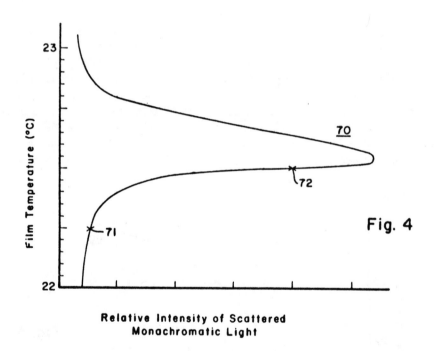

Relative Intensity of Scattered
Monochromatic Light

Fig.5 is an alternate embodiment of the present invention wherein parts corresponding to those shown in Fig.1 are given like reference numbers. A modification has been made in order to provide an additional face 14' on the enclosure 10 so that impinging infrared radiation passing through the face 12 will strike the target 20 on the same side on which the target is illuminated by the lamp 36. The windows 14 and 14' are transmissive to the radiation from the lamp 36. Between the lamp 36 and the input face 14', there is provided a polarizer 52. There may also be provided a pass band filter 37. Between the output window 14 and the viewer 38, there is provided an analyzer 53.

26

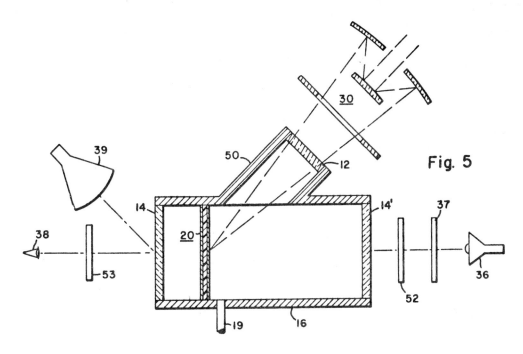

Fig. 5

In accordance with the teaching of copending application Serial No. 821,567, by J.H. Lady, filed June 19, 1959, and assigned to the same assignee as the present invention, a thermal image on a thermally sensitive film may be made visible by the transmission of linearly or circularly polarized light therethrough. For this purpose either white or monochromatic light may be used and is provided by the lamp 36. If monochromatic light is to be employed, the filter 37 is provided. The light is passed through the polarizer 52 before striking the target 20 and transmitted light is passed through the analyzer 53 for viewing.

In Fig.5 the target 20 comprises the same layers 24, 25, and 26 as are provided in the target of Fig.1 and as are shown in Fig.2 Particularly, a thermally sensitive film 26 of a material having a cholesteric liquid crystalline phase is provided in the target. Analogous to the operation of the embodiment in Fig.1, when the film 26 is illuminated with monochromatic light, an intensity image is obtained, and when illuminated with white light, a color image is obtained. Heat stabilization means 39 is provided to maintain the film 26 at a uniform background temperature within the region in which it is liquid crystalline. The operation of the device of Fig.5 is made possible by the optical activity of the thermally sensitive film 26 when it is illuminated by linearly polarized light. The viewed image is obtained by the light transmitted rather than scattered by the film. Therefore, it is necessary that the infrared absorbing layer 25 be transparent to the visible radiation to be transmitted through the film. A layer of evaporated nickel is suitable. The device of Fig. 5 may be operated also by illuminating the target with circularly polarized light. Here the images are achieved by reason of circular dichroism of the thermally sensitive film. In this case it is not necessary to use the analyzer 53. An imprtant point is that the resulting image formed by devices in accordance with this invention is scattered from or transmitted by the thermally sensitive member 26 without frequency change. This is believed due to the fact that essentially no energy transfer occurs upon interaction of the light from the illumination source 36 with the thermally sensitive film 26.

" "

MULTI-ELEMENT ELECTRO-OPTIC CRYSTAL SHUTTER.

Alvin M. Marks and *Mortimer. M. Marks.*
Application Jan. 11, 1960.

...Another form of shutter according to this invention is shown schematically in Fig.14. A light reflecting surface 101 is positioned behind the electro-optic shutter. Immediately in front of the reflector 101 are a plurality of high intensity illuminants 102. The light from the illuminants 102 is converted into a uniform dield by a diffusing plate 103 which is placed between the illuminants 102 and the shutter 104. The diffused light emanating from the plate 103 is polarized by a suitable polarizing sheet 105 before it enters the shutter 104.

The body of this form of shutter is in the shape of a thin rectangular transparent tank 155. Within the tank 155 there may be contained a liquid 106. The liquid 106 contains suitable transparent birefringent elongated dipole particles 107. The length of these particles 107 is critical.

A maximum dipole particle length is desired to increase the dipole moment, to enable easy alignment by means of weak electric fields. The birefringent effect, moreover, is increased in the thicker and longer particles 107. On the other hand, the particle length must not exceed a given size, since the relaxation time must be sufficiently small to provide an adequate response to the control signals. Moreover, the width of the particles must not be great enough to cause substantial light scattering when the light is passing approximately parallel to the axis of the aligned particles 107.

Such requirements are met by colloidal suspensions of anisotropic, birefringent, elongated, dipole particles of substances which have an inherently large dipole moment. These colloidal particles may preferably be suspensions of crystallites in a suitable liquid. The crystallites may be obtained from a widely dispersed class of organic or inorganic chemical compounds; for example, meconic acid, quinine sulphate, certain protein crystallites, quartz, etc. In addition to colloidal suspensions of transparent birefringent crystallite dipole particles, the liquid 106 may comprise a dilute solution, in any suitable solvent such as water, alcohol, etc. of a substance having an elongated molecular structure. This substance must also have a large electric dipole moment and birefringent effect, when a plurality of its molecules are suitably aligned in an electric or magnetic field. Such substances include the class known to form "liquid crystals" in molten, or concentrated solution, and which may exist in the nematic or smectic state. An example of a substance belonging to the class of liquid crystals, is p-azoxyanisol. Many other such well known substances may be alternatively employed.

The front and rear inner surfaces of the shutter 104 are latticed by a plurality of wires 108, 109, which comprise two distinct series of gratings (see Fig.15). The rear grating 108 is formed of spaced vertical wires. The front grating 109 is formed of spaced horizontal wires. The wires which are formed into the gratings 108, 109 are small in diameter compared to the distance therebetween, and consquently will cause a minimum of interference with the passage of light through the shutter 104. The cutaway section shown in Fig. 11 is therefore exaggerated as to the relative size of the wires and width of the tank 155, for the purpose of clarity of illustration.

A polarizing sheet 110 is placed in front of the shutter 104. The plane of polarization of the sheet 110 is at right angles to that of the opposed polarizer 103 located behind the shutter 104. In this manner, all the light which enters the shutter 104 from the illuminants 102 is ordinarily absorbed by the second of the crossed polarizers 110; hence the observer 111 sees only an opaque shutter. However, light passing through region 112 is rotated or depolarized and is thus enabled to pass through the second polarizer 110. The intensity of the light passing through the region 112 may be modulated by an intensity signal voltage e_1 applied to the bank of illuminants 102.

The above mentioned birefringent particles ordinarily may be aligned normal to the gratings 108, 109 by an electrical field 113 applied between the said gratings (see Fig.15). Under these conditions the polarized light 114 from the polarizer 105 (the plane of polarization of which may be at 45° to the horizontal) traverses a path approximately parallel to the long (optic) axis of the particles 107 except in apssing through the region 112. Thus there will be no relative retardation between the horizontal and the vertical components, or depolarization of the polarized light 114 except in passing through the region 112. However, since the electrical field may be reduced to zero as by shorting the wires adjacent thereto within the region 112, the particles 107 within the region will quickly become disoriented. Some of the disoriented birefringent particles will have the effect of randomly rotating the plane of polarization, and hence of depolarizing the light. The result of a rotation or depolarization of the divergent rays of light 114, in passing through region 112 is to enable a substantial portion of the rays 114 to pass through the second polarizer 110; whereas, other light rays 115 from elsewhere within the shutter are blocked by the polarizer. Thus, a modulated spot of light at region 112 will appear...

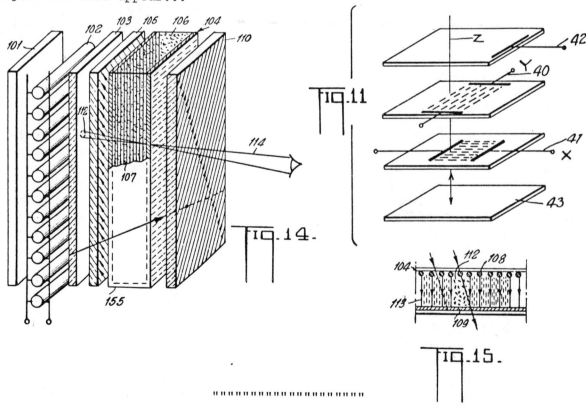

Fig.11

Fig.14.

Fig.15.

""""""""""""""""""""""""

3,322,485 (U.S.)   *Patented May 30, 1967*

ELECTRO-OPTICAL ELEMENTS UTILIZING AN ORGANIC NEMATIC COMPOUND.

<u>*Richard Williams*</u>, *assignor to Radio Corporation of America.*
Application Nov. 9, 1962. Also British Patent No. 1,131,688; 23 Oct., 1968.

This invention relates to improved electro-optical elements useful for making light valves, optical display devices, and for similar applications which involve the modulation of light. The objects of the invention are accomplished by providing an electro-optical element comprising two substrates having adjacent parallel surfaces less than 1/2 - millimeter apart, such as planar plates positioned so that their adjacent opposing faces are substantially parallel. The space between the adjacent faces of the two substrates is filled with an organic nematic mesomorphic compound. Means such as conductive coatings on each of the adjacent faces are provided for applying an electric field between said faces and through the compound. A device may be constructed in which the field is applied selectively to change the light reflective or light transmissive properties of the element.

Mesomorphic materials suitable for the practice of this invention are organic thermotropic nematic compounds. Examples of such compounds are given on the following page.

EXAMPLE I.

An electro-optical device according to one embodiment of the invention will now be described with reference to Fig.1a. The device 10 comprises two substrates 11 and 12, which are preferably plates having plane opposed parallel faces. Substrates 11 and 12 are positioned opposite each other so that their adjacent faces 13 and 14 respectively are parallel. The distance between the inner faces 13 and 14 of the two substrates is critical, as will be explained below, and should be less than one-half millimeter. Preferably, the distance between faces 13 and 14 is about 5 to 300 microns. The substrates are prepared with at least one electrically conductive region or strip 15 on inner face 13 of plate 11, and at least one conductive region or strip 16 on the inner face 14 of plate 12. The two plates 11, 12 and their conductive path or paths are substantially transverse or perpendicular to each other. An electrical lead wire 17 is connected to the conductive path 15 on wafer 11, and another electrical lead wire 18 is connected to the conductive path 16 on wafer 12, using known techniques. For example, the lead wires can be attached to the conductive strips by means of a droplet of silver paste. Lead wires 17 and 18 are connected to a voltage source 19.

At least one of the two substrates or plates 11 and 12 is transparent. Furthermore, the conductive region or paths on the transparent substrate is also transparent. In this example, only

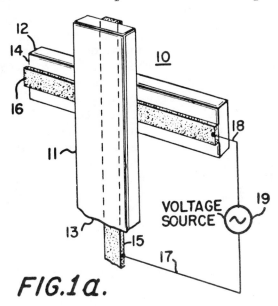

FIG.1a.

Compound	Structural Formula
(1) deca-2,4-dienoic acid	$CH_3(CH_2)_4CH=CH—CH=CH—COOH$
(2) 4,4′ di-n-heptoxy-azoxybenzene	$C_7—H_{15}—O—C_6H_4—NO—N—C_6H_4—O—C_7H_{15}$
(3) 4,4′ di-n-hexoxy-azoxybenzene	$C_6H_{13}—O—C_6H_4—NO—N—C_6H_4—O—C_6H_{13}$
(4) 4,4′ di-n-pentoxy-azoxybenzene	$C_5H_{11}—O—C_6H_4—NO—N—C_6H_4—O—C_5H_{11}$
(5) 4,4′ di-n-butoxy-azoxybenzene	$C_4H_9—O—C_6H_4—NO—N—C_6H_4—O—C_4H_9$
(6) 4,4′ diethoxy-azoxybenzene	$C_2H_5—O—C_6H_4—NO—N—C_6H_4—O—C_2H_5$
(7) Undeca-2,4-dienoic acid	$CH_3(CH_2)_5=CH—CH=CH—COOH$
(8) Nona-2,4-dienoic acid	$CH_3(CH_2)_3CH=CH—CH=CH—COOH$
(9) 4,4′-Dimethoxy-stilbene	$CH_3O—C_6H_4—CH=CH—C_6H_4OCH_3$
(10) 2,5-Di(p-ethoxy-benzylidene) cyclopentanone	$C_2H_5O—C_6H_4—CH=(C_5H_4O)=CH—C_6H_4OC_2H_5$
(11) 2,7-Di-(benzylidene-amino) fluorene	$C_6H_5CH=N(C_6H_4—C_6H_4)—N=CH—C_6H_5$
(12) 2,p-Methoxybenzyl-ideneamino-phenanthrene	$CH_3O—C_6H_4—CH=N(C_{14}H_9)$
(13) 4-Methoxy-4″-nitro-p-terphenyl	$CH_3O—(C_6H_4)—(C_6H_4)—(C_6H_4NO_2)$
(14) p-Azoxyanisole	$CH_3O—C_6H_4—(NO)=N—C_6H_4OCH_3$
(15) 4-p-Methoxybenzyl-ideneamino-biphenyl	$C_6H_5—C_6H_4—N=CH—C_6H_4OCH_3$
(16) 4,4′-Di-(benzylideneamino) biphenyl	$C_6H_5—CH=N—C_6H_4—C_6H_4—N=CH—C_6H_5$
(17) p-n-Hexylbenzoic acid	$C_6H_3—C_6H_4—COOH$
(18) p-n-Propoxybenzoic acid	$C_3H_7O—C_6H_4—COOH$
(19) Trans-p-methoxy-cinnamic acid	$CH_3O—C_6H_4—CH=CH—COOH$
(20) 6-methoxy-2-naphthoic acid	$CH_3O—C_{10}H_6—COOH$

one of the two substrates is transparent. A variety of transparent solids may be utilized for the transparent substrate, including the various types of glass, fused quartz, transparent varieties of corondum, and transparent plastics or resins. In this example, substrate 11 is transparent, and consists of a glass microscope slide. The conductive portion 15 on the substrate 11 is also transparent, as indicated above. This may conveniently be accomplished by depositing thin layers of indium oxide or tin oxide on the desired regions of inner face 13 on transparent plate 11. In this example, plate 12 is also a glass microscope slide, but is made reflecting by any convenient means, for example by depositing a metallic coating such as silver or aluminum on the outer face of plate 12. The conductive region 16 on face 14 of plate 12 need not be transparent, and may for example be a film of copper or gold.

The operation of the device of this example will be described with reference to Fig.1b. The transparent plate 11 and the reflecting plate 12 of this

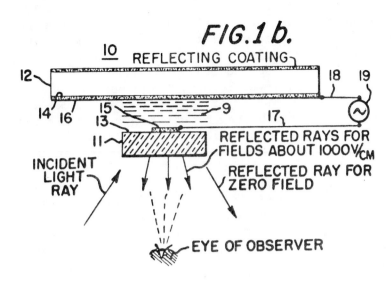

FIG. 1 b.

10 REFLECTING COATING

12

14 16

15
13

11

INCIDENT
LIGHT
RAY

9

17

18 19

REFLECTED RAYS FOR
FIELDS ABOUT 1000V/CM

REFLECTED RAY FOR
ZERO FIELD

EYE OF OBSERVER

example are positioned about 10 microns apart by means of shims (not shown).
Alternatively, the spacing may be maintained by means of clamps or by a suitable frame-like holder. The space between the two plates is filled with an
organic thermotropic compound (nematic) 9 such as p-azoxyanisole. The device
10 is maintained in the temperature range in which the compound exhibits the
nematic mesophase, that is, in the temperature range above the melting point
of the solid compound but below the temperature at which the molten compound
becomes isotropic. It will be understood that in the remainder of this
specification when reference is made to an organic nematic thermotropic
compound, the compound is in that particular temperature range in which the
nematic mesophase is exhibited.

The observer views the device through the transparent plate 11 and the
transparent conductive region or electrode 15. A light source is positioned
so that a collimated beam of light rays is incident on the transparent substrate 11. The angle between the incident light ray and the substrate 11 is
less than 45°, and preferably less than 22°. When the electric field between
the conductive strips or electrodes 15 and 16 is zero, most of the incident
light is reflected by the substrate 12 in a regular manner, so that the angle
of incidence equals the angle of reflection. Under these circumstances, as
shown in Fig. 1b, very little light is reflected to the eye of the observer,
whose line of sight is normal to the transparent plate 11 and transparent
electrode 15 and the layer 9 of organic nematic thermotropic material.
Accordingly, for zero applied field the observer sees the entire area of the
transparent electrode over the organic nematic thermotropic compound as dark.

When a weak field is applied between electrodes 15 and 16 by the voltage
source 19, no change is seen by the observer. If the strngth of the applied
field is slowly increased, there is no visible change in the light intensity
of the device viewing area, that is, the area of the transparent substrate
over the nematic compound, until a certain threshold value is reached. This
threshold value for the applied field varies with the particular organic
nematic thermotropic compound and the particular distance between the two
electrodes, but for most organic nematic thermotropic compounds is of the
order of magnitude of about 1,000 volts per centimeter. When the voltage

applied between the two electrodes reaches this value, there is a sudden change in the optical properties of layer 9 for that portion only of the organic nematic thermotropic compound 9 which is between the two electrodes and subject to the field. As a result of this change, some of the incident light is scattered through the transparent electrode 15 and the transparent plate 11 in the direction normal to the plate 11, and hence this scattered light reaches the eye of the observer. Thus, the observer, who has hitherto seen the entire area of the nematic layer 9 as uniformly dark, suddenly sees a particular portion of this area become brighter than the remainder of the area. The particular area which becomes bright is that area only of the nematic layer 9 which is directly between the intersection of the transparent conductive strip 15 and the conductive strip 16.

Although various experimenters have applied electrical fields to various mesomorphic compounds, this light scattering effect has not hitherto been observed. One reason is that experimenters have been measuring other properties of these compounds. More important, most experimenters have used mesomorphic layers which were more than one-half millimeter thick, whereas, as indicated above, the effect is only observed when the mesomorphic layer is both nematic and thermotropic and is less than one-half millimeter in thickness. In fact, the effect is observed best only when the nematic thermotropic compound layer is less than 300 microns in thickness.

While the exact nature of this light scattering effect is not definitely ascertained, it is theorized that groups of the parallel-oriented molecules of the nematic compound exist and in each group all the molecules tend to move in the same direction at the same time. Such groups or swarms of molecules may be regarded as domains. These domains tend to change their direction when the electrical field across the material reaches a certain threshold value. This change in the direction of groups or swarms of the molecules, all the molecules within each individual group or domain being similarly oriented, is thought to result in the scattering of light be the domain walls.

In the embodiment just described, the effect is obtained by modulating light reflection, and the observer sees a predetermined area of the device become bright, while the remaining area remains dark.

EXAMPLE II.

In the device 20 of this example, both substrates or plates 21 and 22 (Fig.2) are made of transparent materials. Fused quartz is one of the transparent materials suitable for this purpose. The quartz plates 21 and 22 are aligned so that their adjacent faces 23 and 24 respectively are parallel and spaced about 20 microns apart. The conductive region or electrode 25 on face 23 of plate 21 is transparent, as is the electrode 26 on face 24 of plate 22. The transparent electrodes 25 and 26 may, for example, consist of films of indium oxide or tin oxide, and are substantially perpendicular to each other in a manner similar to those of electrodes 15 and 16 in Fig. 1a. An electrical lead wire 27 is attached to electrode 25 and another electrical lead wire 28 is attached to electrode 26. Lead wires 27 and 28 are connected to a voltage source 19. The space between the two substrates or plates 21 and 22 is filled with an organic nematic thermotropic compound, which in this example consists of anisaldazine.

The observer views the device in a direction normal to the two transparent

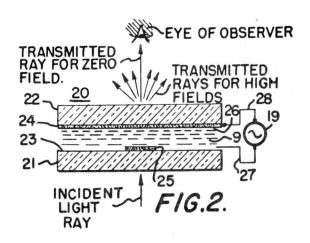

TRANSMITTED RAY FOR ZERO FIELD.

EYE OF OBSERVER

TRANSMITTED RAYS FOR HIGH FIELDS

INCIDENT LIGHT RAY

FIG.2.

electrodes 25 and 26. A light source is positioned to direct a collimated beam of light rays on the side of the device 20 opposite the observer so that the incident light rays pass through the device normal to the transparent plates 21 and 22 and the transparent electrodes 25 and 26 and the layer 9 of the organic nematic thermotropic compound. When the electric field between the two conductive paths or electrodes 25 and 26 is zero, the light rays transmitted through the device are in the same direction as the incident rays. The observer therefore sees the region of the device which contains the organic nematic thermotropic compound layer 9 as uniformly bright.

When the electric field between the two conductive paths 25 and 26 is increased, no effect is observed until a certain threshold value is reached. As indicated above, this threshold value for the applied field is of the order of 1,000 volts per centimeter. When this threshold value for the applied field is reached, there is a sudden change in the optical properties of that portion only of layer 9 which is directly between the two electrodes 25 and 26. This change in optical properties is manifested as a scattering of the transmitted light in all directions. The observer, who has hitherto seen the entire area of the nematic layer 9 as uniformly bright, now suddenly sees a portion of this area become darker than the remaining area. The darker area is that area only which is in the intersection of the two conductive paths or electrodes 25 and 26.

EXAMPLE III.

An optical display device 30 embodying an x-y grid comprises two planar substrates 31 and 32 (Fig.3), which in this example consists of transparent plates of corondum. The two plates 31 and 32 are parallel, and are separated by a distance "d" which is less than one-half millimeter, and preferably about 5 to 300 microns. In this example, the distance d is 40 microns. On the inner face 33 of plate 31 an array of transparent conductive strips are deposited, all running in one direction. In this example, only four such strips or electrodes (35a, 35b, 35c, 35d) are shown for greater clarity, but it will be understood that in practice, a much larger number of electrodes may be utilized. On the inner face 34 of plate 32, an array of transparent conductive electrodes are deposited, all running in the same direction substantially perpendicular to the direction of the conductive strips on plate 31. Again only four such strips (36a to 36d) are shown for greater clarity. The space between plates 31 and 32 is filled with an organic nematic thermotropic compound, which in

35

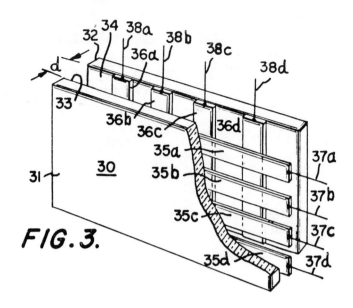

FIG.3.

this example, consists of 4,4'-dimethoxystilbene.

The optical device 30 of this embodiment is utilized in a manner similar to that shown in Fig.2, since both substrates and both sets of electrodes are transparent. A light source is positioned on one side of the device so that a collimated beam of light is directed through the device in a direction normal to the plates 31 and 32. The observer is on the opposite side of the device. For zero applied field, the observer sees the entire area of the nematic thermotropic compound as uniformly bright. Now when a voltage pulse is applied between one electrode strip of the group 35a to 35d and another electrode strip of the group 36a to 36d, then provided the voltage applied is equal to or greater than the critical field, the observer will see a portion of his field become darker than the remaining area of the nematic compound. The portion that becomes darker will be that portion corresponding to the intersection of the two electrodes which have been energized. For example, if the two electrode strips energized are 45a and 36d, the portion of the plate area which will suddenly darken is the area corresponding to the inter- section of the electrode strip 35a and electrode strip 36d.

By energizing more than one electrode strip from each set, a plurality of predetermined areas are thus darkened. Scanning techniques known to the optical display art may be utilized to sequentially and cyclically energize the conductive strips of one array, for example the vertical columns 36a to 36d, at a relatively rapid rate, while the conductive strips of the other array, which are the horizontal rows 35a to 35d in this example, are energized at a relatively slower rate. Row selector circuits and column selector cir- cuits for energizing selected rows and columns of an x-y grid are known to the mural television art, and need not be described in detail here. In this manner various types of information may be optically displayed, for example, a pattern of an alpha-numerical character. Furthermore, by using a large number of narrow electrode strips that are on the order of one mil wide and spaced one mil apart, a photograph or picture can be displayed on a device of this type.

An important advantage of the optical display devices described in this example is that there is very little crosstalk or spurious display, since those portions of the nematic thermotropic compound which are not directly between the two energized electrodes do not receive the threshold field, and hence do not exhibit the optical effect of modulating either the transmission or the reflection of light.

Still another advantage of the optical display devices described in this example is that they do not require polarized light, and may be utilized with any wavelength for which the substrate and the organic nematic thermotropic compound is transparent.

Another important advantage of the optical display devices described in this example is that their relaxation time is sufficiently short so that different displays may be shown at as high a rate as 30 frames per second. Hence the devices are compatible with present day television standards.

EXAMPLE IV.

Another optical display device embodying an x-y grid embodying the invention comprises two planar substrates such as plates 31 and 32 in Fig.3. In this embodiment, only one plate and its associated electrodes or conductive strips are transparent. The transparent substrate in this example is plate 31, and consists of a transparent plastic such as Plexiglass or the like. An array or grid of transparent conductive paths such as 35a to 35d are deposited on one major face of transparent plate 31, all of these paths running in the same direction. The other substrate or plate 32 in this example is preferably made of an opaque and reflecting material. In this example, plate 32 consists of aluminum. Strips of an insulating lacquer (not shown) are deposited on one face 34 of plate 32 so that all the strips are parallel and in one direction. A conductive metal such as silver or gold is then deposited, for example, by evaporation, on the insulating strip so as to form an array or grid of conductive paths 36a to 36d. The plates 31 and 32 are positioned opposite and parallel to each other, so that the array or grid of transparent conductive strips 35a to 35d is substantially perpendicular to the grid of conductive strips 36a to 36d. In this example, the distance between plates 31 and 32 is 60 microns. The space between plates 31 and 32 is filled with an organic nematic thermotropic compound, which, in this example is dibenzalbenzidine. Electrical lead wires 38a to 38d are attached to conductive strips 36a to 36d respectively. Similarly, lead wires 37a to 37d are attached to conductive strips 35a to 35d respectively.

The optical display device of this example is utilized in a manner similar to that shown in Fig.1b. A light source is positioned so that a collimated beam of light is directed against the transparent plate 31 and the grid of transparent electrodes 35a to 35d. The incident light is arranged to make a small angle (less than 22°) to the plate 31. The observer is positioned in front of the transparent plate 31, and sees the entire plate as dark, since the incident light is reflected away from the observer by the opaque substrate 32 in a regular manner with the angle of reflection equal the angle of incidence, while the line of sight of the observer is normal to the transparent substrate. When a voltage is applied between one electrode strip of the group 35a to 35d and another electrode of the group 36a to 36d, then provided the applied voltage is sufficient to attain the required threshold value of the order of 1,000 volts per centimeter, the observer will see a portion of the transparent plate 31 become brighter than the remaining area of the plate. The portion of the plate 31 that becomes brighter is that portion corresponding to the intersection of the two electrode strips which have been energized.

While the optical display devices of Examples III and IV utilized x-y grids which are particularly suitable for displaying information in rectilinear coordinates, optical display devices having other arrangements for the grids may also be fabricated. For example, optical displays may be manufactured as described below with a type of grid which is particularly useful for presenting information in polar coordinates.

EXAMPLE V.

An optical device is prepared utilizing two transparent substrates as in the embodiment of Example III. In the device of this example, the substrates are plates 41 and 42, which are shown in plan view in Figure 4.

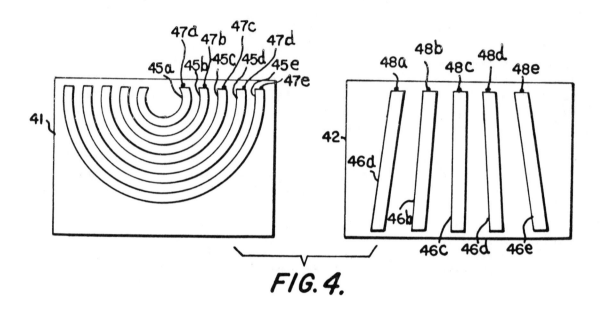

FIG. 4.

Plates 41 and 42 are made of Pyrex glass in this example. A plurality of transparent conductive strips such as 45a to 45e are deposited on one face of plate 41 in the form of a series of concentric circular sections. A plurality of transparent conductive strips or electrodes 46a to 46e are deposited on one face of plate 42 as straight lines diverging from a common central point. Electrical lead wires 47a to 47e are attached to transparent electrodes 45a to45e respectively. Similarly, lead wires 48a to 48e are attached to transparent electrodes 46a to 46e respectively. The plates are positioned parallel to each other and about 80 microns apart. Plates 41 and 42 are aligned so that the two sets of transparent electrodes are opposite each other on the inner faces of the assemblage, and the central point of the concentric circular electrodes 45a to 45e is opposite the central point of the diverging linear electrodes 46a to 46e. The space between the two sets of electrodes is filled with an organic nematic thermotropic compound, which in this example consists of 4,4' di-n-heptoxy-azoxybenzene.

The operation of this device is similar to that of the device in Example III, since the effect obtained depends on the modulation of the transmission of light through the device in a manner similar to that illustrated in Fig.2.

An advantage of the optical display device of this example is that the polar coordinate grid is easily adapted to indicate range and angle information of a body. Energizing the correct circular electrode of the 45 set of electrodes will give the range or distance of the body, while energizing the correct diverging strip electrode of the 46 set will give the azimuth or direction to the body.

EXAMPLE VI.

An optical display device is prepared generally similar to Example V, but utilizing one transparent substrate and one opaque reflecting substrate. In thsi example, plate 41 consists of a transparent material, and the circular electrode strips 45a to 45e on one face of plate 41 are also transparent. Plate 42 may consist of a polished metal, as in Example IV, with the linear conductive strips 46a to 46e being deposited over strips of insulating lacquer (not shown). The plates are positioned opposite and parallel to each other at a distance of about 100 microns apart. The separation between the two sets of electrodes is filled with an organic nematic thermotropic compound, which in this example consists of 4'-di(p-n-alkoxybenzylideneamino)-3-methylbiphenyl. The optical display device of this example operates by modulation of deflected light, in a manner similar to that described in Example IV and illustrated in Fig.1b.

"""""""""""""""""""""

MOLECULAR SWARM LIQUID CRYSTAL OPTICAL PARAMETRIC DEVICES.

Isaac Freund, and *Peter M. Rentzepis*, *assignors to Bell Telephone Laboratories, Inc.   Application March 10, 1967.*

Liquid crystals of the type characterized by molecular swarms, e.g., nematic crystals, can be made to produce harmonics and parametric operation at optical frequencies. When magnetic and electric fields are applied to the crystal, a variable birefringence results, permitting phase matching over a range of frequencies.

The invention is based upon the realization that certain liquid crystals, particularly those of the nematic class can be made to exhibit a large variable birefringence upon the application of a magnetic field, with or without an applied electric field. This arises from the molecular arrangement in the nematic liquid crystal. The molecules exist in swarms having a high degree of orientational order and a direction of very large magnetic susceptibility. Inasmuch as the molecules are not fixed in position, as in a solid crystal, they easily align themselves with an applied magnetic field, thereby producing a large birefringence characteristics. In addition, the electric moments of the molecules cause them to line up with an applied electric field, thereby making the crystal noncentrosymmetric, that is, all molecules are polarized in substantially the same direction, also contributing to the birefringence.

Such characteristics make it possible to generate efficiently the second harmonic of an incident laser beam, since the second harmonic and the fundamental can be made phase matchable. In addition, parametric amplification and oscillation are realizable, as are both frequency and amplitude modulation.

In Fig. 1 there is shown an embodiment of the invention for generating second harmonics from an incident beam. The arrangement of Fig. 1 comprises an electromagnetic wave source 11 which may be, for example, a ruby laser producing a 6943 A. wavelength beam. The output of source 11 which in the case of the ruby laser is a beam of coherent light, is directed through a filter 12 which is designed to pass light of 6943 A. wavelength and to block extraneous light.

From filter 12 the beam passes through a polarizer 13 which imparts a single polarization to the light, shown in Fig. 1 as a vertical polarization. The beam is then directed into a liquid crystal assembly 14 which comprises a container of fused quartz or other suitable material filled with a liquid crystal of the nematic class, such as, for example, p-azoxyanisole or p-azoxyphenetole, or other nematic crystals with suitable properties. The temperature at which the liquid crystal phase occurs varies with the material used. In general, although by no means always, the temperature of the liquid crystal phase is higher than room temperature. To maintain assembly 14 at the proper temperature, an oven 16, which may take any of a number of forms, is provided. Oven 16, shown in dashed outline in Fig. 1 should be such that the light beam may enter and exit therefrom substantially unattenuated.

On either side of assembly 14 are contacts 17 and 18 for applying an electric field to the liquid crystal by means of a suitable source 19. Magnetic field producing means, the poles 21 and 22 of which are shown,

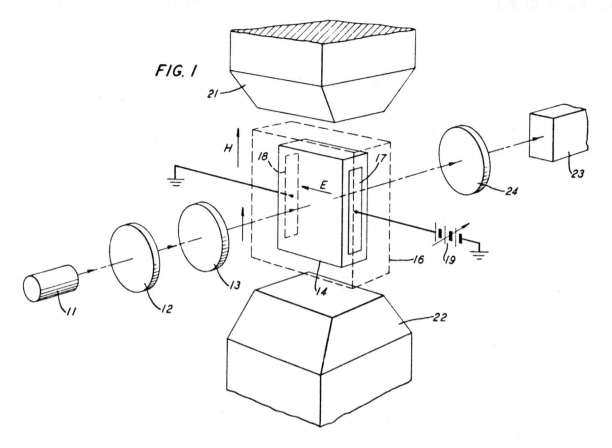

FIG. 1

produces a magnetic field in which member 14 is immersed. Preferably the magnetic field and the direction of travel of the beam are at right angles to each other. In liquid crystals having an electric moment of the molecules perpendicular to the direction of large magnetic susceptibility, the applied electric field E is normal to the magnetic field and beam direction. It is parallel to the magnetic field in those materials where the electric moment is parallel to the direction of large magnetic susceptibility.

When a light beam, such as in Fig.1, passes through a liquid crystal, numerous frequencies are generated which are harmonics of the incident beam. In the case of higher harmonics, they are generally too weak to be of use. The second harmonic, on the other hand, is usually much stronger than the higher harmonics. However, because of the random disposition of the swarms in the liquid crystal, there is a cancellation of the generative effects in the crystal with the net result that even the second harmonic is too weak to utilize.

In a nematic crystal, the molecular swarms tend to align themselves with the magnetic field, thereby imparting to the crystal a birefringent characteristic which in turn makes it possible to phase match the incident wave and the generated second and even higher harmonics. When this occurs, the two waves interact over a large distance, thereby increasing the amplitude of, for ex., the second harmonic to usable levels. In addition, the electric moments of the molecules tend to align themselves in an applied electric field, thereby imparting the same polarization to all generative contributions to the second harmonic. This electric field insures noncentrosymmetry in the liquid crystal and also contributes to the birefringence of the liquid crystal.

In the Arrangement of Fig.1, the magnetic field is varied until the second harmonic output of the liquid crystal is maximum, at which point optimum phase matching is achieved. In the case of a 6943 A. input beam, a magnetic field of an order of magnitude of 1000 to 5000 gauss produces a maximum intensity of second harmonic radiation at 3472 A. wavelength. One of principal advantages of the use of the liquid crystal is its tunability. For input beams of different frequencies, the magnetic field is adjusted to produce the particular degree of birefringence necessary to give optimum phase matching. The differential index of refraction is variable over a range of, for example, zero to 0.3, which makes possible a wide range of frequencies of operation.

Nematic crystals are not optically active and are not doubly refracting, and are optically uniaxial in a magnetic field. As a consequence, a polarized beam entering the liquid crystal normal to the surface and polarized parallel or perpendicular to the magnetic field emerges from the liquid crystal with the same polarization and in the same direction. In addition, the generated second harmonic travels colinearly with the fundamental in the liquid crystal and emerges traveling in the same direction, but orthogonally polarized thereto. In the arrangement of Fig.1, therefore, the output of the element 14 is a beam containing vertically polrized light at 6943 A. and horizontally polarized energy at 3472 A. Where it is desired to use only the 3472 A. wave, a filter 24 may be used to filter out the 6943 A. wave. The beam then passes to a utilization device 23, which may take any one of a number of forms well known in the art, depending upon the particular use to which the beam is to be put.

From the foregoing it can readily be seen that an amplitude modulated second harmonic can be produced by varying the magnetic field H in accordance with modulating signals. This has the effect of varying the phase match and hence the amplitude of the second harmonic output. In like manner, variation of the electric field in accordance with modulating signals varies the output amplitude of the second harmonic.

The foregoing discussion has dealt with second harmonic generation in a liquid crystal. The unique characteristics of the nematic class of liquid crystals makes it possible to produce parametric amplification and oscillation also. In Fig.2 there is shown an arrangement for parametrically amplifying signals.

The arrangement of Fig.2 comprises a crystal assembly 31 comprising a container of fused quartz or other material filled with the liquid crystal material. For simplicity, the magnetic and electric field producing means have not been shown but the fields produced thereby are indicated by the vectors E and H, E being horizontal and H vertical. These means may, of course, take the forms shown in Fig.1, or other suitable forms. In addition, the oven for maintaining the liquid at the proper temperature has, for simplicity, been omitted.

A source of pump energy 32, which as in the case of Fig.1 may be a ruby laser, directs a beam of energy at, for example, 6943 A., through a polarizer 33 which imparts a horizontal polarization to the beam, and into a beam

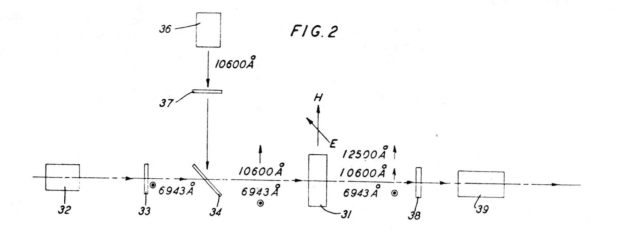

FIG. 2

combiner 34, which may take any one of a number of forms known in the art. In like manner, a source 36 of signals to be amplified directs a beam at, for example, 10600 A. through a polarizer 37, producing a vertical polarization, and to beam combining means 34. The output of combiner 34 is a beam containing horizontally polarized energy at 6943 A. and vertically polarized energy at 10600 A. This beam is directed into crystal assembly 31, as shown.

As in the arrangement of Fig. 1, the magnetic field H and electric field E produce both birefringence and noncentrosymmetry in the liquid crystal. As a consequence, the magnetic field may be varied until a phase match is achieved among the pump, signal and the idler generated within the liquid crystal. Optimum phase match is indicated by the maximum intensity output of the 10600 A. energy.

The polarization of the pump, signal, and idler depend upon the frequencies of these waves. For the frequencies or wavelengths shown, the pump is polarized in the direction of smaller index of refraction in the liquid crystal to counter act the larger index due to the higher frequency of the pump. By the same token the signal is polarized in the direction of high index to counteract the normally smaller index due to the signal frequency being less than the pump frequency. As a consequence, it is possible to match the signal and the pump. The magnetic field is adjusted to produce that birefringence for which the pump, signal and idler satisfy the parametric requirements as to frequency and phase velocity It should be understood that the polarizations of the various waves may differ from those shown for different frequency combinations or for different liquid crystals. Determination of the proper polarizations in accordance with the above principles is within the ordinary skill in the art.

The output member 31 is a beam containing pump signal, and idler frequencies. For the example shown, the idler is at approximately 12500 A., and the sum of it and the signal frequency equals the pump frequency. This beam is directed into a member 38 which, where only one of the frequencies, e.g., the amplified signal, is desired, may be a filter passing only that frequency. On the other hand, where more than one frequency is to be utilized, it may be a beam splitter of suitable form, or a combination of beam splitters, with or without filters. Alternatively, where the multifrequency beam is to be used, member 38 may be omitted altogether. From member 38 the beam passes to a suitable utilization device 39 which may take any of a number of forms.

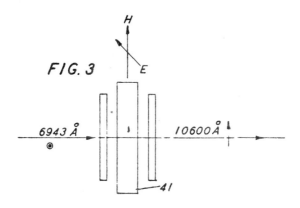

FIG. 3

Parametric oscillation may readily be achieved utilizing the principles of the present invention in a manner similar to which the amplification was achieved in Fig.2.

In Fig.3 there is shown the crystal arrangement for achieving parametric oscillations. For simplicity, the pump source, magnetic and electric field producing means, oven, and utilization device, as well as various polarizers and filters have not been shown. The arrangement of Fig.3 comprises a crystal assembly 41 comprising a suitable container filled with the liquid crystal material. Member 41 is inserted within a resonator formed by a pair of partially transmission mirrors 42 and 43, which may be separated from member 41, or attached thereto. The resonator is designed to be resonant at the frequency to be generated, e.g., 10600 A. wavelength, or for tunable operation may be broadband. Pump energy from a suitable source having, for example, a wavelength of 6943 A. and being horizontally polarized, is directed into the liquid crystal member 41. As is well known, such energy generates within the crystal a large number of frequencies. However, for a set amount of birefringence, two particular frequencies, i.e., signal and idler, will be phase matched to the pump, and hence will grow in amplitude. Varying the electric and magnetic fields, as in the case of the arrangement of Fig.2, varies the birefringence and hence the particular signal and idler waves that are phase matched to the pump. The resonator causes the generated signal to make several or many passes through the crystal, in a manner well known in the art.

When the mirrors and resonator are made broadband, i.e., capable of supporting a range of frequencies, the output of the resonator can be frequency modulated by varying the magnetic or electric field in accordance with a modulating signal.

The output of the crystal and resonator, the generated signal, can be utilized in any suitable utilization device, not shown.

The foregoing discussion has dealt primarily with crystals of the nematic class. Other classes of nonoptically active crystals may also be used to generate second harmonics. For example, second harmonic generation has been observed in liquid crystals of the smectic class which, like nematic crystals, are characterized by molecular swarms. The individual swarms or domains in smactic crystals are so large that each domain functions as a second harmonic generator, and the intensities of the incremental second harmonics add to produce a strong second harmonic output. Even when the various swarms are randomly polarized, the second harmonic grows with length, giving, in effect, a noncentrosymmetrical crystal.

DISPLAY DEVICE.

Juris A. Asars, assignor to Westinghouse Electric Corporation.
Application June 8, 1966; prior U.S. application June 29, 1965.

    The invention resides in a display screen comprising a heat sensitive
layer comprising a cholesteric phase liquid crystal film exhibiting a change
in selective scattering properties in response to temperature changes, and
thermal distribution means for impressing a thermal image on said heat sensitive layer, wherein said thermal distribution means comprises an array of magnetic elements disposed in thermal contact with and extending over the area
of said heat sensitive layer.

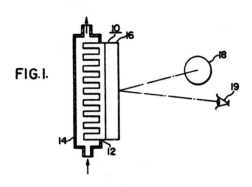

FIG.I.

    Referring to Fig.1, a display system is illustrated. The display system
consists of a display screen assembly 10. The display screen assembly 10 may
include a heat sink member 12 and an associated cooling means 14 in which a
liquid such as water is directed therethrough for controlling the temperature
of the display screen assembly 10. A thermoelectric cooling means may also
be utilized. The display screen assembly includes a display screen 16 that may
be mounted on the heat sink 12 and on which a visible image is presented. A
light source 18 is provided for illuminating the display screen 16 by a suitable
light such as white light. The illumination of the screen 16 by white light
source 18 provides a visible display which may be viewed by an observer illustrated by the numeral 19.

    In the embodiment of Fig.2 the display screen assembly 10 is shown to be
mounted on the heat sink 12. The heat sink 12 may be of any suitable good
thermally conductive material such as a metallic layer of a material such as
copper or aluminum. A thermal barrier layer 20 may be provided on the heat
sink 12 of a suitable thermal insulating material such as polyethylene terephthalate. The termal barrier layer 20 is to reduce thermal conductance from
the sensitive screen portion to the heat sink layer 12 if less excitation
power is desired. The layer 20 may not be required in some applications.

    The screen includes a heat distribution structure that in the illustrated
embodiment is diposed on the thermal barrier layer 20. In the exemplary embodi-

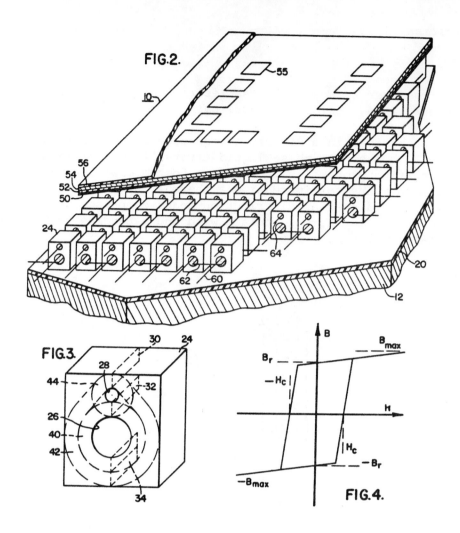

FIG.2.

FIG.3.

FIG.4.

ment shown here, the thermal distribution structure consists of an array of magnetic elements, such as magnetic memory devices, for example, the two-aperture transfluxors 24 illustrated. Each of the transfluxors 24 provides a small area display element and in the normal embodiment, by way of example, about ten of these transfluxors could be provided per linear inch. The thermal distribution structure is made up of a plurality of magnetic elements 24 of a ferromagnetic material. The elements 24 are normally made up and pressed from a mixture of ferric oxide powder and other materials and then baked in an oven. The magnetic memory devices 24 may be in many different shapes and configurations and if desired, may be simply a well known magnetic core if storage is not required. The specific device illustrated herein provides a magnetic structure which has storage features incorporated.

The transfluxor 24 which is shown enlarged in Fig.3 consists of a major aperture 26 and a minor aperture 28. If a section is taken of this transfluxor 24 along the center lines of the two apertures 26 and 28, the cross-sectional area of the region 30 is equal to the cross-sectional area of the region 32 and the sum of these two areas 30 and 32 is equal to the area of the region 34. Fig.4 shows an idealized B-H curve of the material in element 24 where B_r is the residual flux density following maximum magnetization B_{max} and H_c the coercive force of the major hysteresis loop. If it is assumed that I_{40}

48

is the current in a single turn winding necessary for reaching H_c in every part of the shaded magnetic path 40 which encloses only the major aperture 26, that I_{42} is the corresponding current for a shaded magnetic path 42 which encloses both apertures 26 and 28, and that I_{44} is the corresponding current for a path 44 enclosing only the minor aperture 28, then the relationship of these currents may be expressed as $I_{42} > I_{40} > I_{44}$.

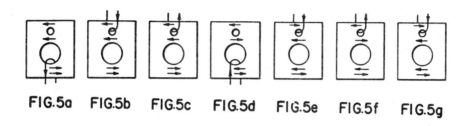

FIG.5a   FIG.5b   FIG.5c   FIG.5d   FIG.5e   FIG.5f   FIG.5g

Referring now to Fig.5 for an explanation of the general operation of the transfluxor element 24. Ig clearing current I_c, which is somewhat greater than I_{42} is passed through the larger aperture 26 in a direction as indicated in Fig.5a, a magnetic flux in all three regions 30, 32 and 34 saturates in a counterclockwise direction about the larger aperture 26. When this current is removed, the flux density is reduced only slightly to the residual value B_r. Complete saturation in each of these areas 30, 32 and 34 is achieved because of the cross-sectional area relationship stated above. When a small excitation current I_r, where $I_{44} = I_r$ is then passed through the smaller aperture 28 as indicated in Fig.5b, no flux reversal takes place because in every portion of the region 32 the material is already saturated in the direction of the magnetic field produced by the current I_r. If the current I_r is passed through the small aperture 28 in the opposite direction as indicated in Fig. 5c, no flux reversal takes place because of the saturation in region 30. In these two cases illustrated by Figs.5b and 5c, only a minute amount of energy is dissipated because flux changes from B_r to B_{max} are only possible and the hysteresis loop illustrated in Fig.4 is not traversed.

If after the clearing current I_c has been applied (see Fig.5a), a writing current I_w equal to I_{40} is passed through the major aperture 26 in the opposite direction as I_c as shown in Fig.5d, flux is reversed in the shaded region 40. I_w is smaller than the minimum current to reverse any residual flux in region 42, and residual flux after termination of I_w is reversed only in the region 32 and not in 30. The result is that a counterclockwise residual flux is found around the minor aperture 28, in region 44. Now, if the excitation current I_r is passed through the small aperture 28, a flux reversal takes place as shown in Fig.5e in the region 44. After the removal of this current, the residual flux around the small aperture 28 is in a clockwise direction and can again be reversed to the counterclockwise direction by an excitation current I_r in the opposite direction as shown in Fig.5f. Such reversals can be continued with current pulses of alternating polarity without affecting the residual flux in region 34 and therefore its memory state. During these flux reversals the hysteresis loop is traversed in the shaded path 44 of Fig.3 and an amount of energy much larger than in cases illustrated in Figs.5b and 5c is dissipated during each current pulse.

The above explanation shows that, if an alternating current pulse I_r is passed through the smaller aperture 28, the amount of energy dissipated in the memory core 24 and therefore its temperature rise is determined by the presence or absence of a writing pulse I_W after a clearing pulse I_C. The characteristics of the core geometry and its material determine the ratio between the dissipations in the two cases, but the absolute power dissipation can be controlled by the choice of excitation current pulse frequency.

The amount of writing current is such as to exceed the switching threshold, that is the minimum drive necessary to switch any remanent flux from counter-clockwise to clockwise as illustrated by Figs. 5c and 5d and determines the amount of remanent flux that is acted upon by the excitation current. It is found that a high degree of linearity can be achieved between the remanent magnetic flux and the applied drive and this information may be stored for an infinite time. Thus, the writing current can determine the regions in magnetic path 44 in which flux reversals occur in response to the excitation current. The larger the extent of these regions, the greater will be the heating found in the transfluxor element 24. The properties of the transfluxor elements 24 are well known in the art and the above-description is given to fully appreciate and understand the operation of the transfluxor as a heating element in the screen structure and the manner in which varying degrees of heating can be obtained for display of information. How this heating property is utilized will be more fully explained with respect to Fig.6.

Referring again to Fig.2, the next layer provided upon the thermal distribution structure is a coating 50 of a suitable material such as a black dye. Positioned on the black coating 50 is a protective film 52 of a suitable material such as polyethylene terephthalate. Positioned on the layer 52 is a layer 54 of a liquid crystalline material of the cholesteric phase which is sensitive to heat. Suitable materials are described in U.S. Pat. No. 3,114,836. A specific material may be a mixture of 60% by weight cholesteryl nonanoate, 20% by weight of oleyl cholesteryl carbonate, and 10% by weight of cholesteryl benzoate. The response of this liquid crystalline material to heat is illustrated by the curve of Fig.7. A protective coating 56 of a similar material as layer 52 may be provided on the layer 54. Heating of selected transfluxor elements 24 results in a display of elemental areas 55 as illustrated in Fig.2.

Referring in detail to Fig.6, a 4 by 4 circuit assembly or transfluxor matrix is illustrated. Two single turn windings 60 and 62 pass through the large aperture 26 and carry the control signal current pulses. The winding 60 is the Y winding and is common to a whole column of transfluxors and permits the selection of an element 24 in the horizontal direction. The winding 62 is the X winding and is common to a whole row of transfluxors and permits the selection of an element 24 in the vertical direction of the display panel. A single turn winding 64 passes through the smaller aperture 28 of the transfluxor elements 24 and is common to all the elements in the matrix and supplies the excitation signal from a source 66.

Each of the Y windings 60 is connected to a separate terminal 72 of a first switching means 70. The switch 70 includes a rotating contact 74 for contacting any of the terminals 72. The rotating contact 74 is connected to the rotating contact of a second switching means 76. The switch 76 includes two termonals 80 and 82 which are in turn connected respectively to current sources 84 and 86. The current source 84 provides suitable value of current, for example a 300 mA positive pulse to provide a pulse to the Y winding 60 during the store operation. The current source 86 provides a current source of about 600 mA which is of negative polarity and is utilized to erase or clear

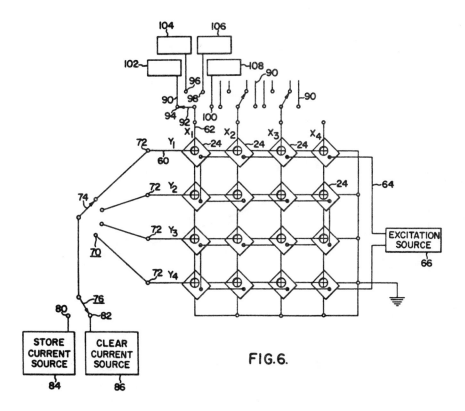

FIG.6.

information from the transfluxors 24.

Each of the X windings 62 is connected to a separate switch 90 and specifically to the rotating contact member 92. The switch 90 consists of four terminals 94, 96, 98, and 100 which are connected respectively to a blue information current source 102, a green information current source 104, a red information current source 108. The current pulse of these respective sources 102, 104, and 108 might be of the values of 150 mA, 100 mA, 50 mA, and 0 respectively.

In the operation of the device, assuming that the switch 76 is connected to the source 86 and all of the transfluxors 24 have been cleared as indicated by the representation in 5a, then the switch 76 would be thrown to the terminal 80 to connect the current source 84 which is the store pulse to winding Y. If the switch 90 is placed on terminal 94 as to connect the blue source to the winding X_1, then an adequate signal will pass through the transfluxor common to X_1 and Y_1 and information will be written or stored on the transfluxor in a manner represented by Fig.5d. Current flowing through the excitation winding 64 from the current source 66 which may provide a current of 250 mA both in the negative and positive direction and at a frequency of about 200 kilocycles, will cause heating of the transfluxor common to X_1 and Y_1 to a point 114 on the curve in Fig.7. This is at a temperature of about 37° C. Light directed from the source 18 onto the liquid crystalline layer 54 will result in light of blue color being reflected from an element 55 of the screen.

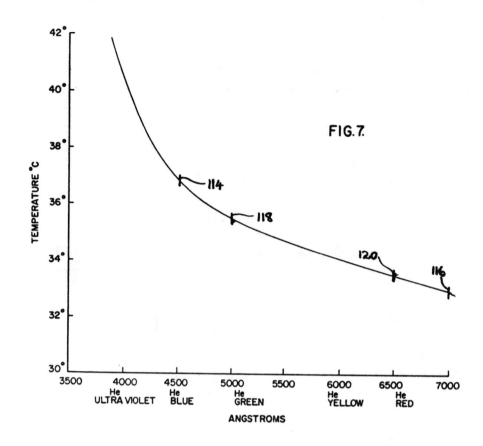

FIG. 7

The transfluxor common to X_1 and Y_1 will continue to reflect this light until a signal from the erase or clear source 86 is applied so as to remove this write information. If the switch 90 is thrown to connect the black source 108, then a point 116 on the black element will be seen by the viewer. In this condition, the transfluxor 24 does not have any flux reversals but simply remains in a clear state due to the erase pulse and the source 84 is inadequate writing current to write any information in the transfluxor. Corresponding switching of the switch 90 to pulse source 104 in the liquid crystal operating on point 118 and source 106 results in operation on point 120. The reflected colors in this instance would be respectively green and red.

In the above manner, a color image may be written onto the display screen and will be stored thereon to provide a visual color image until the informatio is cleared from the transfluxors.

"""""""""""""""""""""""""""

1,120,093 (British)   Patented July 17, 1968

DISPLAY SYSTEM.

Arthur E. Anderson and James L. Fergason, assignors to Westinghouse Electric
Corporation. Application June 8, 1966. Prior U.S. application June 29, 1965.

This invention relates to display systems and, more particularly, to
display systems for the visual display of information by means of a cholesteric
phase liquid crystal film.

The present invention resides in a display system for the visual display
of information by means of a light control element comprising a cholesteric
phase liquid crystal film exhibiting a change in optical properties in response
to temperature changes, wherein said light control element is disposed in the
path of a radiation beam from a control radiation source representative of the
information to be displayed for impressing on said liquid crystal film a thermal pattern corresponding to the information-representative radiation beam.

The described embodiments of the display system according to the present
invention employ illumination of, preferably large area, light control elements by a suitable light source and ambient lighting to provide a high intensity light image by reflection of light from or transmission through the light
control element. Generally, in preferred embodiments the thermal pattern
impressed on the liquid crystal film is utilized for modulation of a high
intensity light source.

Liquid crystals of the cholesteric phase have significant optical properties. The cholesteric phase has an index of refraction which varies with
direction of propagation of light through the material. For light traveling
through a thin sheet of cholesteric crystalline material, the index of refraction will be a minimum for normal incidence. As the angle if incidence
becomes more oblique, the index of refraction will increase.

If linear polarized light is transmitted along the optical axis (the
direction along which the optical index of refraction is a minimum), the plane
of the polarized light will be rotated through an angle which will depend upon
the thickness of the material and upon the particular wavelength with which it
is illuminated. This property is called optical activity. The cholesteric
phase of liquid crystal is found to be the most optically active substance
known. It is found that the plane of polarization may be rotated as much as
up to 18,000°, i.e. up to 50 rotations per millimeter.

Another important property of a cholesteric liquid crystal is the iridescence appearance when illuminated by ambient light. The colors that the crystals exhibit are due to a scattering within the material, which in some ways
bears the resemblance to the scattering of light from an oil film on water.
However, the differences are quite remarkable. An oil film will scatter light
when its thickness is an exact multiple of half of the wavelength. The cholesteric films scatter only one wavelength at one angle. The light scattered from
an oil film is not polarized; however, with the liquid crystal film, the light
becomes circularly polarized when it is scattered. A circularly polarized
wave is one which has two equal components of electric fields that are in space
and time quadrature. It may be either right- or left-hand circularly polarized,

depending upon the type of material used. It is also found that with a cholesteric liquid crystal the circular polarized light is reflected or scattered
in the same sense contrary to the ordinary mirror reflection. That is, right-
hand circularly polarized light when reflected from a cholesteric material is
right-hand when it is scattered. The left-hand circularly polarized light will
not be scattered but will be transmitted through the film. This gives rise
to a property which is called circular dichroism or selective scattering of
right- or left-hand circularly polarized light. It is found that a liquid
crystal absorbs no energy so that the light energy directed thereon is either
transmitted or reflected. It is found that at selected wavelengths and the
normal angle of incidence that about 50 percent of the incident radiation is
scattered. At larger angles the amount of energy reflected increases and the
peak (wavelength of maximum scattering) shifts toward the shorter wavelength.
If the temperature of the film is varied, the peak of the reflection curve will
shift to shorter wavelengths with increase in temperature. This temperature
effect is completely reversible. At any temperature the wavelength of maximum scattering depends on the sum of the incident angle of the light radiations
and the observation angle.

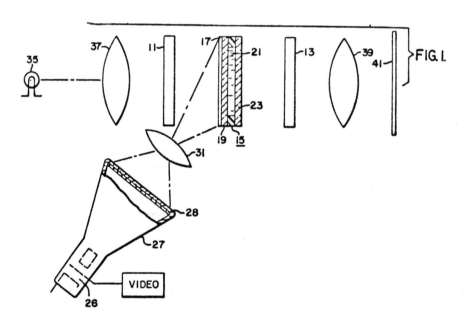

In Fig.1, there is shown a projection system which includes a polarizer 11
and an analyzer 13 which are disposed in parallel spaced relationship. The
polarizer 11 and the analyzer 13 may be of tourmaline, nicol prisms or any other
suitable material which will permit light to pass in only one plane.

A light modulator 15 is provided between the polarizer 11 and the analyzer 13. The modulator 15 includes a layer 17 exhibiting the property of absorbing an input electromagnetic radiation image and converting the radiation
image into a heat or thermal image. The layer 17 absorbs those wavelengths
emitted by a modulation system while permitting radiation of a projection
source to be transmitted. In the specific embodiment shown, the modulation
radiation is in the ultraviolet portion of the spectrum and the projection
source radiation is in the visible portion of the spectrum. A suitable material for the layer 17 is a tartrazine of a thickness of a few microns. Any
suitable dye including organic or inorganic dyes may be used for this purpose.

54

Their suitability is determined by their absorption characteristics. Other materials suitable for ultraviolet range are anthracene and phenantrene. A support layer 19 of low heat capacity and transmissive to at least the visible region of spectrum is provided and supports the layer 17. The layer 19 has a thickness of about 10 microns and may be of a suitable material such as polyvinyl fluoride.

A layer 21 of a suitable liquid crystalline material of the cholesteric phase is provided on the layer 19. The layer 21 is in good thermal contact with layer 19. A suitable material for the layer 21 is a mixture including 20 percent by weight of cholesterol benzoate, 30 percent by weight of cholesterol nonanoate and 50 percent by weight of cholesterol oleyl carbonate. This is only one specific liquid crystalline material of cholesteric phase that will function in this embodiment. Several other suitable materials are described in U.S. Patent 3,114,836. Another layer 23 of polyvinyl fluoride is provided on the opposite surface of the liquid crystalline layer 21 and the resulting structure may be sealed by any suitable means to retain the liquid crystalline material layer 25 confined within between layers 19 and 23.

A cathode ray tube 27 is provided for directing modulation radiation onto the light modulator 15. The cathode ray tube 27 includes a phosphor layer or screen 28 on the face plate which generates ultraviolet radiation in response to electron bombardment. An electron gun 26 is provided for generating an electron beam. Suitable deflection means are provided for scanning the electron beam to form a raster on the screen 28. The video signal is applied to an electrode of the electron gun 26 for modulating the electron beam in well known manner.

A lens 31 may be provided between the cathode ray tube 27 and the light control element 15 for focusing the radiation from the ultraviolet phosphor layer 28 onto the light control element 15. A suitable light source 35 is provided on the opposite side of the polarizer 11 with respect to the light control element 15. In the specific embodiment, the light source 35 is monochromatic and provides radiation of a wavelength of about 5,700 A. Suitable filters may be utilized with the light source 35 in order to provide this substantially single wavelength transmission. Lens elements 37 and 39 may also be provided for focusing of the light from the source 35 directed onto the control element 15 and a viewing screen 41, respectively.

To best explain the operation of the system, reference is made to Fig.3 (see next page). Curves 40 and 42 in Fig.3 represent certain properties of the layer 21 at two different temperatures. If it is assumed that the temperature is 27° C. as represented by curve 40, then the light is rotated about 45 degrees by the layer 21. The polarizer 11 and the analyzer 13 may be adjusted so that substantially no light from the source 35 is projected onto the screen 41 at this temperature. By raising the temperature to 29 ° C. so as to be on curve 42, the rotation by the light control element 15 will be about 15 degrees so that a substantial amount of light from the source 35 will now be transmitted through the system onto the screen 41. By modulating the intensity of the electron beam generated by the gun 26 with the video information, the amount of radiation from the screen 28 may be controlled. The amount of radiation directed on the light control element 15 controls the temperature of the light element control 15 and accordingly the amount of light transmitted from the source 35 to the screen 41. In this manner, a high intensity light image

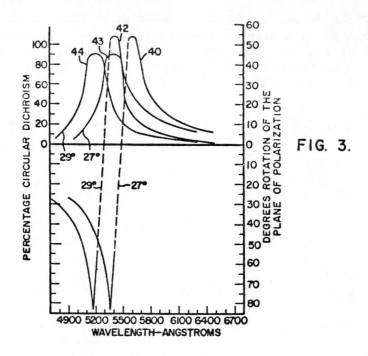

FIG. 3.

may be displayed on the screen 41 corresponding to the video information. The polarizer 11 will linearly polarize the emergent light beam from the source 35. The light emerging from the polarizer 11 will illuminate the light control assembly 15. The temperature pattern is impressed on the layer 21 by means of the cathode ray tube 27. The light control element 15 will be illuminated by a weaker control source in the form of the ultraviolet beam from the cathode ray tube 27. It is normally desirable that the light beam from the cathode ray tube 27 be at different wavelength than the source 35 but it is not essential to the operation of the system. The radiation from the cathode ray tube 27 is directed onto the light control assembly 15. The radiation absorbing layer 17 will absorb the radiation from the cathode ray tube 27 and generate a heat pattern which is impressed on the optically active film 21. The layer 17 will not substantially absorb the visible radiation from the source 35.

The layer 17 may also be of metal such as nickel having an electrical resistance of about 377 ohms per square which absorbs about one-half of the incident radiation including the source 35 and the cathode ray tube 27 and transmits one-fourth of the remaining. Under these conditions, the radiation source 36 together with the radiation of the cathode ray tube 27 can be used to elevate the temperature of the layer 21 to a suitable operating temperature at which temperature the primary radiations of the source 35 are transmitted through the analyzer 13. If one-twentieth of the total power needed to reach the optimum film temperature is provided by the cathode ray tube 27, then this amount of power is more than adequate to modulate the transparency of the system.

It is also possible to use the circular dichroic properties of the film 21 by removing the polarizer 11 and analyzer 13 and positioning a circular polarizer between the light source 35 and the control element 15. The light source 35 would be set at a wavelength of 5,400 A. At a temperature of 27° C. the film transmission will be at one level, as shown on curve 43 of Fig.3. By raising the temperature to 29° C., the film transmission would be at a second

level that is vastly different from said one level, as shown on curve 44 of
Fig.3. The polarizer and the film should be of the same polarization, that
is right- or left-handed.

If the source 35 is modified to provide a given band of wavelengths rather
than a single wavelength as previously described with respect to Figs.1 and 3,
then the system may be utilized in the following manner: The light source 35
in this case would emit radiation from the infrared end of the spectrum to
about 6,250 A. This is represented by curve 49 in Fig.4.

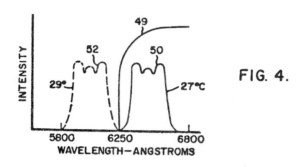

FIG. 4.

Curve 50 in Fig.4 represents the transmission properties of the polarizer 11,
analyzer 13 and light control element 15 for a temperature of 27 degrees Centigrade. The curve 52 represents the transmission characteristics of the same
assembly at a temperature of 29° C. Thus by shifting the temperature of the
control element 15 to a higher temperature, the transmission of light through
the system from the source 35 may be cut off. By lowering the temperature to
about 27° C. light from the source 35 will be transmitted through the assembly
to the screen 41. Only about 50% of the light from the source 35 will be
transmitted through the assembly. This is due to the fact that within the
optical activity range of the material in layer 21, the circular dichroism
effect is also found such that only the right- or left-hand portion of the
light will be transmitted and the other portion will be reflected from the
liquid crystal layer 21.

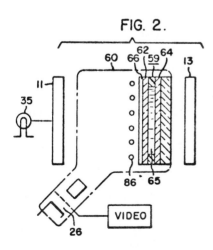

FIG. 2.

In Fig.2 a modified light controlled
unit is shown in which a light control
assembly 59 is provided within an evacuated envelope 60 so that the electron
beam bombards the light control assembly
59. The target assembly or light control structure 59 in this embodiment
consists of light transmitting layers
62 and 64 of polyvinyl fluoride with a
thin layer 65 of a cholesteric liquid
crystalline material positioned between
the two layers 62 and 64. A layer 66
of a material such as tin oxide or gold
is provided on the layer 62. The electron
beam bombards the layer 66 and generates
a heat image which is impressed on the
layer 65. In this manner, the electron
beam is utilized directly on the light

control structure 59 rather than through the radiation as illustrated in Fig.1. Under this condition the gain of the system can be at least 100.

The operation of the system is similar to Fig.1. The speed of response of the device can be optimized by coating the inner surface of the cathode ray tube with a plastic film of sufficient thickness to provide the right amount of heat conductivity to reduce the thermal time constant of the system. This can be accomplished without a great sacrifice in the power sensitivity of the liquid crystal film which is sandwiched between these films. It is also possible to provide a plastic film on the target facing the electron gun of a material having a second crossover in its secondary emission characteristics at a high voltage so as to absorb maximum energy from the bombarding beam. The maximum transparency of the composite layer in this case should be made as high as possible to the wavelength of the light from source 35 to be amplified. By locating the writing gun 26 at an angle with respect to tube face, the polarized light from the high intensity source 35 may be modulated by projecting the light through the face of the tube as illustrated in Fig.2.

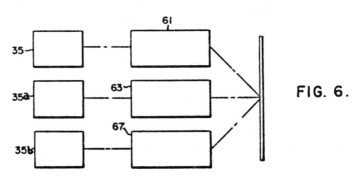

FIG. 6.

In Fig.6 there is illustrated a projection system utilizing three separate systems 61, 63 and 67 similar to Fig.1 and in which the three light sources 35, 35a, 35b would be sources capable of radiation respectively in the red, green, or blue band of the spectrum. In this manner, the light projected from the system 61 would project a red image onto a viewing screen corresponding to the light modulation or red video signal applied to the cathode ray tube of the system 61. In a similar manner, the source 35a would provide a green image by system 63 and 35b a blue image by system 67. The video information of these three colors would be applied to their respective cathode ray tubes. The resulting image of the viewing screen could be a sequential type of display or simultaneous type of display to provide a high intensity color television image.

In Fig. 5 there is illustrated a display tube capable of presenting an image by utilizing the reflection properties of the liquid crystalline layer. The display tube is of substantial conventional cathode ray tube design and consists of a face plate portion 70, a flared portion 72 and a neck portion 74. An electron gun 76 is provided within the neck portion 74 of the envelope. The electron gun 76 may be of any suitable design for producing a pencil-like beam and is well known in the art. The videa signal may be applied to a control grid 77 of the electron gun 76.

The screen 81 includes a coating 78 of an electrically conductive light transmissive material such as stannic oxide provided on the inner surface of the face plate 70. A layer 80 of a liquid crystalline material of a mixture

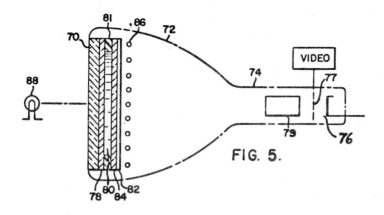

FIG. 5.

such as 45 percent by weight of cholesterol nonanoate, 45 percent of oleyl
cholesterol carbonate and 10 percent of cholesterol benzoate is provided on
the electrically conductive coating 78 of a thickness of about 25 microns.
Provided on the inner surface of the liquid crystal layer 80 is a layer 84 of
polyvinyl fluoride having a black coating provided on the surface facing the
liquid crystal layer 80. A layer 82 similar to layer 66 of Fig.2 is provided
on the inner surface of the polyvinyl fluoride layer 84. An electrically
conductive grid 86 may be provided between the screen 81 and the electron gun
76 for acceleration and focusing of the electron beam. A suitable light
source 88 of white light is provided exterior of the envelope for illuminating
the screen 81.

During the operation of the device, the electron beam from the electron
gun 76 is directed onto the surface and generates a heat pattern in layer 82
corresponding to the video intelligence applied to the control grid 77 of the
electron gun 76. Suitable deflection means 79 are provided for scanning the
electron beam over the screen 81. The heat image established in the layer 82
is impressed in the layer 80 and a visual image is obtained when illuminated by
the source 88. By proper design, the target will provide the proper amount
of heat conductivity and speed of response. By adjustment of the video signal,
the color may be selected. The intensity of the color can be varied by simple
modulation of the electron beam to provide a multi-color image. The screen
may be veiwed in high ambient light condition. The brighter the ambient
light the brighter will be the display on the display screen. It is also
possible to provide a single color on a black background by utilizing a monochromatic light from the source 88.

" "

ELECTRIC FIELD DEVICE.

James L. Fergason, assignor to Westinghouse Electric Corporation.
Application June 8, 1966; prior U.S. application June 29, 1965.

This invention relates to electric field responsive devices for the
detection and visual indication of electric fields.

In many applications, it is desirable to provide an electric field sensitive device for giving a visual indication of the fact that a field is present
and also visual indication in response to a change or different values of the
field thereacross. Certain organic materials have been found that modify their
optical properties in response to an electric field. These materials are
liquid crystalline materials of the cholesteric phase.

The unique molecular architecture of the cholesteric liquid crystals give
rise to a number of optical properties which differ from the smectic or nematic
phase. The characteristic properties of the cholesteric structure may be summa-
rized as follows:

(1) It is optically negative, while smectic and nematic structures are
optically positive. An optically negative layer provides that light entering
perpendicular to the molecular layers has a maximum velocity.
(2) The structure is optically active. If linearly polarized light is
transmitted perpendicularly to the molecular layers, the direction of the
electric vector of light would be rotated progressively to the left along the
helical path. Thus the plane of polarization, which is determined by the
electric vector in the direction of propagation, will be rotated to the left,
to an angle that will be proportional to the thickness to the transmitting
materials. The magnitude of the rotation of the plane of polarization is also
a function of the wavelength input. This property may be referred to as wavelength dependent optical activity.
(3) It selectively scatters light directed onto the molecular structure.
The term scattering is used rather than reflection in order to distinguish
from the effect occurring on a mirror surface wherein light is reflected at an
angle equal to the angle of incidence. A scattered light ray may leave the
scattering material at an angle unrelated to the angle of incident light. A
selectively scattering film when observed with light impinging on the film
from the same side as that which is viewed, has an apparent color which is the
complement of the color of the light transmitted by the film. That is, the
light scattered from the film is within a wavelength band which, if added to
the light transmitted through the material, would form white light, if white
light was incident on the film. The terms light and color as used herein have
a broad connotation of referring to electromagnetic radiation generally,
rather than to solely visible radiation. Most materials do not selectively
scatter light in that light transmitted through them is not complementary to
light scattered by them but rather is within the same wavelength band. The
difference in effect between selectively scattering materials and ordinary
materials is believed due to the fact that in ordinary material some light is
absorbed by electron photon interaction while in selectively scattering materials there is very little absorption. A cholesteric material exhibits a scattering peak having a narrow bandwidth over the electromagnetic spectrum. The

bandwidth in the visible spectrum is about 200 angstroms. The phenomena of selective scattering as exhibited by cholesteric liquid crystal films is independent of whether the light illuminating the film is polarized or not. This is the property that gives the iridescence appearance of the material under ambient light.

(4) Another optical property exhibited by the cholesteric liquids is circular dichroism. When ordinary white light is directed onto cholesteric material, the light is separated into two components, one with the electric vector rotating clockwise and the other with the electric vector rotating counterclockwise. Depending upon the material, one of these components is transmitted and the other is scattered. This gives the property of circular dichroism or the selective scattering of right or left-hand circularly polarized light.

(5) Another property is that when circularly polarized pight is directed onto cholesteric materials, the sense of polarization of the scattered light is unchanged from the incident light.

(6) The mean wavelength of the scattering band depends upon the angle of incidence of the light. The type of material and the temperature also affect the mean wavelength of the scattering band.

The molecular structure of a cholesteric liquid crystal substance is very delicately balanced and can be easily upset. Thus any small disturbance that interferes with the weak forces between the molecules and produces marked changes in such optical properties as scattering, transmission, birefringence, circular dichroism, optical activity and color.

One of the most striking optical transformations that occurs in certain cholesteric substances is in response to changes in temperature. Although most cholesteric substances are colorless as liquids, they pass through a series of bright colors when they are cooled through their liquid crystal phase. All cholesteric liquid crystals do not respond in the same way to fluctuations in temperature. The colors may vary and the sequence of colors with cooling may vary. It is also possible to obtain certain materials that have very little reaction at all to changes in temperature. The properties of the liquid crystal materials of the cholesteric phase with regard to response to thermal changes is discussed in U.S. patent 3,114,836.

Another effect that has been noted with certain cholesteric liquid crystals is its response to certain chemical vapors. The addition of extremely small amounts of certain chemical vapors can change the basic molecular structure and thereby affect the optical properties, such as the selective scattering effect.

The present invention is based on the observation that electric fields can affect the structure of cholesteric liquid crystals so that one or more optical properties thereof is changed. The device according to the present invention may be utilized for detection of a field with an indication by color of the value or a voltage or a current impressed thereon. It may also be utilized for display of a visual image. Various embodiments of the devices may be constructed to bring about and utilize this phenomenon. The optical property readily utilized in the practice of this invention is that of selective scattering since it does not require polarization for observation. The change in transmission properties of light through the liquid crystal device may be utilized and controlled. This transmission shift is in the same direction and to the same extent as the scattering band.

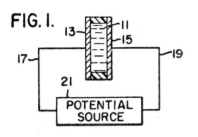

FIG. I.

POTENTIAL SOURCE

Referring to Fig.1, there is illustrated a simplified voltage sensitive device including a layer 11 of a mixture of liquid crystalline materials of the cholesteric phase that exhibit a change in optical properties in response to an electric field impressed across the layer 10. Examples of liquid crystal materials of the cholesteric phase exhibiting a change in optical properties in response to an electric field include cholesterol, cholestanol, sitosterol, cholesteryl halide, e.g., cholesteryl iodide, cholesteryl chloride and cholesteryl bromide, cholestanyl halide, e.g., cholestanyl chloride, cholestanyl bromide and cholestanyl iodide, sitosteryl bromide and sitosteryl iodide, or mixtures thereof. Usually these materials or mixtures thereof may be mixed with other substances such as sterol derivatives, and up to 20% of fatthy acids and compounds thereof. The following Table gives a listing of specific mixtures of materials by per cent weight which exhibit the field effect. These materials are stable at room temperature.

MIXTURE:	COLOR AT ROOM TEMPERATURE:
20% Cholesteryl Chloride (CC) 80% Cholesteryl Oleyl Carbonate (OCC)	Blue
25% Cholesteryl Chloride 75% OCC	Green
30% CC 70% OCC	Red
20% CC 20% Cholesteryl Nonanoate (CN) 60% OCC	Blue
25% CC 75% Cholesteryl Oleate (CO)	Green
25% Cholesteryl Bromide (CB) 75% OCC	Green
30% CB 70% OCC	Red
25% CC 25% OCC 25% CO 25% CN	Green

In Fig.1 thereis shown a voltage-sensitive device including a layer 11 of a suitable liquid crystal material of the cholesteric phase exhibiting a change in optical properties in response to electric fields impressed there- across. The layer 11 may consist of 20% by weight of cholesteryl chloride with 80% by weight of cholesteryl oleyl carbonate. The percentage of cholesteryl chloride may vary from 15% to 50% by weight of the mixture.

The layer 11 is snadwiched between two transparent electrical conductive layers 13 and 15. Electrical conductive leads 17 and 19 from the respective conductive layers 13 and 15 provide means of applying an electric potential illustrated as source 21.

The application of a voltage across the layer 11 by the source 21 results in a field across the layer 11. The electric field modifies the optical properties of the layer 11. These properties include optical rotation, selective scattering and selective transmission. The apparatus and the methods of visual display of these effects will be discussed with respect to the following embodiment.

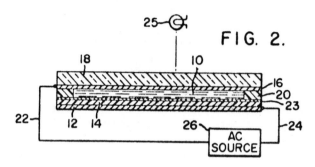

FIG. 2.

Referring to Fig.2, there is illustrated a voltage sensitive device including a liquid crystalline material of the cholesteric phase. This device utilized the selective scattering properties of the liquid crystalline layer. The device consists of a layer 10 of suitable liquid crystal materials, for example a layer consisting of 45% by weight of cholesteryl bromide, 30% cholesteryl oleate and 25% cholesteryl nonyl-phenyl carbonate. This layer 10 when illuminated by white light, which provides uniform intensity over the spectrum, exhibits properties as best illustrated by the curves in Figs. 3 and 4. The electric field sensitive device illustrated in Fig.2 consists of a layer 12 of suitable electrically conductive layer of a material such as aluminum, a layer 14 of suitable insulating material such as aluminum oxide, a suitable black coating 23 of a suitable dye, the layer 10 of a suitable liquid crystalline material, a layer 16 of a suitable electrical conductive material transmissive to visible light of a suitable material such as stannic oxide and a support layer 18 of a suitable material transmissive to visible light such as glass and supporting layer 16. The function of the layer 14 is to provide a carrier for the light absorbing layer 23 and to insure against electrical breakdown of the cell. In some applications, the layers 14 and 23 could be omitted.

The specific device shwon in Fig.2 may be constructed by providing a sheet of commercial grade aluminum of about 0.5 inch in thickness. The sheet of aluminum may be of any desired thickness and may be of any desired dimensions, such as about 3 inches in diameter. The sheet of aluminum may be cleaned in an aqueous solution of ammonium nitrate 3% by weight and anodized to provide the desired thickness of aluminum oxide by the adjustment of voltage. An electrode of lead may be utilized for the cathode in this operation. By this procedure, an aluminum oxide coating 14 of a desired thickness of about 1 micron is formed on both surfaces of the aluminum sheet simultaneously. The anodized aluminum sheet is then removed from the electrolyte and washed in distilled water and then pure acetone. Next, the anodized layer on one side of the aluminum layer 12 is removed by treatment with a suitable caustic reagent, such as sodium hydroxide. After the sodium hydroxide has had an opportunity to act on one of the aluminum oxide films, the aluminum mat be washed in distilled water and the aluminum oxide film on one surface of the aluminum layer 12 is removed leaving the other layer 14 of the aluminum exide. The resulting structure provides an aluminum oxide layer 14 of a thickness of about 1 micron and a suitable electrical conductive layer 12 of aluminum of a thickness of about .5 inch. The aluminum oxide layer 14 is then treated with a suitable dye to provide a black coating 23 for light absorption.

The other electrically conductive electrode 16 is provided by evaporating a coating of a suitable material such as stannic oxide to a thickness of about 0.1 micron onto a substantially transparent sheet of glass of a suitable material and of a thickness of 0.125 inch. An annular spacer 20 of a suitable electrically insulating material such as polyethylene terephthalate is positioned on the aluminum oxide surface and the liquid crystalline material is deposited on the coating 23. Since this liquid crystalline material may be squeezed onto the surface from a container, applied by a dropper, painted or by other means applied onto the exposed surface of the layer 23. The other electrode 16 is then positioned over the liquid crystalline layer 10 and the structure may be sealed by a suitable sealing compound such as epoxy to mechanically secure the structure.

Electrode leads 22 and 24 connected respectively to the layer 16 and the layer 12 are connected to a voltage source 26. A suitable light source 25 such as a tungsten filament light source is provided to illuminate the liquid crystalline layer 10 through the substantially transparent layers 16 and 18 with white light. It should be noted that ambient lighting can provide this white light illumination or at least supplement.

Referring to Fig.2, on application of potential across the layer 10 by means of a voltage source 26 the light from the source 25 will be selectively scattered back from the layer 10 in accordance with the voltages applied. For example, as illustrated in Fig.3, with no voltage or a very small voltage from source 26 applied, light will be scattered from the liquid crystalline layer 10 to give a red color to an observer as illustrated by curve 30.

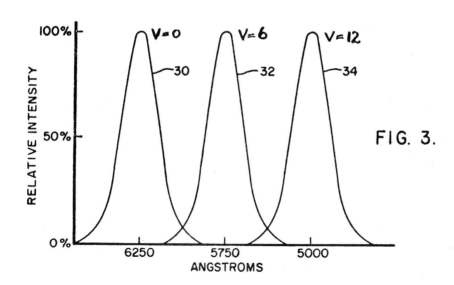

FIG. 3.

With a field of about 6 volts per micron applied across the layer 10 the light scattered from the liquid crystalline film 10 will be in the range as indicated by curve 32 so as to give off a green light. On application of a higher voltage of about 12 volts per micron light will be scattered from layer 10 so as to give a blue color and in the range indicated by curve 34. The bandwidth of scattering is about 200 angstroms. In Fig.4 there is a plot of the dominant wavelength of scattering with respect to the electric field for the device shown in Fig.2.

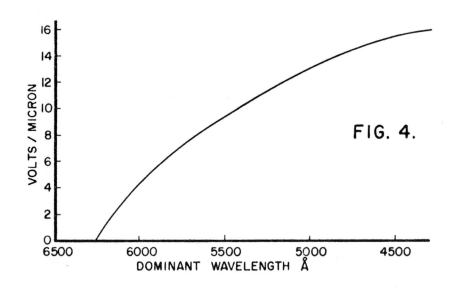

FIG. 4.

The molecular structure of the layer 10 is illustrated in Fig.5. The molecules are arranged in layers 31 substantially with the molecules within each layer oriented in aprallel alignment. The molecular layers 31 are very thin with the long axis of the molecules parallel to the plane of the layers. Because of the peculiar shape of the cholesteryl molecules, the direction of the long axis of the molecules in each layer 31 is displaced slightly from the corresponding direction in the adjacent layers. The overall displacement traces out a helical path as indicated by the line 33. In Fig.5, about every three hundredth layer is illustrated. The line 35 is the optical axis of the crystal. It is found that when selected liquid crystals are placed in an electric field parallel to the direction of alignment or optical axis, the wavelength of maximum scattering or colr will be shifted from long wavelengths to short wavelengths that is from red toward blue. The effect appears to be associated with substituted sterol molecules containing polar functional groups.

Another suitable mixture that may be used in Fig.2 is one consisting of 27% cholesteryl chloride and 73% cholesteryl oleate. In the absence of any electrical field and at room temperature 28° C.±15° C., this material is yellowish-green appearing at normal incidence of white light. When placed between the conducting electrodes 12 and 16, the color will change from yellow-green to blue as the electric field is increased. For example, with a smaple 20 microns thick, this change occurs between zero and 100 volts or the range of color occurs over zero to five volts per micron. This material has a resistivity in excess of 10^{12} ohms centimeters so that a charge may be placed across this material which will maintain a steady state field, the liquid crystal material behaving as a dielectric of a capacitor. The energy estimated to change the color a maximum amount is less than 10^{-6} joules per square centimeter for a 20 micron thick sample.

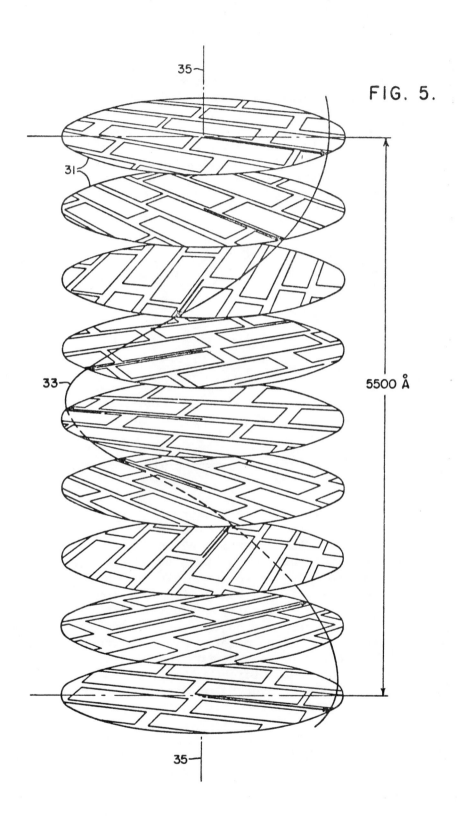

FIG. 5.

It is found that such a device as illustrated in Fig.2 is usable as a volt meter, having a very high impedance in excess of 500 megohms. It can also store charge for several seconds thus retaining its color once charged. By placing an a.c. field on the material, it was found that the liquid crystal could change its color at a rate in excess of 20 cycles per second indicating a response time as fast or faster than the human eye. Further, it has been shown that only fields in the direction of the liquid crystal axis are effective, thus making very high definition possible. That is, if two areas of charge are very close together only that part of the fields which are in the normal direction parallel to the optical axis will have an effect on the liquid crystal, thus improving resolution. It is estimated that the resolution of a 20 micron thick film would be in excess of a thousand lines per inch. The properties of this device make this material ideally suited to a number of high resolution and fast display systems. The material is ideally matched with an electron beam since both are of very high impedance.

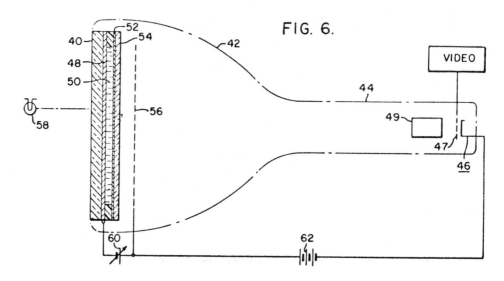

FIG. 6.

In Fig.6, there is illustrated a storage tube incorporating a liquid crystal display screen. The storage tube is of suitable design and consists of a face plate portion 40, a flared portion 42 and a neck portion 44. An electron gun 46 is provided within the neck portion 44 of the envelope. The electron gun 46 may be of suitable design for providing a pencil-like beam and is known in the art. The video signal may be applied to a control grid 47 of the electron gun 46. A coating 48 of electrically conductive light transmissive material such as stannic oxide is provided on the inner surface of the face plate 40. A layer 50 of liquid crystalline materials of a mixture such as described with respect to Figs.2, 3 and 4 is provided on the electrical conductive coating 48 and of a thickness of about 25 microns. Provided on the inner surface of the liquid crystal layer 50 is a layer 54 of dielectric material having a black coating 52 provided on the surface facing the liquid crystal layer 50. The dielectric may be of a suitable material such as glass or resinous material (for example polyethylene terephthalate). The thickness of the dielectric material layer 54 is about 6 microns. Provided between the screen structure and the electron gun 46 is an electrically conductive mesh 56, which forms the second electrode for the layer 50. A suitable light source 58 of white light is provided exterior of the envelope for illuminating the screen assembly including layer 50. A suitable voltage source 60 is provided between the conductive coating 48 and conductive mesh 56 and a voltage source 62 is connected between the conductive mesh 56 and the cathode of the electron gun 46. The potential of the source 60 may be about zero to 200 volts and the potential of the source 62 may be about 500 volts to 15 kilovolts.

During the operation of the device, an electron beam of several hundred volts is directed onto the surface of the dielectric layer 54 and generates a charge pattern at the surface corresponding to the video intelligence applied to the grid 47 of the electron gun 46. Suitable deflection means 49 are provided for scanning the electron beam over the screen. The charge pattern may be established by secondary emission and the surface will tend to approach the potential of the conductive mesh 56. If it is desired to write in a negative direction then the conductive mesh 56 would be operated at a sufficiently negative potential by control of voltage source 60 and the secondary electrons emitted from the dielectric surface will be returned thereto. The beam current in this case will determine the amount of charging. It is also possible to operate with the dielectric member at a more negative potential than the mesh 56 in which case the writing will be in a positive direction. In this case, the electron beam will cause the emission of secondary electrons which will be collected by the mesh 56. This tube will be able to hold a charge for long periods of time thus displaying the charge or electric field image established on the dielectric surface. The charge established on the dielecctric surface will establish an electric field across the liquid crystal layer 50 and vary the color of the scattered light from the source 58 in a similar manner as described with respect to Figs. 2, 3, and 4.

The charge image may be erased by changing the potential on the mesh 56 and flooding the target with electrons from the gun 46 or by a separate flood gun. This device will provide fast write time and long storage capability. The screen may be viewed in high ambient light conditions such as in an aircraft. Since the material has the property of scattering the light incident thereon, the brighter the ambient light the brighter the display will be on the display screen. It is, of course, obvious that any means of providing a charge image on the dielectric layer 54 will be successful in displaying a color image with the color dependent upon the magnitude of electric field. A plurality of horizontal and vertical conductors with associated switches could be used in a well known manner. It is also possible to provide a single color on black background by using a monochromatic light source. Several colors could be presented by providing a plurality of monochromatic light sources of different colors. A white source with selective filters could also be utilized.

Because of the extremely low power needed to activate the liquid crystal material, several other devices not related to electron beam writing can be adapted to use liquid crystals. The material exhibits the ability to respond in the same manner independent of the polarity of the field. In Fig. 7, a radiation image converter is illustrated. The radiation sensing device illustrated in Fig.7 consists of a glass support member 70 having an electrical conductive coating 72 of a suitable material such as stannic oxide thereon. The layers 70 and 72 are of a material transmissive to the radiation input. A layer 74 of a suitable photoconductive material sensitive to input radiations such as cadmium sulfide in the case of visible light is deposited on the conductive coating 72. A layer 76 of a suitable liquid crystal material exhibiting field effects and of similar material as used in layer 10 of Fig.2, is deposited and the photoconductive layer 74. An electrical conductive coating 78 of a material such as stannic oxide is provided on the liquid crystal layer

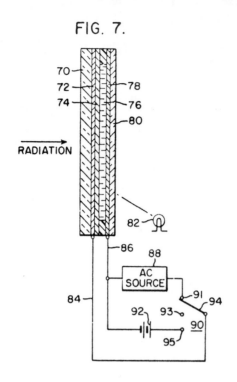

FIG. 7.

RADIATION

AC SOURCE

76 and a support member 80 of a suitable
material such as glass is provided on th[e]
conductive coating 78. The layers 78 an[d]
80 are transmissive to light radiations
from a source 82 which may provide illu-
minations of white light. It is general[ly]
desirable to utilize materials in layers
78 and 80 that are transmissive to the
ambient lighting to obtain the benefit
of this illumination also. Lead-in mem-
bers 84 and 86 are connected respectivel[y]
to layers 72 and 78 for providing the
necessary potential across the liquid
crystal layer 76 and the photoconductive
layer 74. The lead 86 is connected to
the first termainal of an alternating
current source 88 connected to a fixed
contact 91 of a switch 90.

A d.c. potential source 92 is connected from the first terminal of the
source 88 to a fixed contact 95 in the
switch 90. The lead 84 is connected
to the movable member 94 on the switch
90 and may engage contacts 91, 93 or 95.
In the specific embodiment shown, the contact 93 is left open.

In the operation of the device, the movable member 94 of switch 9o is connected to contact 91 and the radiation input such as visible light is directed
onto the radiation detector. The photoconductive layer 74 will become conductive and form a conductivity image corresponding to the radiation image and,
therefore, more voltage from source 88 will be applied across the liquid crystal layer 76. In this embodiment, the photoconductive layer 74 serves simply
as a capacitance voltage divider. When the light is directed onto the phot-
conductive layer 74 more voltage is applied across the liquid crystal layer 76
and the optical properties of the liquid crystal will be modified in accordance
with the voltage.

Here again, as previously described with respect to Figs. 2, 3 and 4, the
light source 82 may be white light. One could obtain a blue or green image
on a background of red with materials used in layer 76. By proper selection
of materials, one could obtain various color displays. By use of monochromatic
light for the source 82, one would be able to provide a black background for
color images. Since the source 88 provides an alternating voltage across the
layer 76 there will be no permanent charging. In the case where the contact 95
is connected to the movable member 94 of switch 90, a direct current field will
be placed across the layers 74 and 76. When the input signal is directed onto
the photoconductive layer 74 the structure will become conductive and a charge
image will be established across the liquid crystal 76 and will be maintained
thereon until removed by application of the source 88.

The optical effect utilized in the devices in Figs. 2, 6 and 7 is the light
scattering property of liquid crystal materials of the cholesteric phase. It
is also possible to utilize the transmission properties of the liquid crystals.

70

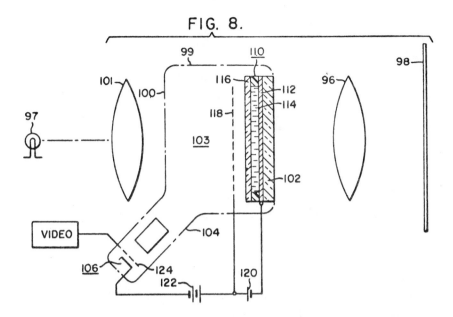

FIG. 8.

In Fig.8, there is illustrated a projection system utilizing liquid crystalline materials. The liquid crystalline materials of the cholesteric phase exhibiting the field effect are largely temperature insensitive and do not absorb light. High light intensities may be controlled by an electron beam by the system shown in Fig.8. In Fig.8, there is illustrated a light source 97, a lens system 101, a control tube 103 and a lens system 96 for focusing the light into a viewing screen 98. The control tube 103 includes a body portion 99 with an input window 100 and output window 102. A neck portion 104 extends from the body portion 99. The input window 100 is transmissive to the radiations from light source 97 and the output window 102 is transmissive to radiation transmitted through the tube. An electron gun 106 is provided within the neck portion 104 with means for directing and scanning a raster over a light control structure 110. The light control structure 110 consists of an electrically conductive electrode 112 provided on the inner surface of the face plate 102 and transmissive to radiation passing through the output window 102. A suitable material for the layer 112 is stannic oxide. A liquid crystal layer 114 is provided on the conductive layer 112 and a radiation transmissive dielectric layer 116 is provided on the surface of the liquid crystal layer or coating 114. Here again the materials in layer 114 may be the same as those described with respect to Figs.2, 3 and 4. The layer 116 may be of a suitable material such as glass. The control structure 110 is similar to the screen structure shown in Fig.6 with the omission of the black coating 52. A control grid 118 is positioned in front of the dielectric layer 116. A voltage source 120 is connected between the conductive coating 112 and the control grid 118. A voltage source 122 is also connected between the cathode of the electron gun 106 and the control screen 118. This tube operates in a similar manner to that described with respect to Fig.6 as far as the electrostatic charge written onto the dielectric coating 116 and the establishment of a field across the liquid crystal layer 114. The video intelligence is applied to the control grid 124 of the electron gun 106. Suitable deflection means, not shown, are utilized for the deflecting of electron beam over the dieledctric surface. The light source 97 is monochromatic such as red

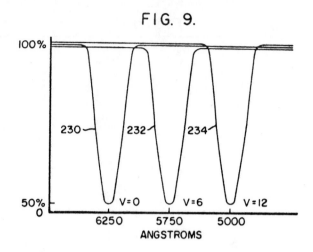

FIG. 9.

of about 6250 angstroms.

The materials in the liquid crystalline layer 114 may be the same as in Fig.2. The transmission characteristics of the layer 114 with different voltages applied are illustrated in Fig.9. These curves 230, 232 and 234 are substantially the reverse of those of Fig.3. By varying the voltage across the liquid crystalline layer 114, the amount of red light from the source 97 passing through the layer 114 and through the output window 102 can be controlled. As can be seen from Fig.9, with no voltage applied the light from source 97 would be substantially scattered and only 50% of light would be transmitted through. As the voltage across the layer 114 is increased the layer would allow more transmission of the red light. If the light source 97 is circularly polarized then 100% of the light would be reflected at 6250 A.

It is also obvious that other monochromatic light sources could be utilized such as green and blue to taje advantage of the nontransmissive portions of curves 232 and 234 of the layer 114 in these regions. It is, therefore, possible to provide a multicolor projection television system in which a separate system, as illustrated in Fig. 8, would be provided for the red, green and blue colors. In a specific example shown in Fig. 8, a red color is obtained By providing a second system with a blue light source and a third system with a green light source, a three color projection system would be available. The three separate color images projected through the liquid crystal layers could then be combined by well known optical means to superimpose the three images. Representative video signals of the representative three colors would be provided to the separate control tubes for each color. The images could be projected simultaneously or sequentially onto the screen.

It is also possible to use the selective optical rotational properties of the liquid crystals. This can be accomplished simply by providing a polarizer between the source 97 and the control tube 103 and an analyzer between the control tube 103 and the screen 98.

In Fig. 10, there is illustrated another arrangement for displaying a multicolor image by using the light scattering properties of the liquid crystals. This device or arrangement consists of a flying spot scanner which is comprised of a substantially conventional type cathode ray tube 130. The tube 130 includes an electron gun 134 and a phosphor screen 132 of a suitable material which in this case may be of a type which emits ultraviolet light in

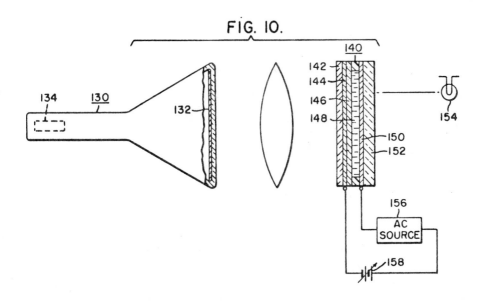

FIG. 10.

response to electron bombardment. Suitable deflection and scanning circuitry
well known in the art may be utilized to scan a raster on the screen 132. The
light generated by the acthode ray tube 130 is projected through a suitable
lens system onto a liquid crystal control structure 140. The liquid crystal
control structure 140 consists of a layer 142 of glass transmissive to the light
from the cathode ray tube 130, a layer of electrically conductive material 144
also transmissive to radiations from the cathode ray tube 130, a layer 146
deposited on the conductive layer 144 of a suitable photoconductive material
which exhibits the property of conduction in response to ultraviolet light
excitation. A suitable material for the layer 146 is selenium. A liquid
crystalline mayer 148 is provided on the photoconductive layer 146 and may
be of a suitable liquid crystalline material as described with respect to Fig. 2
and which exhibits the properties as represented by Figs. 3 and 4. On the
opposite side of the layer 148, a layer 150 of electrically conductive material
is provided transmissive to light directed onto the layer 148 from a source 154.
The layer 150 may be of a suitable material such as stannic oxide. A glass
support member 152 is provided on the exposed surfaces of the conductive layer
150. The light source 154 is provided for illuminating the liquid crystal layer
148 through the transmissive layers 150 and 152. The light source 154 should
be of the type that emits white light. An alternating current source 156 is
connected across the two conductive layers 144 and 150. A direct current
potential source 158 is also provided in series with the source 156.

In the operation of the device, the cathode ray tube 130 would project a
blank raster through the layers 142 and 144 and excite the photoconductive
layer 146 causing it to become conductive. This would, in turn, permit the
voltage from the source 156 to be applied primarily across the liquid crystal
layer 148 and by varying the amplitude of the source 156, the overall color
of the screen could be varied. Thus, using liquid crystal materials that follow
or respond at 90 cycles per second, three frames may be projected each lasting
a thirtieth of a second with a different color set by the level of the bias
provided by the direct current voltage source 158. This would provide in
effect a field sequential type color display. In the operation of the device,

the light from the cathode ray tube 130 would cause the photoconductive layer 146 to become conductive. The application of a suitable d.c. potential from the voltage source 158 across the liquid crystal layer 148 would cause the layer 148 to scatter red, green or blue and the particular color selected would be modulated with video intelligence by the source 156 to modulate the intensit of the relative colors. For this particular application, it would ne advisable to utilize a light source 154 in which the source provides maximum intensities in three bands namely red, green and blue, each about 200 angstroms in width or by providing filters in with a white light source to provide a black background.

The arrangement could also be operated with a video intelligence applied across the two conductive layers 144 and 150 such that the video signal would include both a d.c. component to change the selective scattering of the liquid crystal layer 148 from red, green or blue and also provide an a.c. component which includes the necessary video intelligence for the color. In this manner, the color from the screen could be changed on a line-to-line basis or element-to-element if so desired. It is also possible to apply a suitable signal to the liquid crystal layer 148 to determine the proper color and utilize or apply video information to the cathode ray tube 130 to modulate the conductivity of the photoconductor in accordance with the intensity of the particular color at that instant.

While there has been shown and described what are at present considered to be the preferred embodiments of the invention, modifications thereto will readily occur to those skilled in the art. For example, a piezoelectric layer of a suitable material such as barium titanate may be used to generate the electric field necessary to activate the liquid crystal layer. In this manner, sound or other mechanical energy may be detected and converted to a visible pattern.

"""""""""""""""""""""""""

RADIATION SENSITIVE DISPLAY SYSTEM UTILIZING A CHOLESTERIC LIQUID CRYSTALLINE PHASE MATERIAL.

James L. Fergason, and Arthur E. Anderson, assignors to Westinghouse Electric Corporation. Application June 29, 1965. Also British Patent No. 1,118,227.

This invention relates to a radiation sensitive display device which includes a heat sensitive display screen of a liquid crystalline material of the cholesteric phase with a radiation sensitive screen incorporating heating elements in thermal contact with the heat sensitive display screen which the heating is due to current flow. The radiation sensitive screen responds to input radiations to cause a current flow which in turn provides heat for impressing a thermal image on the heat sensitive display screen.

Referring to Fig.1, a display system is illustrated. The display system consists of a cathode ray tube 10 for directing a radiation image onto a display screen 12. A suitable lens 11 may be provided for focussing the radiation image onto the screen 12. The other surface of the display screen 12 is illuminated by a viewing light source 14 and a viewer 16 may observe the visible pattern or image on the display screen 12. The cathode ray tube 10 is of any suitable design and includes an electron gun 20 and a luminescent screen 22 of suitable phosphor material which emits visible light in response to electron bombardment by the gun 20. A video signal is fed to the cathode ray tube 10 from a source 24 and may be connected to any suitable electrodes of the electron gun 20. Suitable deflection means, not shown, are provided for scanning of the electron beam generated by the gun 20 over the screen 22. The intensity of the electron beam is modulated by the video signal from the source 24. It may be desirable to utilize a long time persistent phosphor in the screen 22. A radiation image thus is generated on the face of the cathode ray tube 10 representative of the video information applied from the source 24 and this radiation image is directed onto the display screen 12.

The display screen assembly 12 is shown in detail in Fig.2 and is comprised of the following layers. The display screen assembly 12 is supported by a substrate layer 30 which is also the heat sink for the display screen assembly. Temperature control of the display screen 12 may be obtained by any suitable means such as directing air along one surface of the layer 30 by the air source 28. The support layer 30 is transparent to the input radiation

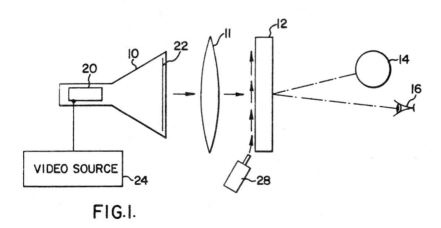

FIG.1.

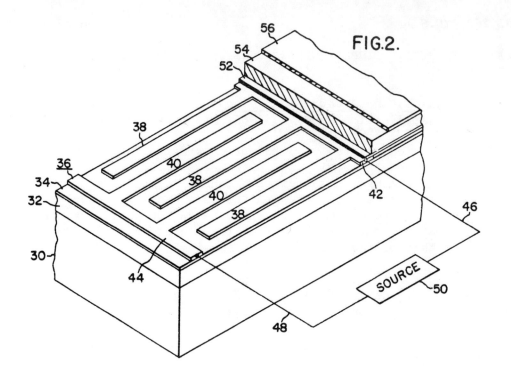

FIG.2.

from the cathode ray tube 10 and may be of a suitable material such as glass for visible radiation, barium chloride for infrared radiation or quartz for ultraviolet radiation. In the specific embodiment illustrating a visible radiation input, the thickness of the glass support layer 30 may be of a thickness of about 1 centimeter. The device may be used to convert X-Ray pattern to visible light pattern. A thermal barrier layer 32 of a suitable thermal insulating material such as polyethylene terephthalate is provided on one surface of the glass substrate 30. The layer 32 may be secured to the substrate by any suitable adhesive and may be of a thickness of about 25 microns. This material is suitable for both the visible and ultraviolet. In the case of infrared, a layer of polyethylene or polypropylene may be utilized. The thermal barrier layer 32 is to reduce thermal conduction from the sensitive screen portion of the heat sink layer 30. The thermal time constant of the layer 32 should provide a time constant for the sensitive screen layer adjacent thereto of about 1/30th of a second.

A layer 34 of photoconductive material is evaporated onto the layer 32 and may be of a thickness of 1 to 25 microns and of a suitable high impedance photoconductor having a resistance of about 10^{10} ohms-centimeters. Suitable materials for visible light are cadmium sulfide or arsenic triselenide. A suitable material for ultraviolet is selenium and a suitable material for infrared is lead sulfide.

A layer 36 consisting of a plurality of electrically conductive strips 38 and 40 is provided on the layer 34. The conductive strips 38 are connected to a common bus bar 42 and the strips 40 are connected to a common bus bar 44. Suitable leads 46 and 48 are connected respectively to the conductive bus bars 42 and 44 for providing a voltage between the conductive elements 38 and 40. This potential is supplied by a potential source 50 connected across the lead-ins 46 and 48. The potential source 50 may be an AC or DC potential and may be of the order of about 50 volts. In the specific embodiment shown, the electrode strips 38 and 40 may be evaporated onto the photoconductive layer 34 by well known techniques such as evaporating through a mask to provide strips of thickness of about 100 angstroms. The width of strips 38 and 40 may be about 50 microns and with a spacing between strips of about 200 microns.

An optical isolation layer 52 is provided on the conductive layer 36. The optical isolation layer 52 prevents radiations from the light source 14 affecting the photoconductive layer 34. The optical isolation layer 52 may be provided by spraying a coating of a water soluble black aniline dye of a thickness of about 1 micron.

Positioned on the optical isolation layer 52 is a liquid crystalline layer 54 of cholesteric material and responses to heat by changes in the light reflective properties thereof. Several suitable materials are disclosed in U.S. Patent 3,114,836 by Fergason et al and a specific material for this specific application may be 60% by weight of cholesteryl nonanoate, 30% by weight oleyl cholesteryl carbonate and 10% by weight of cholesteryl benzoate. A protective film 56 may be provided upon the surface of the layer 54 of liquid crystalline material of a suitable material such as polyethylene terephthalate and of a thickness of about 6 microns. It should be noted that the radiation assembly 12 may function as a simple detector simply by providing the photoconductive layer 34, the electrode layer 36 and the liquid crystalline layer 54.

In the operation of the device, the cholesteric liquid crystal film 54 and the photoconductive layer 34 are held at a constant operating temperature by the heat sink 30 and the associated temperature control system 28, in the absence of a projected light image from the cathode ray 10 onto the display assembly 11. The temperature of the liquid crystal layer 54 may be about 32° C. so as to provide a background color of black to the viewer 16. With the white light source directed onto the liquid crystal layer 54 at the temperature of 32° C. the viewer will simply see a uniform black background due to light reflected from coating 52. When a light image is focused onto the photoconductive layer 34 by means by means of the cathode ray tube 10 and with the potential source 50 connected across the conductive electrodes 38 and 40, current carriers are introduced into the illuminated areas. The amount of illumination directed onto the photoconductive layer 34 determines the amount of current flowing in the illuminated areas of photoconductive material positioned between the electrode strips 38 and 40. The video source 24 can control the intensity of the electron beam striking the phosphor 22 and accordingly the amount of current and heating by the photoconductive layer 34. Power dissipation from the resulting photocurrent is localized to only the illuminated areas by the electrode structure design, which limits the length of the current path to a fraction of the smallest resolvable image distance and the high resistance of the photoconductive layer 34 that is not illuminated. The thermal insulator 32 between the heat sink 30 and the photoconductive layer 34 permits a temperature rise in the illuminated area of a photoconductive layer 34 and the closely coupled liquid crystal film 54. The amount of illumination determines the amount of current flow and heat generated. Due to this temperature rise, the reflection band of the liquid crystal film 54 in those areas is shifted toward a shorter wavelength part of the spectrum. This is illustrated in Fig.5 and for example if the teperature is raised to 33.5° C. the reflected color will be red. At 34.1° C. the color will be yellow, at 35.5° C. the color will be green, at 37° C. the color will be blue and at 40° C. the color will be in the ultraviolet region and appear black to the observer.

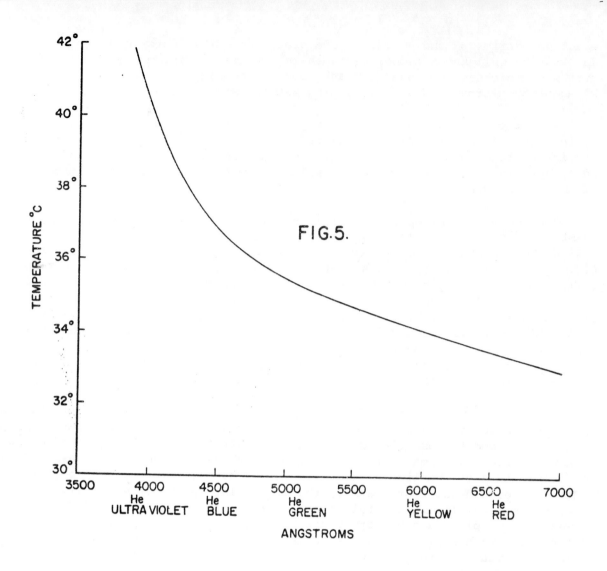

FIG.5.

The optical isolation layer 52 between the photoconductive layer 34 and the liquid crystal film 54 permits heat transfer between the two. The layer 52 blocks light from the light source 14 used for illuminating of the viewing side of the panel from effecting the photoconductive layer 34. This isolation layer 52 also serves as a black background for the liquid crystal film 54.

As indicated if the liquid crystal display is illuminated with white light from source 14, the liquid crystal film 54 provides a color display of the temperature pattern or image. Such a display is inherently compatible with high ambient illumination because reflective light, which is proportional to the incident light rather than internal generative light, produces the image. In this manner a large amplification of the input signal from the cathode ray tube 10 may be obtained so as to obtain an amplification greater than 100. If the display is illuminated with a monochromatic light from the source 14 rather than white light, a single color display with gray scale capabilities results.

The temperature rise required to activate the liquid crystal is created when light impinges on the photoconductive layer 34, resulting in photocurrent. The photocurrent is generated by applying a voltage from source 50 across the

78

interlaced comb-like electrodes consisting of alternate conductors 38 and 40. The conductive electrode system 38 and 40 consists of parallel conductors whose width is a fraction of a spacing to obtain maximum active surface area and whose spacing is determined by the desired display panel resolution. The length of the photoconductive current path, which is equal to the electrode spacing, must be a fraction of the smallest resolvable distance on the display.

The liquid crystal film 54 may be of various materials and is selected for the required sensitivity and the operating temperature range. The operating temperature may be chosed arbitrarily within the limits compatible with the temperature control method. The sensitivity of the film is determined by the application of the display. A liquid crystal film with high temperature sensitivity will result in a display with high overall sensitivity, but will also require a much better temperature control system and layer uniformity to eliminate color variations in the reflected light image due to small temperature variations over the surface and to sensitivity and normal resistance variations in the various layers.

The protective film 56 is provided on the liquid crystal to reduce contamination of the liquid crystal film by dust and chemicals in the atmosphere. It also minimizes temperature variations due to air flow in front of the image intensifier panel 12. If chosen properly, the film material provides additional enhancement for the molecular alignement in the liquid crystal film and does not contribute significantly to lateral heat spread. The chemical composition of the film 56 and the optical isolation layer 52 must prevent contaminating substances from being released into the liquid crystals, whose optical properties are very sensitive to the presence of various chemical substances as well as temperature variations.

In Fig.3 a modified photoconductive and electrode system is illustrated. In this embodiment, two conductive bus bars 60 and 62 are provided and parallel strips 64 of photoconductive material are evaporated across the space so as to be in electrical contact with both of the conductive bus bars 60 and 62. The photoconductive strips 64 may be provided with conductive elements 66 interspersed in the photoconductive strips to limit the range of carriers to provide high resolution.

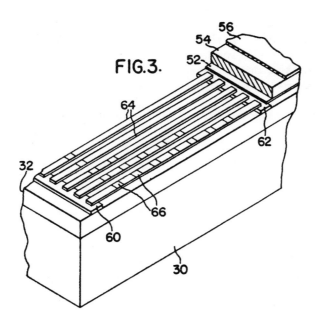

FIG.3.

In this type of configuration a lower impedance photoconductive material may be utilized, that is one having a dark resistance, of less than 10^3 ohms-centimeters and such materials as lead sulfide, lead telluride and indium antimony. Here again, the conductive bus bars 60 and 62 may be evaporated onto the thermal insulating layer 32 and the photoconductive elements 64 evaporated onto the substrate 32 by well known procedures in which evaporation is provided through a mask. The source 50 would be connected to the bus bars 60 and 62. The remainder of the device is similar to that already described and the operation is also similar and will not be described again.

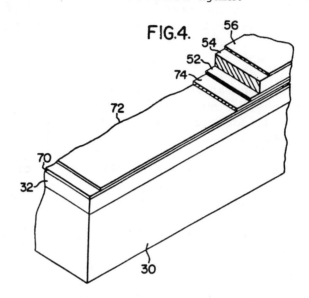

FIG.4.

Fig.4 illustrates another possible modification of the photoconductive and electrode system in which a large area of electrically conductive layer 70 is deposited on the thermal barrier 32. A layer 72 of photoconductive material 70 is deposited on the layer 70 and another electrically conductive layer 74 is provided on the photoconductive layer 72. The optical isolation layer 52 would be provided on the conductive layer 74. Here again, the operation is similar to that previously described. The layer 70 should be transmissive to the input radiations and may be of a material such as stannic oxide. The source 50 would be connected to the electrodes 70 and 74. If desired, the photosensitive element may be used to control the current through a resistive heating element in contact with the heat sensitive screen. It is also possible to convert sound energy into visible energy by detecting the sound on an element whose resistance is modified and therefore permitting control of current and associated through the detecting element per se or an associated resistive heating element in thermal contact with the heat sensitive screen.

"""""""""""""""""""""""""

3,409,404 (U.S.)   *Patented Nov. 5, 1968*

ANALYTICAL METHODS AND DEVICES EMPLOYING CHOLESTERIC LIQUID
CRYSTALLINE MATERIALS.

<u>*James L. Fergason*</u>*, assignor to Westinghouse Electric Corporation.*
Application Nov. 13, 1963. Equivalent of 1,041,490 (British), Sep. 7, 1966.

It has been discovered, and it is on this discovery that the present
invention is in large part predicated, that gases, liquids and solids can
affect the structure of cholesteric liquid crystals so that one or more optical properties thereof is at least temporarily changed. It has further been
discovered that, upon providing a comparable basis, the resultant change is
specific for the unknown involved which is thereby determined. By utilizing
these general principles an utterly new mode of analysis is provided.

The optical property most readily utilized in the practice of this invention is that of selective scattering since it requires no polarizers, or
analyzers for observation. Each cholesteric liquid crystal, at a given temperature and composition, exhibits, when exposed to white light, a scattering
peak. In accordance with this invention, the shift in the scattering peak may
be utilized for the analysis if unknown materials since the direction of the
shift is a qualitative indication of the unknown and the extent of the shift
is an indication of the quantity of the unknown. However, it is also possible
to utilize changes in other optical properties of the liquid crystals.

For example, it has also been found that the circular dichroism and optical rotation of cholesteric materials are similarly affected by foreign matter.
The component of circularly polarized light that is affected by the choles---
teric material has a waveband of minimum transmission. This waveband shifts
in the same direction and to the same extent as the scattering peak.
Similarly, the waveband of peak optical rotation exhibits such a shift. Since
cholesteric liquid crystalline materials have negligible optical absorption,
the transmitted radiation may be utilized for the purposes of this invention
as well as the scattered radiation.

In general, a material that is at least partially intersoluble with the
cholesteric liquid crystalline material will affect the optical properties of
the liquid crystal in a reversible manner. Also it is the case that a material that chemically reacts with the cholesteric liquid crystalline material
will affect its optical properties in an irreversible manner. In instances
in which the effect is reversible, the liquid crystal provides an optical
indication of the nature and quantity of the foreign material present at that
instant. Because of the reversible nature of the effect, the liquid crystal
may be continually reused. In instances in which the effect is irreversible,
the liquid crystal provides an optical indication of the same type that is
cumulative. Hence, each type of effect has advantageous applications and the
present invention is concerned with both reversible and irreversible effects.

Referring now to the drawing, numeral 10 indicates a support or substrate
member upon which a cholesteric liquid crystal can be deposited and supported.
Generally, the criterion for the use of any material as a substrate is only
that it not interfere, as by reacting with the crystal that is to be deposited thereon or masking the optical properties of the crystal. Typical materials that have been used include halogenated hydrocarbon resins such as poly-

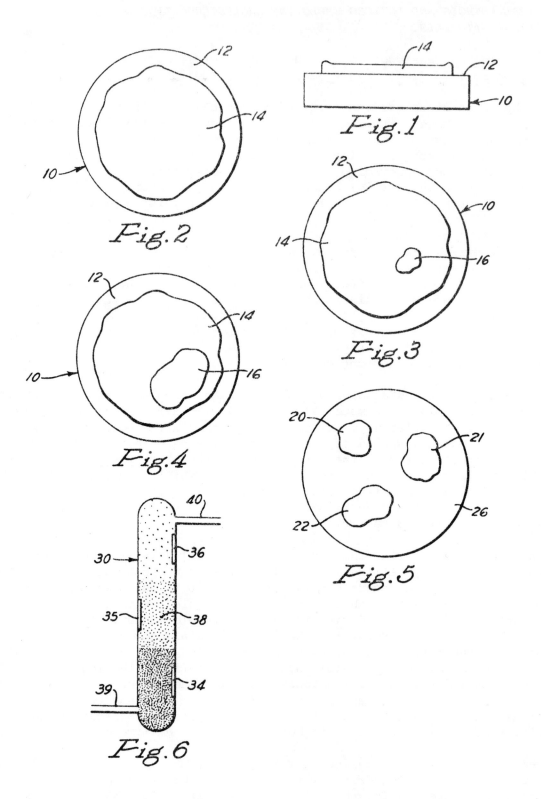

Fig.1

Fig.2

Fig.3

Fig.4

Fig.5

Fig.6

tetrafluoroethylene, polyethylene terephthalate and the like, glass, methyl methacrylate resins, ceramics generally, etc. The substrate 10 may be any thickness desired. In instances where transparent substrates are used, it may be useful to limit the thickness so that the substrate does not contribute unnecessary scattering of light that may be employed. On the upper surface 12 of the substrate 10 is shown a cholesteric liquid crystal 14. As is evident from the wide number of materials that have a cholesteric liquid crystalline phase and therefore can be used in the invention, it will be evident that a wide variety of ways of applying the liquid crystal to the substrate is possible. For example, the crystal can be cast thereon, "buttered thereon," applied from a dropper, painted, sprayed or otherwise applied. A quite common method of application is to pour a solution containing the liquid crystal thereon and allow the solvent to evaporate.

When the crystal is deposited from a solvent as just indicated, an irregular shape normally occurs and such is shown in the top view thereof in Fig.2. In Fig.2, the irregular shape 14 is the cholesteric liquid crystal and the circular shape 12 is the surface of the substrate 10.

Optical properties, such as color, of a liquid crystal change when a vapor is allowed to permeate the crystal. In Fig.3, there is shown a small irregular shape 16 within the irregular shape 14 which constitutes the liquid crystal supported on the surface 12 of the substrate 10. The irregular shape 16 constitutes a color area brought about by permeation by a vapor into the cholesteric liquid crystal 14. As more of that vapor is added, the irregular shape 16 expands correspondingly as is shown at 16 in Fig.4.

Since each liquid crystal is distinct and its reaction or response to an unknown is distinct, an array of liquid crystals can be devised to give an immediate determination of the unknown. Such an array is shown in Fig. 5. Thus three distinct liquid crystals 20, 21, and 22 are supported on a substrate 26. The liquid crystals being of known characteristics and known response to a given vapor, can be simultaneously exposed to an unknown vapor. Observation of all crystals will, upon comparison with standard information, indicate through optical change the identification of the unknown. Of course, such an array need not be limited to three cholesteric liquid crystals, but any larger or smaller number of crystals can be used as well.

As indicative of the results that can be achieved in accordance with the present invention, the following demonstration was made... All percents given are by weight. Ten liquid crystalline compositions were made, each consisting of a mixture of cholesteryl chloride and cholesteryl nonanoate. The amount of cholesteryl chloride in the compositions varied from 18% to 30%. Films, of substantially uniform thickness, of each composition were made by mixing the constituents in a solvent of 20% chloroform and 80% petroleum ether. The solutions were poured on polyethylene terephthalate film having a black coating on the opposite surface formed by spraying with a black acrylic lacquer available under the name "Krylon." The solvent was then permitted to evaporate. Each film was then axposed, at 27° C., to a group of common organic solvents including acetone, butyl acetate, benzene, chloroform, trichloroethylene, n-heptane and pyridine. The solvent concentration varied from about 1 part per thousand to about 50 parts per million. The concentration was sufficient to produce color changes readily apparent to the human eye. Where no color change was observed, the detecting element eventually became colorless due to a phase change. These solvents reversibly affected the film color

% Cholesteryl Chloride in Cholesteryl Nonanoate

Solvents	18%	19%	20%	21%	22%	23%	24%	25%	27%	30%
Acetone	red to blue	red to green	green to blue →→→→→→→ green to slightly red							red (no change)
Butyl Acetate	← red to blue →		← green to blue →					green (no change)	green to red	red (no change)
Benzene	← red to blue →		← green to blue →			green (no change)			green to red	red (no change)
Chloroform	← red to blue →				green to red					red (no change)
Trichloro-ethylene	← red to blue →		← green to blue →				green to red			red (no change)
N-Heptane	← red to blue →		← green to blue →		green to blue				red to blue	
Pyridine	← red to blue →		green to blue			green to red			red to blue	red (no change)

(i.e., the scattered waveband with the film exposed to white light) in the manner shown to the left...

The data in the Table illustrates that each solvent had a unique effect on the set of ten liquid crystals. Thus if an unknown solvent of the group described were exposed to the set of liquid crystals, it could be readily identified. For example, acetone is unique in producing a red to green shift in the 19% crystal; butyl acetate is unique in producing no change in the green color of the 25% crystal; benzene is unique in causing no change in the green color of the 23% or 24% crystals; chloroform is unique in producing a green to red shift in the 20% crystal; trichloroethylene is unique in producing different effects in the 21% crystal (green to blue) and the 22% crystal (green to red); n-heptane is unique in turning all of the liquid crystals blue; and pyridine is unique in producing a green to red shift in the 21% crystal that is readily distinguished from the slightly red appearance of that crystal when exposed to acetone.

Consequently, an array of the seven compositions having from 19% to 25% cholesteryl chloride in cholesteryl nonanoate permits the specific identification of the abovementioned seven solvents.

The foregoing demonstrates the feasibility of forming an array of cholesteric liquid crystals that have a unique pattern in response to any of the materials that alter the optical properties of the liquid crystals, thus providing a "fingerprint" of each of those materials.

Another application of this invention is in gas chromatography, to which reference can be made in conjunction with Fig. 6 There a vertically disposed transparent tube 30 can be adapted to have a plurality of liquid crystals of predetermined composition along its inside surface. In the embodiment shown three liquid crystals 34, 35 and 36 are used, though any other number could be employed. Within the tube 30 is a mass of gas absorbents 38. At its oower end, tube 30 is provided with a gas inlet 39 and a gas outlet 40 extends from the upper end of the tube. Upon passing a gas into the system, it is absorbed on the absorbent until the latter is saturated, at which time it passes onwardly. By appropriate placement of specified liquid crystals length-wise or vertically along the tube 30, the effective absorbency, or more correct-ly the failure to absorb possibly due to saturation, is promptly indicated be-cause the gas would pass by that portion of the absorbent, permeate the liquid crystal, for example liquid crystal 34, and thereby change its optical proper-ties which would be visible through the transparent tube, or could be measured. Similar action in due course will be evidenced by crystals 35 and 36 vertically disposed from crystal 34. Consequently, the liquid crystals can be used to indicate absorbent effectiveness, and visually show when regeneration or replace-ment should take place.

The cholesteric liquid crystals as such can be employed as the packing for a gas chromatograph column. This is possible for gases to permeate and diffuse through each crystal in a distinct manner. This property permits gas resolution; and the conditions at all times in the column would be directly observable be-cause of the light scattering effects accompanying the diffusion.

In another contemplated use for the present invention, a cholesteric liquid crystal would be disposed within a controlled atmosphere reaction zone. If the reaction to be carried out were, for example, to be accomplished in the absence of oxygen or air, a liquid crystal particularly sensitive thereto could be used. Upon observing changes, if any, in the liquid crystal an operator would immedi-ately know if his conditions of oxygen concentration were no longer tolerable. He could accordingly take appropriate action. Where this system is used in connection with a vacuum pump. a photocell can be focused on the crystal and be adapted to start the pump when the crystal indicated an undesirable oxygen concentration. For example, a mixture of 30% by weight of cholesteryl eleo-stereate, 20% by weight of cholesteryl nonanoate and 50% by weight cholesteryl oleyl carbonate, which is red at 24° C., would change to a blue color upon absorption of oxygen. A typical reaction in which such a system may be par-ticularly useful is that in which organo-metallic compounds, such as an alkyl lithium, are involved. Numerous similar applications are possible in view of the great number of controlled atmosphere reachtion and processes that are presently practiced.

Another example of the invention was: A liquid crystal was made from equal parts by weight of cholesteryl acetate and cholesteryl benzoate. At room temperature in ordinary light, a 10 micron thick film of this crystal was red. Benzene vapors changed it to blue. Chloroform vapors deepened its red color. Trichloroethylene caused a change to blue. The optical property most frequently used to observe change (and therefore the presence of an unknown) in the cholesteric liquid crystal has been color. Other optical properties are similarly affected, such as optical rotation, shift of circular dichroism, birefringence, and the like, and changes in those proper-ties can be used in the analysis system. Conventional optical instruments, recorders and the like, such as a photomultiplier, a photocell and so on can be used also to read out the detector in addition to direct visual observation. These may be indeed be necessary for remote operations.

Mixtures of compounds also can be used. For example, one such mixture was 45% of cholesteryl acetate and 55% of cholesteryl benzoate. It had a

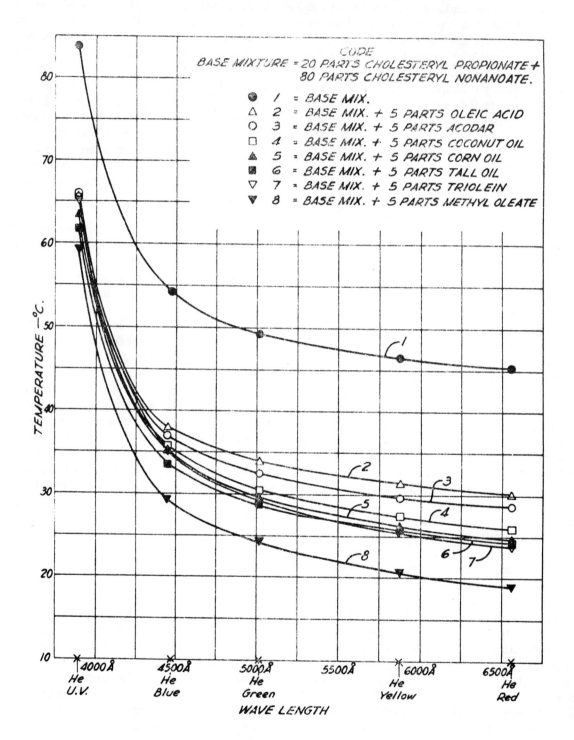

Fig. 7

deep red color at room temperature. The composition of this mixture was varied in five percent steps in both directions. It was found that the color was shifted further toward the red for either direction of composition change.

In Fig.7 there are plotted data obtained on a cholesteryl liquid crystal varied by the presence of a small amount of different commercial oils. The various liquid crystals were illuminated with a helium lamp. The color of maximum reflected intensity, corresponding to the strong spectral lines of helium, was observed at various temperatures and plotted for each system. The base cholesteric liquid crystal in all instances was, by weight, 20 parts of cholesteryl propionate and 80 parts of cholesteryl nonanoate. Data for the first (top) curve were obtained on that mixture free of oils. Then a crystal was formed by adding 5 parts by weight of oleic acid to the 20:80 mixture of the propionate and nonanoate, and pouring to a substrate in the usual manner. The third mixture was made by adding 5 parts of acodar (commercial oil with high percentage of free fatty acids) to the base mixture. Number 4 was 5 parts of coconut oil and 100 parts of the base. Similarly, 5 parts of corn oil, of tall oil, of triolen and of methyl oleate were used with base mixes to provide, respectively, the 5th through 8th liquid crystals. Temperature - wave length data were taken on each and plotted. It is to be noted that Fig.7 is substantially to scale, and direct reading can be made from it.

The curves of Fig.7 show many of the unique characteristics of the discovery. The substantial effect of temperature on any of the given crystals is plain. The unique effect of any of the additives in the same liquid crystal also is plain, and shows at once that these materials, which have some chemical similarity, can be detected and distinguished. For example, if any of these materials is known to be present in the base crystal mixture, temperature scanning to give a characteristic color will immediately show which it is. Or at constant temperature, the maximum reflection of helium light can be noted, thereby showing which additive is involved. Thus if maximum reflectance of the crystal is red at 26° C., the additive is cocnut oil, while if, at the same temperature, it is yellow, the curves show it to be corn oil.

Further, a constant temperature line can be projected across this graph and the sharply differing colors noted for several compositions. For example, the 26° C. line crosses the curves for mixtures 4, 5, 6, 7 and 8 and the colors indicated will range from red to blue.

The data in Fig. 7 can be replotted. Thus if the ratio of the slopes of any of the curves 2 through 8 to that of curve 1 be replotted versus the wave length, a curve characteristic of the effect of the additive in the particular liquid crystal (the base mixture) is found. Any other amount of that additive in this liquid crystal will give another curve of this type having the same general characteristics as this particular curve. Identification is possible through this, and by standardization procedures quantities can also be recognized. This same procedure of forming standard references can be accomplished with any other cholesteric liquid crystal and with any other series of chemically similar additives with similar results.

For analysis or detection system where continuous monitoring is undesirable or not possible, an irreversible detector may be more useful than those of reversible systems. In the irreversible system, interaction of the cholesteric liquid crystal and the unknown occurs bringing about a permanent change in optical properties because, in effect a new cholesteric liquid crystal results from the interaction. The effect on optical properties depends on the specific materials reacted and their concentrations. In this manner, cholesteryl nonanoate, or any cholesterol derivative, can be used to detect free halogens such as chlorine or bromine. Ozone, oxygen and the halogens can be detected and determined by cholesteryl allyl ether or cholesteryl eleostearate.

In any analysis procedure, standardization is practiced to insure reproducibility and that the results achieved can be appropriately interpreted. In this invention, substrates can affect the intensity of a color (dark substrates reflect better) and must be considered to that extent. Temperature in most instances has a striking effect (see Fig.7), and can bring about a color change or change in other optical property. This can occasionally be utilized to further refine the analysis system. Generally, however, this must merely be noted so that changes resulting will be attributed to the proper influence. A dipole field can affect the dipolar character of cholesterol derivatives. A shear stress applied to a cholesteric liquid crystal can change the optical characteristics. Radiation can affect the chemical constitution thereby providing a different cholesteric liquid crystal and, consquently, different optical properties. The angle of incidence and the character of light used can also be significant. For example, with polarized or unpolarized light, the scattering maximum (50%) is all circularly dichroic at normal incidence, but decreases as the angle of incidence increases. In any of the foregoing instances, no adverse effects will result in any analysis procedure if, for example, the test temperature is the same as that at which the standard was determined, or but a single angle of incidence is used and so on.

From the foregoing discussion, description and data it is evident that the present invention constitutes a unique and highly effective analysis discovery. Its sensitivity can be compared to that of the human nose in scope. Data have shown that with it, changes in concentration on the order of but a few parts per million can be detected, as well as chain characteristics, isomerism and other slight variations in chemical structure. It may be noted that quantities of material used are not critical, and are generally important only for quantitative analysis. In the practice of the invention it has been the usual practice to use about one to 50 parts by weight of the unknown per 100 parts of liquid crystal, though other weight ratios could be used as well. When it is considered that a determination can be readily made with very minor amounts of the cholesteric liquid crystal, the economy available with this invention becomes apparent.

" "

3,410,999 (U.S.)   *Patented Nov. 12, 1968*

DISPLAY SYSTEM UTILIZING A LIQUID CRYSTALLINE MATERIAL OF THE CHOLESTERIC PHASE.

James L. Fergason and *Arthur E. Anderson*, *assignors to Westinghouse Electric Corporation. Application June 29, 1965.*

A large area display screen is provided which includes a layer of liquid crystalline material of the cholesteric phase in which a temperature image is applied thereto according to electrical information by means of lossy elements provided in intimate contact with the liquid crystalline material. The lossy elements may be in the form of resistive elements of nonlinear characteristics.

Referring to Fig.1, a system is shown including a display screen assembly 10. The screen assembly 10 is provided with a heat sink 12 on one surface with an associated temperature control means 14. The temperature control means 14 consists of an enclosure on one surface of heat sink 12 with means for permitting flow of a liquid medium such as water over the surface of the heat sink 12. The temperature of the water may be controlled to the desired operating temperature. A thermoelectric temperature control system may be employed for controlling the operating temperature.

The display screen 10 is illuminated with a light source 16. The source may be of white light or monochromatic depending on the particular application. The display on the screen 10 may be observed by an observer 18.

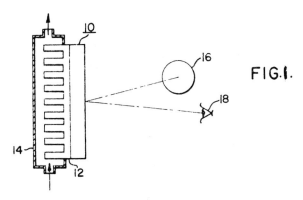

FIG.1.

The display screen structure 10 is shown in detail in Figs.2 and 3. The screen structure 10 included a support layer which is the heat sink 12. The heat sink 12 is comprised of a suitable material such as aluminum and having a thickness of about 2 cm. A thermal barrier layer 20 is provided on the support layer 12 and may be of a suitable material such as polyethylene terephthalate and known under the trade name Mylar. This film or layer 20 may be applied and secured to the support layer 12 by a suitable adhesive. The thickness of the layer 20 may be about 25 microns. The function of the thermal insulating layer 20 is to provide a thermal barrier layer to provide a time delay in thermal conduction from the heat sensitive screen to the heat sink 12 so as to provide a proper time constant for the screen structure. The material and thickness of the layer 20 may be varied to obtain a desired time delay.

A plurality of electrically conductive strips 22 shown as vertical columns are provided on the layer 20 and may be of a suitable electrically conductive material such as aluminum. The conductive strips 22 should be of

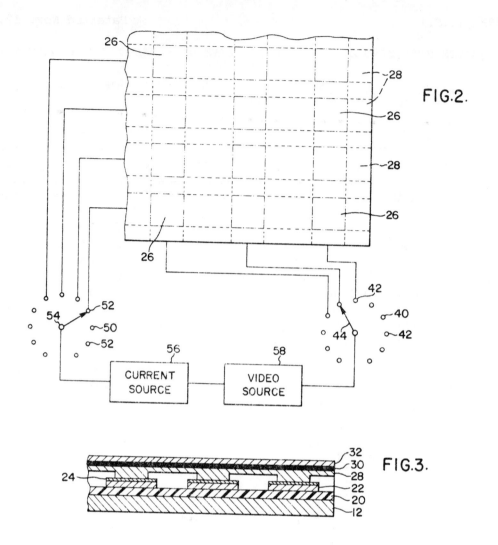

FIG.2.

FIG.3.

a thickness of about 100 angstroms and the width of about 400 microns. The spacing between the conductive strips 22 should be about 100 microns. Positioned on the conductive strips 22 is heating layer 24 of a suitable lossy material. In the specific embodiment a resistive material such as selenium, magnesium oxide or aluminum oxide is provided in the layer 24 and having a thickness of about 25 microns. The coating 24 may be evaporated and provided on the entire conductive 22, as a continuous layer or simply on active areas 26 of the screen as illustrated in Fig.2. Positioned on the exposed surface of the resistive layer 24 are electrically conductive strips 28 to provide a non-linear resistor within the active areas 26. The resulting structure consisting of the conductive electrodes 22 the resistive layer 24 and the conductive electrode 28 is to provide the matrix of non-linear resistive elements or active areas 26.

A coating 30 is provided on the conductive strips 22 as a continuous coating and may be of a suitable black paint such as India ink to provide a black surface. A layer 32 of a liquid crystalline material of cholesteric phase is provided on the black coating 30. A suitable material for the liquid crystalline layer 26 is a mixture including 60% by weight of cholesteryl nonanoate, 30% by weight of oleyl cholesteryl carbonate and 10% by weight of

90

cholesteryl benzoate. There are other suitable materials and mixtures that exhibit the change in reflecting properties in response to heat such as described in the U.S. Patent 3,114,836.

The conducting strips 22 are connected to a switching member 40 and as indicated each of the conducting strips 22 would be connected to a separate terminal 42 of the switching device 40 with rotor 44 provided for making contact to selected terminals 42. A similar switching system 50 is provided in which terminals 52 thereof are connected to the conducting strips 28 with a rotor 54 provided for connecting to any of the desired terminals 52 and associated strips 28. The rotors 44 and 54 are connected together through a suitable current source 56 and a video source 58. In this manner, the necessary current may be applied across a selected active area 26 to provide heating. The switching units 40 and 50 have been shown as simple mechanical switching arrangements for convenience of illustration and it is understood that any suitable scanning or selecting arrangement might be utilized. The scanning system for a display would normally require that it be capable of providing a standard television scan. It might be desirable to utilize a simple cathode ray tube with special fiber optics face plate to provide the desired control signals to actuate semiconductor devices or glow discharge switches associated with the conductive elements 22 and 28. Various other switching devices might be used to control the current flow through selected areas 28.

In the operation of the device shown in Figs.1, 2, and 3, the active elements 26 are heated by coincident technique. The ambient temperature of the display screen 10 is controlled by the control means 14. The ambient temperature of the liquid crystal layer 32 associated with the element 26 for this specific material will be at 32° C. Light directed onto the display screen 10 from the viewing light source 16 will cause the screen 10 to look black to the observer 18 due to the fact that the light is not reflected from the liquid crystal layer 32 but from the black coating 30. In order to display an image, heat must be applied to the elements 26. The heat may be applied a given middle resistive active element 26 and specifically the element 26 in the bottom row, the switch 50 would be connected to the terminal 52 as shown in Fig.2 and the switch 40 would be connected to the terminal 42 as shown in Fig.2. A current corresponding to the source 56 and the video source 58 would be applied across the element 26. The current flowing in the resistive layer 24 of the element 26 would cause heating in accordance with the amount of current. Since a resistance of the area 20 is non-linear, the ratio of power dissipated will be 100 or more. If the temperature of the elemental area 26 is raised to a temperature of 33.5° C. then a red color will be reflected by the screen 10, at a temperature of 34° C. a yellow color, at a temperature of 35.5° C. a green color, at a temperature of 37° C. a blue color and at a higher temperature the structure will again be black to the observer. By the amount of the current flow, the color may be controlled.

This property of the screen 10 is illustrated by the curve shown in Fig.5. In this manner, a color visual image can be displayed of contrasting colors or by controlling the temperature by current flow, the image may be made to appear in a single color on another color background. The above description is directed to the use of a light source 6 of white light. If a monochromatic light source is used then a single color can be obtained so as to obtain a brightness variation within a single color on black background.

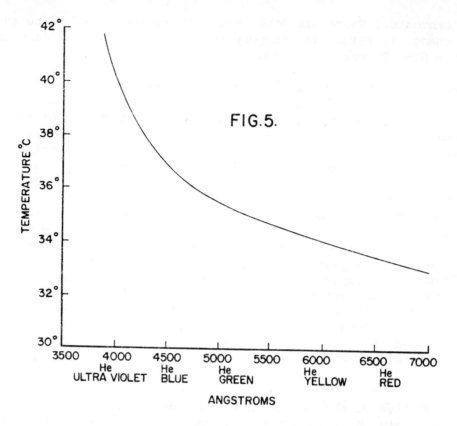

FIG.5.

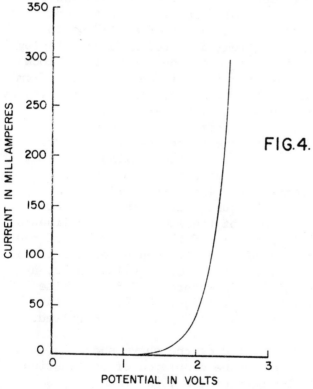

FIG.4.

A typical characteristic curve for the non-linear resistive element 24 is illustrated in Fig.4. By utilization of the non-linear device, one is able to insure that power will not be dissipated in adjacent elements but will be applied across the single element where substantial conduction is found due to the fact that a greater voltage is applied across the single element rather than the other elements. By providing the temperature barrier layer 20, one is able to control the amount of time that the heat image is applied to the liquid crystalline layer 32. Although the suggested scanning method does not provide for a storage type display, it is recognized that the propsed display screen is adaptable to other scanning structures which incorporates both storage and selective erase.

"""""""""""""""""""""""""""

VISUAL DISPLAY DEVICE.

D. Churchill, J.V. Cartmell and *R.E. Miller*, assignors to *The National Cash Register Company.*
Application May 22, 1967; prior U.S. application June 17, 1966.

This invention relates to temperature-sensitive visual display devices and, more specifically, relates to arrays of encapsulated liquid crystal material which iridesce whenever temperature changes occur on the arrays.

Up to this time, the utility of cholesteric mesomorphs in temperature-sensitive systems has been severely limited due to a number of reasons, the following points being some of the assigned faults:

(1) Such systems containing a mixture of one or more intermingled meso-morphic compounds as a film are subject to crystallization of large areas at the desired working temperatures. This undesirable crystallization tends to concentrate one of the active materials at each crystallization site to there-by separate it from the other components of such a mesomorphic mixture. This component separation results in (a) loss of precision and efficiency in color change at the desired temperature, and (b) anomalous color change activity at other temperatures;

(2) mesomorphic cholesterol derivatives are oily liquids at and above their melting temperatures. When they exist as a film on any surfaces, the film, being wet, is subject to injury of many types from ageing, and contact with the environment. Dust particles are easily entrapped by the liquid surface and can serve as undesirable nuclei for crystallization. Such films are exposed to the danger of contact with any material in the vicinity, with resultant disorganization of the mesomorph and possible change in thickness in localized areas, which would alter the response of the system; and

(3) the subject wet-film mesomorphic systems are prone to anomalous color change behavior upon the event of only slight contamination of the system by various solutes. This contamination can cause iridescence by itself at a given temperature not otherwise associated with the yield of color in the film generally, or it can produce large shifts in the color producing temper-ature, either higher or lower.

The present invention provides for the isolation and protection of these thermotropic liquids as droplets as the cores of minute transparent-walled capsules, and the distribution of those capsules in a film-layer onto a suitable substrate for use as a temperature sensing device.

Thus, according to the invention, there is provided a visual display device comprising a substrate coated with a mass of minute capsules each having a liquid nucleus including one or more materials capable of assuming a choles-teric mesophase in a predetermined temperature range, said nucleus being re-tained by a capsule wall material which transmits light incident on and reflected from the capsule contents.

By the term "minute" it is meant that the capsules range from 1 micron to 5000 microns in average dimension, being of such small size as to make the

93

individual manufacture thereof impossible or impracticable.

It should be understood that the capsule product of this invention can be attained by any suitable encapsulation technique which is capable of producing capsules of the required small dimensions. The final form of the capsular material to be coated is preferably ten-to-fifty-micron capsules, but it has been found that any size of capsules can be successfully utilized, the larger capsules only showing a decreased degree of visual resolution when used in a data display system. Encapsulated mesomorphic-compound film layers appear to be free of the, heretofore, limiting disadvantages associated with exposed continuous wet films of the materials. Layers cast from an aqueous slurry of the encapsulated material and dried are dry to the touch, are relatively un-affected by brushing contact with foreign bodies, are substantially immune to solute contamination, and are not subject to rapid deterioration by selective crystallization on contaminating foreign bodies; and, in cases where crystal-lization does begin, it is stopped from further areawise development by the boundary of a capsule wall.

The invention also provides for the distribution in such a film-layer of mixed capsules distinguished by their different content and performance which system of mixed capsules can serve the purpose of sensing temperature or displaying data at several temperature levels. Such a system, in one case, may consist of layers, each layer comprising one, two, or more types of cap-sules having different characteristics. These characteristics may involve:
  a) temperature response range;
  b) size of liquid core;
  c) type and thickness of capsule wall material;
  d) kind of mesomorphic materials,
and the like, all to the purpose of choosing an exact response suitable for the proposed use.

The wall of the mesomorph-containing capsules may be of colored material and such capsule walls serve also as color filters for light traveling to and from the mesomorphic materials. Capsule walls are easily tinted by the use of stains. Such a controlled system would find use in devices where the broad iridescent effect is objectionable.

The substrate 1 can be any suitable material, thick or thin, transparent or opaque, colored or not. Figs. 1a and 1b show a film-thickness of material as a substrate, but the use of a film material is optional. If it is more convenient or to the intended use, any firm body can be utilized to provide a surface for material. As an alternative method, the encapsulated, temperature-responsive materials can be utized as a liquid slurry, the color change phenom-enon remaining the same as with the dried film material. Fig. 1a is intended

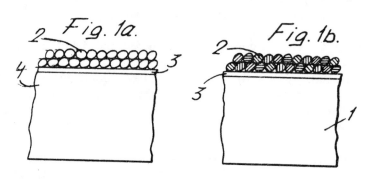

to represent the capsule coating at a temperature above or below that which is required for the color change effect of the mesomorphic material, while Fig. 1b is intended to represent the same capsule coating within the temperature range of the color change effect. The cross-hatching of the capsules in Fig.1b is used only to depict a color change and not to suggest particular colors. Capsules having an average diameter of 5 to 1,000 microns or perhaps slightly larger can be used for the coating; and one capsule layer or a number of super-imposed layers can be used, depending upon conditions and requirements of the intended coating application. Different areas of the same surface may contain different kinds of capsules. Figs. 1a and 1b show a colored layer 3 on the base 1, the use of which is optional.

Figures 2 and 3 illstrate the use of a display screen 4 comprising a coating of capsules containing but one system of cholesteric material, which has been coated onto a substrate of self-supporting material. An onfrared energy source 5 is directed at the display sheet and is controlled by a stencil 6. Infrared rays which pass the stencil 6 are absorbed on the display screen 4 and thereby raise the screen surface temperature in such a manner as to cause a color change having an outline similar in shape to the stencil cut-out. In Fig.3, the encapsulated material has been coated onto a display screen substrate 7 which has the same color and texture as the un-heated, encapsulated material. As infrared rays are directed from an energy source 8 in a beam, through the focusing lens system 9 provided, the capsules in the beam-image area are warmed, causing the characteristic iridescence and visual appearance of the image. Of course, it is understood that any appropriate source of energy can be used in the practice of this invention, heat lamps being shown in the figures only as a convenient means of depicting an energy source.

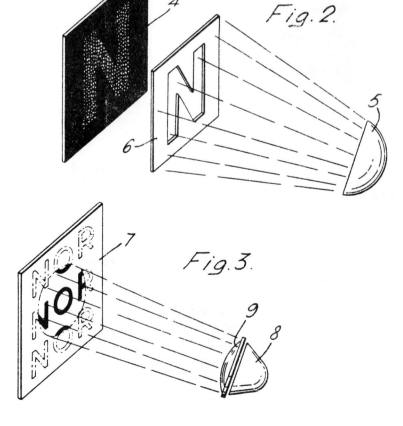

Fig.2.

Fig.3.

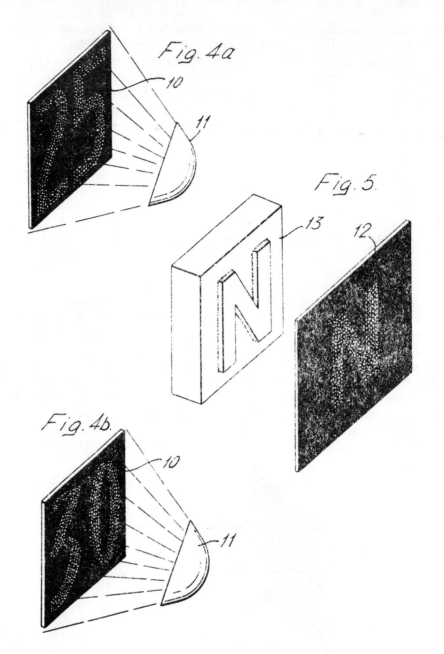

Figures 4a and 4b illustrate the practice of this invention as a direct-reading temperature display device 10 employing more than one responsive system. The device has, coated on its front surface, individually responsive layers of encapsulated mesomorphic materials, each layer being applied in the outline of the numerals which represent the temperature at which the layer undergoes a color change. In Fig. 4a, the surface has absorbed infrared radiation emitted from source 11 of an amount required to bring the temperature of the capsules up to about 25 degrees, the temperature at which color change occurs in the (first) outline layer of the numerals "2" and "5". The result of this heat absorption is a visual indication of the surface temperature. In Fig. 4b, more radiation has been absorbed, and the temperature has been raised above the coloration temperature of the first kind of encapsulated material and up to the coloration temperature of a second kind of material in another layer represented by "3" and "0". The result, as shown, is disappearance of the numerals "25" and subsequent appaearance of the numerals "30" - a direct temperature indication created by the selection and preparation of different areas with appropriate encapsulated mesomorphic materials.

Figure 5 illustrates a further aspect of this invention in the use of encapsulated mesomorphic materials for data display. Capsules are coated onto a display sheet 12 and display characters are caused to appear by contact with or proximity to a warmed character, such as an embossed type 13. There can be prepared, by proper selection of mesomorphic systems, sensing devices and display devices which yield their visual color advent at temperature levels considerably above or below room temperature.

Example I.

1.25 grams of acid-extracted pigskin gelatin, having a Bloom strength of 285 to 305 grams and an isoelectric point of pH 8-9, and 1.25 grams of gum arabic, were stirred with 125 grams of distilled water at 55 degrees Centigrade in a Waring Blendor to yield a solution, which was about pH 4.5. When the solution was formed, the pH was adjusted to 6.0 by the drop-by-drop addition of 20% by weight, aqueous sodium hydroxide solution. To the above system was added a solution of 2 grams of cholesteryl propionate in 8 grams of cholesteryl oleate. The cholesterol derivative materials were emulsified in the Waring Blendor vessel to an average droplet size of 10 to 50 microns, and the pH of the system was slowly reduced by the dropwise addition of 14%, by weight, aqueous acetic acid solution. Addition of acid was continued until the single, liquid walled, capsules clustered to form aggregates having diameters of about 25 to 100 microns. At this final state, the system pH was about 5.

The entire liquid was then chilled with an ice bath to below 10 degrees Centigrade, while the agitation was continued. At 10 degrees Centigrade, 0.6 milliliter of a 25%, by weight, aqueous solution of pentanedial, a chemical hardening agent for the gelatin, was added to the Blendor vessel, and the system was stirred for about 12 hours while slowly returning to room temperature. At the end of that time, the capsule walls were firm and hardened, and the capsular system was poured through a wire mesh sieve having openings of 74 microns. That which passed the screen was suitable for coating the intended substrate. Capsules, along with the equilibrium liquid which passed through the sieve were coated, using a drawdown applicator, to a wet thickness of more than 2 but less than 10 mils onto a blackened, 5-mil-thick, polyethylene therephthalate film and then were dried in air at about 25 degrees Centigrade. If temperature was raised at a point on the coated layer, concentric rings representing a temperature gradient pattern appeared outwardly from a central ring of blue, thence spectrally in order through red, as the temperature gradient decreased. As the temperature of the point was increased or decreased, the effect was evidenced by expansion or contraction of the rings. The system of Example I. first exhibited the mesophase coloration transition at about 25 degrees Centigrade and continued to about 25 to 30 degrees Centigrade. Systems of adjacent expanding and contracting rings intersected, and the resultant color was a function of the temperature of a given area.

Example II.

The encapsulation process of this example is identical with that of Example I. except that a different mixture of cholesterol derivatives was employed. In this example, the cholesteric mesomorphic materials were 5 grams of cholesteryl propionate and 5 grams of cholesteryl nonanoate to be substituted for the cholesteryl propionate and cholesteryl oleate used in Example I. With regard to color change and transition temperatures, this system behaved much like the system of Example I., the proportions being selected with the end in view of making the behavior of the system aligned with ordinary living-environment temperatures, as was also the objective of Example I.

Example III.

In this example, two different cholesterol derivative mixtures were separately encapsulated by the method described in Example I., and the capsules were coated, as a mixture, onto a blackened substrate film. The cholesteric mesomorphic mixtures were (a) Oleyl cholesteryl carbonate and cholesteryl nonanoate in a one-to-one ratio, and (b) Oleyl cholesteryl carbonate and cholesteryl nonanoate in a one-to-three ratio, respectively. Maximum response to incident light (strong in 5500 A. components) was at 34.5 degrees Centigrade in one system (a) and at 48.8 degrees Centigrade in the other system (b).

The visual effect of such a coated mixture of capsules was much the same as that of the previous examples, except that the iridescence occurred in two sequences beginning at two different temperatures. In warming a test point on the coated layer, the first sequence of concentric rings of color appeared circling the point of heat application. When the spot on the coated layer was further heated above the first color producing temperature but below the color producing temperature of the second encapsulated material, the test point again appeared black with only a ring of color remaining, at the time, a fixed distance from the center of heat source, due to the static temperature gradient. Upon further heating of the test point on the coated layer, a second set of color rings began to appear and move outwardly, but never reached the first rings, giving rise to a visual indication of the temperature at two different locations on the coated substrate. So much for point application of heat. When the coated substrate film, as a whole, was heated, the film reflected changing colors, not in rings, but all over colors first appearing due to one encapsulated material and then, on further heating, due to the second encapsulated material, the film appearing black for a time at temperatures intermediate to the different color producing temperatures. The color changes appeared in reverse order on cooling the film. If capsules of differen cholesteric mesomorphic materials which have overlapping color-change temperature ranges are combined, then the reflected colors will be combined to alter the visual appearance, depending on the relation of the different responses and the resolution of the capsular system. As discussed previously, smaller capsules yield systems with higher resolution.

"""""""""""""""""""""""

MULTI-FREQUENCY LIGHT DEFLECTORS.

Kurt M. Kosanke, Werner W. Kulcke and Erhard Max, assignors to International Business Machines Corporation. Application Oct. 6, 1967; prior U.S. application Jan. 16, 1967.

The present invention relates to a method for separating a polychromatic light beam into two or more spaced output beams, each comprising one or more of the component light frequencies of the original polychromatic light beam. In accordance with the invention a multifrequency light deflector comprises beam forming means adapted to produce a beam of plane polarized light including a plurality of wavelengths, polarization control means for orienting the polarization plane of at least one of the wavelengths perpendicular to the polarization plane of the other wavelengths, and beam splitting means adapted to separate wavelengths having mutually perpendicular polarization planes into spatially separated light outputs... A polarization control apparatus which may be used is comprised of a series of electric field controlled liquid crystal cells.

... The device shown in Figure 5 enables a single light frequency to be changed in its polarization direction such that it will be perpendicular to the remaining light frequencies in a polychromatic light beam. The device consists of a transparent vile or cell 72 filled with a liquid crystal material 74. A first electrode pair 76 and 78 is secured to the cell and is connected to a source of high potential 88 by means of the switch 90. If a voltage is applied to a first electrode pair 76 and 78 by closure of the switch 80, as shown in Fig.5, the molecules of that liquid crystal material will align in the direction of the electric field, as shown by the arrow, which is perpendicular to the light direction. Giant molecules of elongated structure often exhibit birefringence if they form a microscopic structure known as liquid crystals. The optic axis of such liquid crystals coincides with the elongated axis of the molecules. Many kinds of such molecules have a considerable dipole moment which makes them align in an external electrical field. This property is made use of in the cell of Fig.5.

Therefore, the light that passes the liquid crystal of said orientation gets split in two components, the ordinary and the extraordinary ray which has polarization rotated 90° with respect to the ordinary ray. Both have the same direction, but different speed, thus getting out of phase. Upon recombination, this phase shift causes, in general, an elliptic polarization state. Due to the dispersion of the indices of refraction, the total phase difference in a cell of given length, depends on the light wavelengths. There can always be found a length of the cell whereby at least one wavelength is polarized perpendicular to all other wavelengths upon leaving the cell. If in Fig.5 the voltage is applied to the second pair of electrodes 84 and 86, instead of to the electrodes 76 and 78, the liquid crystal molecules will align parallel to the light beam. This is now the direction of the optics axis and therefore, no birefringence occurs. All light of whatever wavelength now passes without change of its polarization state.

The effect of putting several such cells in series leads to a binary selection rule for the polarization direction of the wavelength passing the device. To describe the result of the combined cells, the birefringent state

TABLE

The light wavelength λ_1 λ_2 λ_3 λ_4 enter Cell—1 all with the same linear polarization direction.

Cell—1	Cell—2	Cell—3	Result
$(\lambda_1 \perp \lambda_2 \lambda_3 \lambda_4)$	$(\lambda_2 \perp \lambda_1 \lambda_3 \lambda_4)$	$(\lambda_3 \perp \lambda_1 \lambda_2 \lambda_4)$	
0	0	0	$\lambda_1 \lambda_2 \lambda_3 \lambda_4$
1	0	0	$\lambda_1 \perp \lambda_2 \lambda_3 \lambda_4$
0	1	0	$\lambda_2 \perp \lambda_1 \lambda_3 \lambda_4$
0	0	1	$\lambda_3 \perp \lambda_1 \lambda_2 \lambda_4$
1	1	0	$\lambda_1 \lambda_2 \perp \lambda_3 \lambda_4$
0	1	1	$\lambda_2 \lambda_3 \perp \lambda_1 \lambda_4$
1	1	1	$\lambda_4 \perp \lambda_1 \lambda_2 \lambda_3$
1	0	1	$\lambda_1 \lambda_3 \perp \lambda_2 \lambda_4$

of a cell, that is when the molecular orientation in the cell (the arrow in the diagram) is in a direction perpendicular to the light beam, will be designated as "1" and the state at which it is nonbirefringent will be designated as "0". That way we can list the possible polarization combinations according to the cell states. This is done in the Table shown above.

As one sees from the Table the number of combinations of polarization directions which can be achieved by three of the described liquid crystal cells is eight. This is true for four light wavelengths, switched to two mutual perpendicular polarization directions. However, sixteen different combinations may be obtained by the addition to the system of three cells of an electro-optical switch 100, which is achromatic, to switch any polarization state to its perpendicular direction. Such a system is shown in Fig.6.

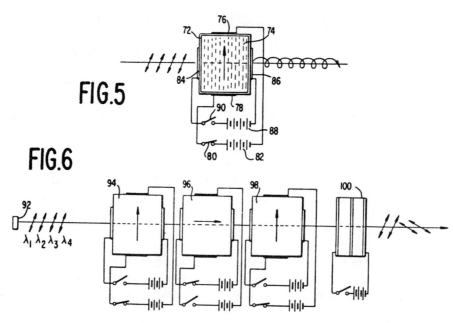

FIG.5

FIG.6

FIG.7

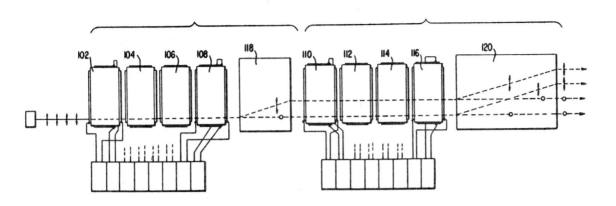

In a case where six light frequencies are to be controlled in the same way, one would need five cells similar to the cell shown in Fig.5, the functions of the cells being analogous to the former example. The number of combinations of wavelengths achieved by five cells is $2^5=32$. The use of an additional achromatic electro-optical switch increases the number of combinations to 64. In general n wavelengths require $n-1$ cells to perform the maximum number of 2^{n-1} different wavelength combinations in the two mutually perpendicular polarization direction.

The device shown in Fig.7 consists of electric field controlled liquid crystal cells in combination with beam splitting means which separate light beams according to their polarization direction. In the example shown by Fig.7 four light frequencies are used and the two stages of the device give four output beams.

The cells used for the polarization control 102, 104, 106, 108, 110, 112, 114 and 116 are each a cell as has been described above with reference to Fig.5. The combination of four cells is similar to the arrangement shown in Fig.6 but with the electro-optical switch 100 of Fig.6 being replaced by a fourth cell which would give to all wavelengths a phase shift of 90° if switched to state "1". Thus, if switched to "1" cell 102 makes the polarization direction of the light wavelength λ_1 perpendicular to all others, the cell 104 makes the polarization direction of the light wave λ_2 perpendicular to all others, cell 106 makes the polarization direction of the light wave λ_3 perpendicular to all others and cell 108 makes all wavelengths to change their polarization direction by 90°.

" "

1,148,724 (British)   Patented Apr. 16, 1969

LIQUID CRYSTAL OPTICAL DEVICE.

George H. Heilmeier, assignor to Radio Corporation of America.
Application April 18, 1966. Prior U.S. application April 26, 1965.

We have discovered that by controlling the molecular orientation of a nematic "host" material with a suitable means, e.g. an electric or a magnetic field, molecular ordering of any "guest" materials, capable of being molecularly dispersed within the nematic host may be controlled. When certain dyes for example are mixed with a nematic substance, their absorption spectra are influenced by the molecular ordering of the nematic substance and can be controlled. Moreover, small particles of a guest material tend to assume an ordered orientation similar to the nematic host. When an electric field is applied to the nematic host which includes a guest material the resulting orientation of the host molecules results in a corresponding ordering of the guest material. This effect enables a control of the optical properties of the guest material. If flake-like particles of aluminum, for example, are mixed with a nematic host the long dimensions of the flake-like particles tend to align themselves parallel to the molecular axes of the molecules of the nematic substance when the electric field is applied.

The absorption spectrum of a guest pleochroic dye mixed with a host nematic substance may be controlled with an applied field. The absorption spectrum of a pleochroic dye is a function of the direction of polarization, with respect to the molecular axes of the molecule, of the light incident upon it. Virtually all dyes exhibit pleochroism to some extent. However, the degree of pleochroism is greater in some dyes than in others. Dyes in which the pleochroic effect is pronounced are well known in the art. Two examples are methyl-red and indolphenol-blue. The color exhibited by a methyl-red guest mixed with a p-n butoxy bezoic acid host varies from orange to yellow depending upon the direction of polarization of the incident light with respect to the axes of the dye molecules. The color of indolphenol-blue in the same host varies between a very deep blue and a pale blue.

When a pleochroic dye is mixed with a nematic substance the orientation of the dye molecules may be controlled by controlling the orientation of the nematic host molecules. Thus the color exhibited by the dye in plane polarized light may be controlled.

The absorption spectra of many materials are functions of the local electric field in the vicinity of the molecules of such materials. Therefore, if the local electric field in the vicinity of the molecules is controlled the absorption spectrum may be controlled. We have found that a nematic substance under the influence of an external electric or magnetic field may be used to control the local fields in the vicinity of guest molecules mixed with the nematic substance. When a material whose absorption spectrum varies with local electric field is mixed with a nematic substance control of the orientation of the molecules of the host nematic substance results in a control in the electric field in the vicinity of the guest molecules and thus a control in the absorption spectrum of the material.

An example of a material whose absorption spectra varies with local molecular field is methyl-red. As noted above methyl-red exhibits pleochroism to a

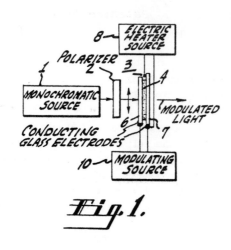

Fig. 1.

significant degree. It can be shown, however, that the absorption spectrum of methyl-red also varies as a function of local molecular electric field.

Any of the above-mentioned effects may be employed to modulate the intensity of a light beam. Fig.1 shows a light modulator constructed according to the present invention and employing a pleochroic guest in a nematic host. A source 1 of monochromatic light, for example a laser, generates a light beam which is passed through a polarizer 2. The light from the polarizer 2 passes through a modulator 3 which is constructed according to the present invention. The modulator 3 includes a mixture 4 of a nematic liquid crystal and a pleochroic dye supported between two transparent conducting electrodes 6 and 7. The mixture 4 may be a thin film held between the two electrodes 6 and 7 by surface tension. Alternatively a suitable enclosure may be used to contain the mixture 4. The thin film construction has the advantage that low control voltages may be used. The particular liquid crystal and dye combination will depend on the particular application and the frequency of the source 1.

The emission line of the monochromatic source 1 matches the absorption spectrum of the dye mixed with the nematic substance. A suitable dye for use with a given monochromatic source will have an absorption spectrum which, due to the pleochroic characteristic, is variable at the emission line of the monochromatic source. One suitable combination of source and dye is a neodymium laser generating a second harmonic at 5,300 A. and a methyl-red dye with p-n butoxy benzoic acid in a concentration of about one tenth to one percent dye by weight. Since the absorption spectrum of methyl-red includes 5,300 A. and is variable at this wavelength due to the pleochroic effect, it is a suitable dye for use with the second harmonic of a neodymium laser.

The preparation of the mixture 4 of nematic substance and pleochroic dye depends in part upon the type of nematic substance used. Where the molecular axes of the nematic substance are parallel to the dipole moments of the molecules, a condition exhibited by butyl anysilidene amino cinnamate for example, no special preparation is required and the mixture may merely be placed between the two electrodes 6 and 7. However, where the molecular axes of the nematic substances are perpendicular to the dipole moments as in p-n butoxy benzoic acid, then it is desirable to establish an initial orientation of the molecular axes by the following procedure.

One of the transparent electrodes, e.g. the electrode 6, is treated with an acid such as HCL to form a roughened surface which provides many points at which the liquid crystal molecules may attach themselves. The mixture of nematic substance and dye is then applied to the roughened glass surface in a manner such that a preferential direction of the molecules is obtained. This may be accomplished by wiping the electrode in one direction with a cotton swab soaked with the mixture of the nematic material and the dye. The second electrode 7 is then placed over the mixture deposited on the first electrode.

This procedure establishes a preferential orientation of the molecules of the mixture. The molecular axes tend to align in a direction parallel to the direction of wiping. Further orientation of the molecules is established when the field is applied across the mixture from the modulating source 10 establishing an alignment of the dipole moments.

The electrodes 6 and 7 are of conventional construction an example being tin oxide coated glass. One of the electrodes 7 serves as a heating element to maintain the temperature of the nematic substance at a proper value. Where the host is nematic at ambient temperatures, heating is not required. Where p-n butoxy benzoic acid is used as the nematic host the temperature is maintained between 147 and 163 degrees centigrade. Heating is accomplished by passing a current from the heating source 8 through the conductive coating on the electrode 7. A source of modulating signals 10 is connected to the conducting portions of the electrodes 6 and 7 to establish an electric modulating field across the mixture 4.

The light beam from the polarizer 2 which enters the modulator 3 is polarized in a direction parallel to the paper as indicated. When no field is applied across the mixture 4 its color in plane polarized white light may be described as orange. The orange color is due to the lack of ordering of dye molecules in the host. As a voltage is applied across the mixture 4, its color in white light polarized in a direction parallel to the molecular axes changes from orange to yellow as the electric field changes from zero volts to approximately 1,000 volts per centimeter. The change is caused by the alignment of the dipole moments of the dye molecules parallel to the applied field. By varying the field applied across the mixture 4 with the source 10 the amount of ordering of the dye molecules is varied and therefore the amount of light absorbed by the material at any one frequency in the absorption band is varied. Since the source 1 is essentially monochromatic, the beam passing from the source 1 through the mixture 4 is intensity modulated by the modulating signals from the modulating source 10.

The p-n butoxy benzoic acid used in the above-described embodiment is a nematic material whose optic axis aligns in a direction perpendicular to the applied electric field. Other nematic materials such as butyl anysilidene amino cinnamate align with their optic axes parallel to the applied electric field. Either type of nematic substance is suitable for use in the modulator shown in Fig.1. It should also be noted that while methyl-red has been described in the above embodiment in general any pleochroic dye may be employed, due consideration being given to matching the dye with the source of monochromatic light and to possible chemical reactions between the dye and the liquid crystal itself. Furthermore, while the modulator of Fig.1 has been described with respect to an electric control field a magnetic field may also be used.

Fig.2 is a diagram of an intensity modulator where a dye whose absorption spectrum is a function of the electric field in the vicinity of the molecules of the dye is mixed with the nematic host. The construction of the modulator of Fig.2 is similar to that of Fig.1 except that no polarizer is required. The same reference numerals as used in Fig.1 are used for corresponding elements in Fig.2. As noted above, methyl-red exhibits an absorption spectrum which is a function of the electric field in the vicinity of the dye molecules and therefore methyl-red is suitable dye for use in the modulator of Fig.2. Other dyes which exhibit this effect may of course be used. The monochrome source 1 may be the same as that used in the modulator of Fig.1, i.e. a neodym-

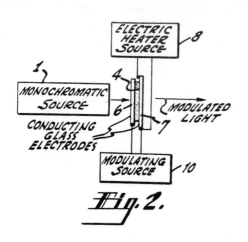

Fig. 2.

ium laser with a second harmonic output frequency at approximately 5,300 A. A suitable nematic host is p-n butoxy benzoic acid. The same concentration and temperature of the mixture 4 as used in the embodiment of Fig.1 may be used here. Also, the same procedure for obtaining an initial ordering of molecules on one of the glass electrodes as described above may be used here.

As the electric field is applied from the source 10 across the mixture 4 the absorption spectrum of the mixture is changed. This may be explained by noting that with no field applied, the dipolemoments of the nematic substance are not ordered. The electric fields in the vicinity of the dye molecules therefore are not ordered and in general the dye molecules experience different electric fields throughout the mixture. As the electric field is applied across the mixture 4 more ordering is achieved and the electric fields in the vicinity of the dye molecules become more ordere The absorption spectrum of the mixture with ordered electric fields is differen than the absorption spectrum with random electric fields. Since the absorptio spectrum of the mixture 4 varies with the applied field, the intensity of the light beam passing through the modulator is a function of the electric field applied across the mixture 4. As signals are applied from the modulating sourc 10 across the mixture 4, the output beam of the modulator is intensity modulate in accordance with the signals supplied.

A modulator employing particles dispersed in a nematic substance may be constructed along the same lines as the modulator of Fig.2. For example, the mixture 4 in Fig.2 may comprise flake-like particles of aluminum and are mixed with p-n butoxy benzoic acid in a mixture of about ten percent particles by volume. Where particles are dispersed in the nematic host the source 1 need not be monochromatic but rather any source of light may be used. As an electri field is applied across the mixture of particles and nematic substance the amount of light transmitted through the mixture will depend upon the orientatio of the particles in the mixture. Maximum transmission will be obtained when th flake-like particles align with their long dimensions in a plane parallel to th direction of the light beam. This will occur when a field gradient of approximately 1,000 volts per centimeter is applied across the mixture. When no fiel gradient appears in the mixture the flake-like particles will assume a more or less random distribution due to the random distribution of the ordered regions of the nematic host material. The light beam passing through the modulator is therefore intensity modulated by the modulating signals from the modulating source 10 applied across the mixture. Reflecting particles dispersed in a nematic material may also form the basis for a reflective modulator. Instead of causing the light beam which is to be modulated to pass through the mixture, it maybe reflected from the mixture.

Fig.3 shows a third embodiment of the present invention. In Fig.3 a mixture of a nematic host and a suitable pleochroic guest dye is employed as a display device. A mixture 50 of nematic host and guest material is supported between two conducting transparent electrodes 51 and 52 by surface tension to

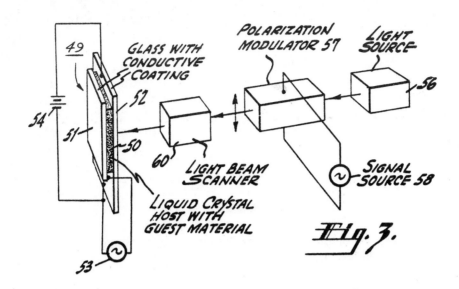

POLARIZATION MODULATOR 57
LIGHT SOURCE
49
GLASS WITH CONDUCTIVE COATING
52
54
51
50
60
LIGHT BEAM SCANNER
LIQUID CRYSTAL HOST WITH GUEST MATERIAL
53
56
SIGNAL SOURCE 58

Fig. 3.

form a display panel 49. The molecular axes of the molecules of the mixture 50 are essentially parallel to each other and to the electrodes 51 and 52. The process for obtaining this orientation is the same as that described with reference to the modulator of Fig.1, i.e., methyl-red mixed in p-n butoxy benzoic acid, is suitable here. The transparent electrodes 51 and 52 may be tin oxide coated glass. A source of voltage 53 is applied across the two transparent conducting electrodes 51 and 52. The source 53 may be either a.c. or d.c. but the former is preferred because it tends to eliminate electro-chemical decomposition of the dye. The maximum field gradient established by the source 53 is approximately 1,000 volts per centimeter. Since the mixture 4 is very thin, the maximum value of the voltage generated by the source 53 may be less than 100 volts. The electrode 52 is used as a heater to maintain the nematic substance at its proper value, i.e., between approximately 147 and 163 degrees centigrade where p-n butoxy benzoic acid is employed. A source 54 of electric energy is applied across the two ends of the electrode 52 to provide a resistive heating effect by passing a current through the resistive coating on the electrode 52. A light source 56 generates a light beam which enters a polarization modulator 57 of the type which can vary the plane of polarization and across which is established a video signal which will determine the intensity of the image established on the display 49. The source 56 generates light whose emission spectrum includes the absorption spectrum of the pleochroic dye of the mixture 50. For example, the source 56 may generate white light. The polarization of the light beam from the polar-ization modulator 57 depends upon the value of the video signals applied across the modulator 57 from the source 58. The beam from the output of the polarization modulator 57 is supplied to a scanning device 60 which causes the beam of light to scan electrode 52. The scanning device 60 may take any suitable form, for example, a rotating mirror scanner.

In the operation of the display device of Fig.3 the electric field pro-duced by the source 53 across the mixture 50 causes an ordering of the dye molecules mixed with the nematic liquid crystal in addition to the ordering established when the mixture was wiped onto one electrode. The electric field provided by the source 53 aligns the molecular dipole moments of the nematic host. This alignment causes a corresponding alignment of the dye molecules. The color exhibited by the panel 49 in plane polarized white light will therefore depend upon the direction of polarization of the light passing through the mixture 50 due to the pleochroism of the dye molecules.

The scanning device 60 causes a light beam to scan the transparent electrode 52 and thus pass through the mixture 50. The polarization of the light beam scanning the electrode 52 is controlled by the polarization modulator 57 in accordance with the video signal applied to the modulator from the source 58. Thus, as the signal applied to the polarization modulator 57 varies the color of the beam passing through the mixture 50 will vary. Where the mixture of methyl-red and p-n butoxy benzoic acid is employed as the mixture 50, the color may be controlled from orange when the incident light beam is polarized in a direction parallel to the molecular axes of the dye molecules to yellow for a polarization at right angles to this direction. Synchronization between the video signal applied to the polarization modulator 57 and the scanning of the light beam across the electrode 52 may be accomplished by conventional television techniques.

Where a larger color variation than is obtainable by using one dye alone is desired, a plurality of display panels, each with a different dye mixed with the nematic substance, may be employed. The panels are stacked so that the ligh beam passes through each plate. A suitable choice of dyes will result in the desired range of color variation.

While one particular embodiment of a display system has been described many other arrangements are pssible. For example, instead of varying the polarization of the light beam which scans the display device, the polarizatio may be fixed at a constant value and the field across the mixture of the dye an nematic substance may be varied. Furthermore, an electron beam may be employed to scan the mixture of nematic liquid crystal an d dye rather than the light beam scanning the liquid crystal. The intensity of the electron beam would then be controlled to produce local variations in absorption spectrum across the display area in accordance with a video signal.

Furthermore, instead of employing a pleochroic dye mixed with a nematic liquid crystal, a dye whose absorption spectrum is a function of local molecula field may be mixed with a suitable nematic substance. In this case the light beam used to scan the display area need not be polarized. The electric field across the mixture would be controlled to produce the desired color variation.

Particles of a reflective material, for example, aluminum, may be mixed with a nematic substance to form a display device. A display device employing such a mixture may be operated with a scanning electron beam the intensity of which is controlled by a video signal. The amount of light reflected from the display panel would then be a function of the intensity of the electron beam impinging upon the mixture of particles and nematic substance.

" "

3,439,525 (U.S.)   *Patented Apr. 22, 1969*

NONDESTRUCTIVE TESTING METHOD USING LIQUID CRYSTALS.

Gary L. Waterman and Wayne E. Woodmansee, assignors to The Boeing Company.

This invention involves a method of applying liquid crystal materials to a surface to be tested for discontinuities. Test areas on the surface are defined through utilization of a hollow, loop-forming tubular member through which a vacuum is applied, and which produces a thermally responsive contact between the crystal holding medium and the surface within the test area.

A flexible application device has been devised and is shown in Fig.1 in an elliptical view wherein a hose 14 is joined at point 17 and permanently bonded (connected) to form a hollow tubular shaped member 14 capable of being shaped in different configurations. Typical materials used for this have been polyvinyls, rubber and Tygon. A multiplicity of holes 15 are made on the inside circumference of the hollow member (ring). At least one pitot opening 16 capable of being adapted to fit into vacuum systems is inserted into the member 14. The hose is assembled so as to include sufficient area within its circumference to enable adequate testing to be done within this defined area.

In Fig.2, the member 14 is placed on the object 10 to be tested and connected with vacuum drawing means (not shown) at the pitot opening 16 so that air is evacuated through the openings 15 inside the inner circumference of the member 14. Thereafter at least one solid film layer 19 suitably coated with a selected cholesteric medium 20 is placed upon the member 14, the top of which has thereon a bonding agent 21 such as an adhesive, vacuum grease, double back or adhesive tape. It is also possible to have a retaining hoop placed over the film layer. In Fig.2, as a vacuum is drawn, film 19 is drawn inward in the middle region of the area defined by the circumference of the member 14. Eventually as more vacuum is drawn, film 19 and medium 20 make a thermally responsive contact with the substrate 10 and as the vacuum becomes more complete the hose turns, as shown by the arrows in Fig.2; eventually leaving the film in thermally responsive contact with the article 10 in the area defined by the inner circumference of the member 14. The vacuum is maintained during testing and released when the testing is completed.

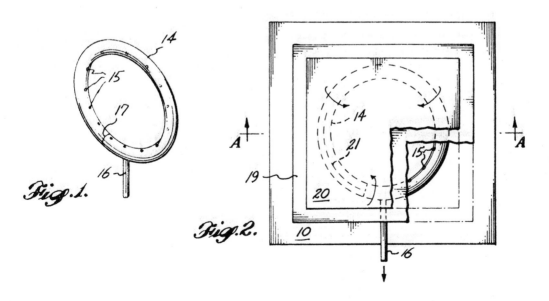

Fig.1.   Fig.2.

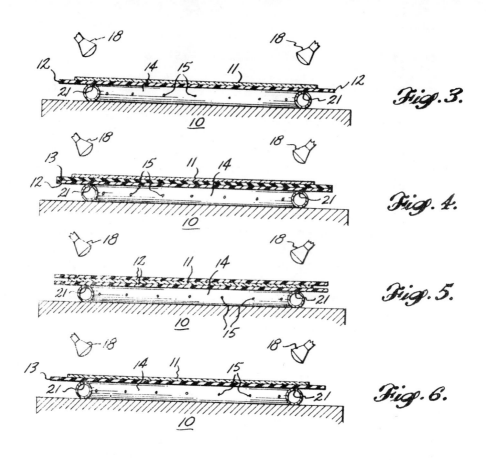

Fig.3.

Fig.4.

Fig.5.

Fig.6.

Fig.3 (cut along line A-A of Fig.2) shows a film 12 being placed upon member 14 held in place by adhesive 21 which member 14 rests on a substrate 10 to be tested. The film 12 is coated with a filled cholesteric compound layer 11. Typical embodiments of film 12 are saran, Teflon, polyethylene, polyvinyl alcohol and clear plastics. Another arrangement possible for Fig.3 is an unfilled cholesteric material layer 11 when the substrate 10 is a dark article which of its own accord will bring out the color patterns of the unfilled cholesteric material 11.

Fig.4 sets forth a combination of film 12 with the member 14, the film 12 being held in place by adhesive 21 upon which film 12 is a dark opaque film 13 followed by a topmost coating layer of an unfilled cholesteric medium 11. A typical embodiment of film 13 would be a black carbon filled polymeric film.

A further embodiment is shown in Fig.5 in which substrate 10 has a member 14 resting thereon with a film 12 being held in place by adhesive 21 upon which film 12 is filled liquid crystal layer 11 followed by a topmost film 12. Typical embodiments of such a film 12 would be saran, Teflon, etc. Another arrangement possible for Fig.5 is using an unfilled cholesteric material 11 when the substrate 10 is a dark article which of its own accord will bring out the color pattern of the cholesteric material 11. Again layer 12 is the topmost film with a second layer being the bottommost film thus surrounding layer 11 and layer 12 is constituted as set forth above. It is also possible to have the layer 12 which comes in contact with the substrate 10 when vacuum is applied comprised of a dark opaque layer when using an unfilled cholesteric medium on a light colored substrate 10. (Typical embodiment as per Fig.4)

110

Fig.6 shows a dark opaque film 13 resting on the hollowmember 14 with an unfilled cholesteric layer 11. The dark opaque layer 13 can be of the same materials as listed for layer 13 in Fig.4.

After a thermally responsive contact has been achieved between the cholesteric medium and the article to be tested, application of heat is commenced by a number of means such as heat lamps, circulating fluids, enclosed heating ovens, electrical resistance setups and any device for impinging hot air currents so that the temperature of the article 10 and the cholesteric medium 11 are heated to a temperature producing at least a first color transition for areas of the cholesteric medium. At this point it should be noted that any discontinuities in the substrate 10 will have different thermally responsive characteristics being shown in the cholesteric layer 11 so that discontinuities will be defined by a color discontinuity within the cholesteric layer 11. Heating can further be conducted until a multiplicity of color transitions takes place within the cholesteric layer at the point of the discontinuity in the substrate (that is, depending on the composition of the liquid crystal mixture being employed, the color changes will normally be from clear to red to yellow to green to blue on heating and vice versa on cooling).

It is also possible to record the thermal patterns which develop by means of motion pictures, sketches, etc. Such recordings can be used to very accurately form overlays on the part and precisely locate the exact configuration of the discontinuity detected.

We have also studied the feasibility of preparing (by encapsulation) sandwiches of liquid crystals using very thin (in the order of 0.001 inch) film (typically saran wrap, Teflon or polyethylene films) to permit inspection of surfaces without the necessity of painting them each time they are tested. The objective of this preparation is to obtain an encapsulated cholesteric film which can be easily manipulated without coming off on the person's hands who is handling the film or being left on the part being tested. To produce such thin films, we use the vacuum member 14 described above to draw the thin film, for example, saran wrap, tight and then paint the film with liquid crystals. The first film is then cut to the inner dimensions of the vacuum frame (member 14) and a second film is placed on the frame. The frame is next placed over the first film so as to have the edges of the film within the circumference defined by the vacuum frame. When the frame is re-evacuated, the second film is pressed against the liquid crystal layer and forms an air-free sandwich. The sandwich can then be placed on the surface of an article for testing and reused repeatedly. Such sandwiches have very high, efficient thermal responsiveness when molded to said substrate. It is readily apparent that such permanent sandwiches are easily handled and add an efficiency factor to any nondestructive testing applications.

"""""""""""""""""""""""

3,440,620 (U.S.)   *Patented April 22, 1969*

ELECTRO-OPTICAL MEMORY.

Larry J. French, assignor to Radio Corporation of America.
Application Jan. 10, 1966.

This invention relates to data memories. More specifically, the present invention relates to random-access memories.

In accordance with the present invention, an optical memory comprises a matrix of selectively energizable discrete electromagnetic radiation producing elements and means to produce a plurality of images of the array. These images are directed onto corresponding storage cells of a stacked plurality of memory plates wherein the stored information is represented by incremental selectively transparent and opaque areas. The storage plate is made opaque to the radiation from the element by an externally applied field except in pre-selected incremental areas which are retained in a transparent condition. An individual sensing device for each of the cells aligned in the stack is arranged to provide an output signal representative of radiation passing through the cell area.

Referring to the single figure, there is shown an optical memory comprising a plurality of photographic storage plates 1 and 2. These plates are each subdivided into sub-areas hereinafter referred to as cells 3, 4, of the plates 1 and 2, respectively.

The storage plates 1, 2, may be any suitable devices which may be selectively made opaque to incident radiation by the application of an external control signal. Such a device is shown in the copending application by George H. Heilmeier, Ser. No. 450,949, filed on Apr. 26, 1965. As shown therein, the operation of the device is achieved by the molecular orientation of a nematic liquid crystal such as p-n butoxy benzoic acid between 147 and 163 degrees centigrade. A "guest" material, such as aluminum flakes or a pleochroic dye such as methyl-red or indolphenol-blue is mixed with the nematic "host" and is oriented therewith by the externally applied field. The nematic liquid crystal and the guest material may be arranged as a thin film between two transparent electrically conducting electrodes, e.g. glass sheets with tin deposited electrodes. In the event that the nematic crystal does not exhibit its nematic properties at ambient temperature, a heating element may be provided to heat the crystal to the desired temperature.

The incremental areas of the storage plates which are to remain transparent during the presence of the applied external field are free from the nematic crystal and the "guest" substance. Such areas may be provided by elevating these areas over the storage plate electrode surface having the liquid crystal coating or by drilling holes through the storage plates. Since the nematic crystal is in thin film form, it will be held between the plates without loss through the drilled holes. Another form which the storage plates 1 and 2 may take is a photographic plate with one of the electrode coatings forming the photographic representation of the stored data. The transparent areas, accordingly, would be provided by an omitted section of the photographically deposited electrode. The other electrode would be uniform since it would affect the liquid crystal only in the area between the two existing electrode surfaces.

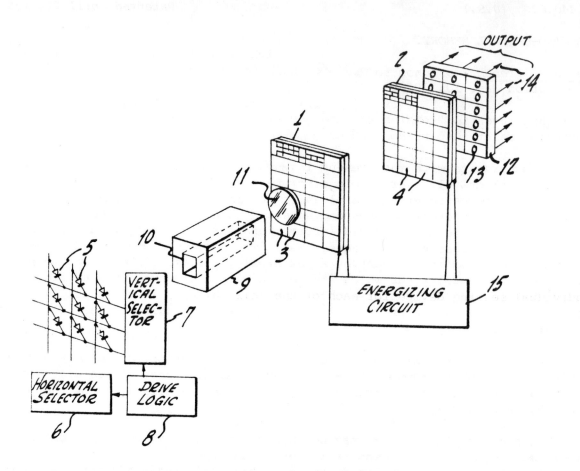

Each cell 3, 4, in turn, is subdivided into incremental areas for storing binary information as either opaque marks 16 for storing one kind of data 17 or transparent marks for storing another kind of data. Thus, the plate 1 has a number of cells 3, 4, with each cell being divided into the same number of incremental areas. The number of areas in each cell is determined by the number of individual illuminating means for each cell. In the embodiment shown in the drawing, the illuminating means comprises an array of photo-emissive elements, such as GaAs (gallium arsenide) diodes 5 which produce electromagnetic radiation at the p-n junction in response to an applied current. The frequency of this radiation is dependent on several factors including the temperature of the environment. These diodes 5 are arranged across the intersections of a matrix having independently scanned X and Y connecting wires. A horizontal selection means 6 is used to selectively energize a desired X wire while a vertical selection means 7 is used to select a Y wire. A diode 5 at the intersection of the selected wires is energized and a beam of radiation is emitted therefrom. A suitable drive logic 8 is used to operate the selection means 6 and 7 to select a desired diode 5.

The radiation from the selected diode 5 is directed into an optical tunnel 9. The optical tunnel 9 may be a device as shown and described in Pat. No. 3,191,157 of Parker et al. which issued on June 22, 1965. Briefly, this device comprises four blocks of optical glass, as shown, placed together to form a central longitudinal tunnel 10. The inside surfaces of the tunnel are arranged to form internal reflecting mirror surfaces by suitably coating the walls with a reflecting material, e.g. aluminum.

The light beam from the selected diode 5 is admitted into one end of the tunnel 10 while the other end of the tunnel 10 is arranged adjacent to a focusing lens 11. The lens 11 is effective to focus the images of the diode array 5 onto the memory plates 1, 2. A light sensitive matrix 12 comprising a plurality of photo-detectors 13 equal in number to the number of sub-areas 2 on the plate 1 is positioned behind the plates 1, 2. The photo-detectors 13 are connected to individual output lines 14 to provide a parallel output representative of the information read out from the memory plates 1, 2. An energizing circuit 15 is provided to selectively energize the electrodes of the storage plate which is to be read.

In operation, the optical tunnel 9 is effective to provide a plurality of images of the array of diodes 5 in an image plane. Since each image comprises a reproduction of the entire array, these images are each focused by the lens 11 onto corresponding cells, 3, 4. The individual diodes 5 are, thus, arranged to illuminate identical respective incremental areas in each of the cells 3, 4. The photocells 13 are each arranged to view an entire corresponding one of the cells 3, 4. Accordingly, any energy reaching a photocell 13 through a transparent incremental area in the corresponding one of the cells 2, 3 is converted to an output signal on a corresponding one of the output lines 14. The diodes 5 are selected by the horizontal and vertical selection means 6 and 7 to provide an energy beam at a particular location in the array. This beam is, then, distributed by the optical tunnel 9 and the lens 11 onto a corresponding incremental area in all of the cells 3, 4. Each cell that has a transparent incremental area at that location is represented by an output signal from the corresponding one of the photocells 13. The combined output from the sensing matrix 12 is a representation of the stored information on the memory plates 1, 2 at the incremental area selected by the diodes 5.

The memory plate that is to be read is selected by the energizing means 15. This selection is effective to render the selected plate opaque to the incident radiation except in the transparent incremental area. This opacity may be evidenced by either an interference with the radiation path in the case of "guest" aluminum particles or a selective color filtering by a dye "guest" which is made to cooperate with the substantially monochromatic radiation from the diodes 5. In either case, only the transparent areas transmit the radiation to the photocells 13. Of course, the unenergized storage plates are entirely transparent and do not enter into the data reading of the selected plate. While, for purposes of illustration, the array of diodes 5 has been shown as a 3 x 3 array, this may be expanded to a number dependent on the optical resolution of the system and the physical dimensions of the diodes 5 or other suitable energy sources, e.g. an array of 60 x 60 has been found to be practical with available diode element packing technique. The number of diodes, of course, is determinative of the number of incremental areas in each of the cells 3, 5. However, the number of cells 3, 4 is determined only by the number of usable images provided by the light tunnel 9. In other words, the image must supply enough radiation to produce an output signal from the photocells 13. Thus, the memory plate 1 illustrated has a 4 x 4 matrix, but it has been found that the usable images would allow, at least, an economical expansion to a 20 x 20 matrix. The further physical consideration is the reduction in radiation energy level in passing through the energized and unenergized storage plates. This may be conveniently limited to any arbitrary number, e.g. 10 storage plates, depending on the ability of the information signal to be extracted from the photocells 13.

"""""""""""""""""""""""

THERMOMETER.

*William J. Jones, assignor to Westinghouse Electric Corporation.
Application Sept. 9, 1966.*

It is a prime object of the present invention to provide an improved
clinical thermometer which is relatively inexpensive, fast-acting, simple
to read, unbreakable, as well as otherwise harmless, and thereby particularly
suited for throw-away use.

Referring to Fig.1, the embodiment of the invention shown therein comprises
a plurality of hollow, substantially-cylindrical sensor cells, ten such cells
being illustrated and numbered 12a to 12j, containing temperature responsive
liquid compositions 14a to 14j, such as hysteretic cholesteric liquid crystalline compositions of the type such as set forth, for example, in copending
U.S. patent application Ser, No. 557,060, Filed June 13, 1966 and assigned to
the assignee of the present patent application. These compositions exhibit
a certain color, green for example, when initially in a cholesteric phase
below a precise threshold temperature, turn colorless upon reaching such temperature and increasing thereabove, and retain such colorless condition for a
significant interval of time following return to and below such threshold
temperature. By controlling the formulation of such compositions 14a to 14j,
precise different threshold temperatures can be obtained for the several sensor
cells 12a to 12j. For example, cells 12a to 12j can be made responsive to body
temperatures ranging from 98°F to 102.5°F in steps of 1/2°. This spans a range
from subnormal body temperature to fever temperatures. The sensor cells 12a
to 12j when containing such liquid crystal compositions and disposed within
a patient's mouth are fast-acting and susceptible to threshold-temperature-
response within ten seconds.

As is apparent from the showing in Fig.1, the several different prime-
temperature responsive cells 12a, 12c, 12e, 12g, and 12j are arranged in groups
of two with their 1/2° complements and are spaced apart in such groups to
afford ready identification and differentiation of those temperature sensor
cells which have responded to their threshold temperatures from those cells
which have not so responded. In the chosen example, those sensor cells 12a
to 12j which have not been subjected to their threshold temperatures will
retain their initial color, green, for example, while those sensor cells which
have been subjected to their threshold temperatures will have changed to the
colorless state.

In the case of use of such liquid crystal compositions, the initial color
is enhanced by a dark background, such as black, for example, so that in their
non-responsive condition the sensor cells 12a to 12j will exhibit their initial
color condition, while in their threshold-temperature-responsive condition in
which the liquid crystal composition turns clear, such sensor cells will appear
black, in accord with the black background as is observed through the then-
clear liquid crystal composition filling such cells.

In accord with the Fig.1 construction and as is apparent also from Fig.2,
the sensor cells 12a to 12f each comprises and elongated transparent rounded
upper wall 16 through which the color state of the liquid crystalline composition within such cells may be observed; such rounded walls serving to mag-

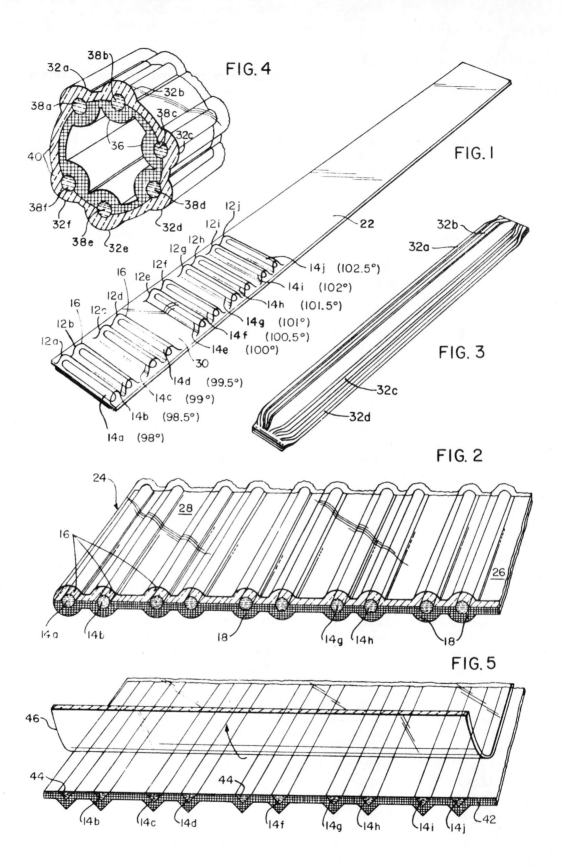

FIG. 4

32a
38b
38a
32b
38c
40
36
32c
38f
32d
38d
32f
12j
38e 32e
12i
12h
12g
16
12f
12e
12d
16
12c
12b
12a
14j (102.5°)
14i (102°)
14h (101.5°)
14g (101°)
14f (100.5°)
14e (100°)
30
14d (99.5°)
14c (99°)
14b (98.5°)
14a (98°)

FIG. 1
22

FIG. 3
32b
32a
32c
32d

FIG. 2
24
28
16
14a 14b
18
14g 14h
18
26

FIG. 5
46
44
44
14b 14c 14d 14f 14g 14h 14i 14j 42

118

nify the appearance of such compositions, as well as to provide separating indentations on the surface of the thermometer which can be recognized visibly in assist to distinguishing the several cells, one from the other, and thus facilitate counting of the number of cells from one end of the thermometer which have experienced threshold-temperature-response.

Also in accord with use of such liquid crystal compositions, each of the sensor cells 12a to 12j will have a dark or black pigmented layer or background therebeneath. In behalf of economy in manufacture of fabrication such dark background may be furnished by dispersal of pigmentation throughout the thickness of the bottom wall 18 of each cylindrical sensor cell as shown, or sprayed on as a coating on such wall.

The thermometer configuration in the embodiment of Fig.1 is tab-like, with the array of sensors 12a to 12j arranged at one end of an elongated support means in the form of a thin rectangular tab 22. The overall dimensions of such tab-like thermometer may be, for example, a quarter of an inch wide and about two inches long; with the array of ten sensors extending about three quarters of an inch along one end of the tab 22, which is relatively small, relatively conservative in material, and readily insertable in the patient's mouth.

In behalf of economy of fabrication, the walls of the sensor cells 12a to 12j can be formed integrally with the tab 22 of a suitable thermoplastic material, such as an ionomer resin, by extrusion. Referring to Fig.2, the tab 22 and the walls 16 and 18 of the cells 12a to 12j can be formed integrally by extrusion and filled with the liquid crystal compositions to gorm a continuous sheet 24 having a handle part 26 and a sensor cell part 28. Subsequent to such formation of the sheet 24, such sheets may be subjected to indentations (not shown) by a heated roller, or other suitable joining means, transversely of the Direction of extension of the continuous liquid-crystalline-composition-containing convolutions or cylinder parts to obtain sealing of the ends of such cylinders to form the discrete sensor cells, simultaneously with or following which the sheet is separated along such indentations to obtain individual thermometers. In the use of liquid crystalline compositions according to the present state of the art and formulation of such compositions where the cell sealing is obtained by application of heat, a thermoplastic material needs to be chosen which will soften sufficiently to obtain such heat sealing and fusion between layers at temperatures which will not alter or destroy the temperature responsive properties of such compositions.

In accord with the preferred feature of the invention, the material of which the thermometer is composed should be somewhat nonrigid, or flexible, in order to enjoy the advantage of such thermometer being unbreakable.

The number of sensor cells 12 which the thermometer may employ is somewhat arbitrary. For example, perhaps only two or three response temperatures may be desired to merely give indication of above, normal, and/or below normal body temperatures, or even a single response temperature to indicate an above normal condition, following which more precise information as to the specific body temperature could be obtained by use of an auxiliary thermometer of the conventional type. In this latter case, use and interpretation of such a thermometer is simplified, and will satisfy the majority of hospital needs. Further investigation of the patient's temperature need be made only when abnormal.

In the configuration shown in Figs. 3 and 4, six temperature cells, 32a to 32f respond to respective body temperatures of 98°F to 103°F, for eaxample. Circumferential spacing between cells can be employed to readily identify and distinguish between such cells and between groups of such cells.

Referring to Fig.4, the cylindrical configuration also can be fabricated by extrusion to provide a black inner layer 36 for dark-background-color-enhancement of liquid crystalline compositions 38a to 38f between inner layer 36 and outer clear layer 40 which is rounded in the region of the sensor cells for magnification of appearance of the liquid crystalline compositions thereunder as well as for distinguishment of the sensor cells from each other. The Fig.3 configuration is one which would accomodate oral as well as rectal use, but would tend to be somewhat more difficult to read than the tab-like configuration of Fig.1.

Referring to Fig.5, a third concept of fabrication of tab-like thermometers somewhat similar to that of Fig.1 can be arrived at by provision of a dark-pigmented bottom sheet 42 having a plurality of parallel-arranged troughs 44 formed in an upper surface thereof which could be filled with the liquid crystalline materials 14a to 14j and covered for containment by a transparent upper sheet 46 of clear plastic material bonded to such bottom sheet. Following this, the sandwich assemblage of sheets could be indented and sealed along lines transverse to the direction of extension of the troughs to form discrete sensor cells similar to those of the Fig.1 thermometer and severance of the thermometers along the lines of seal indentations.

Where the temperature responsive liquid composition employed for the sensor cells of the thermometer of the present invention are hysteretic cholesteric liquid crystalline compositions, the desired threshold temperatures can be obtained by those versed in the art of formulating such compositions with a relatively high degree of accuracy, such, for example, as within a tenth of a degree Fahrenheit. By way of example, a threshold temperature of 98°F. can be obtained by a composition including 26% cholesterol chloride, 73% cholesterol oleyl carbonate and 1% triolein, and a threshold temperature such as 101°F. might be obtained by a composition including 26% cholesterol chloride and 74% cholesterol erucyl carbonate. The rate of response of these materials to increase in temperature to their threshold values can be a matter of several seconds, as compared to three minutes for the usual prior art clinical thermometers. Once having experienced a color change upon temperature increase, these materials retain their color-altered state for a sufficient period of time, for at least a matter of minutes, upon return to subbody temperature, thus affording ample time for reading the thermometer without erasure by the room temperature conditions to which the thermometer becomes exposed after removal from the patient.

" "

LIQUID CRYSTAL COMPOSITIONS.

Wayne E. Woodmansee,   *assignor to The Boeing Company.*
Application Aug.5, 1966.

This invention relates to a series of compositions of cholesteric materials of two or more components which have increased sensitivity in temperature responsive color patterns.

Testing of adhesively bonded structures is conveniently carried out with filled cholesteric liquid crsytals. A filled cholesteric liquid is a composition of cholesterol which has incorporated and dispersed therein various other substances. The test surface is initially warmed to facilitate spreading of the cholesteric film. The filled material is then brushed or sprayed (with approximately 10% benzene added) onto the surface and brushed until a uniform color pattern is observed when the surface is slowly heated to a temperature to which the cholesteric material responds. The bonded structure is then rapidly cycled through the range of temperature to which the cholesteric materials respond. Heating is generally accomplished with a bank of 1000 watt photoflood lamps positioned to provide even heating of the test surface. The intensity of the lamps is controlled by variable autotransformers. Convective cooling is used to lower the temperature of the panel following application of heat from the flood lamps. As the bonded panel is quickly heated and cooled, voids, lack of adhesive and other flaws are revealed as temperature anomalies which produce a color contrast over the flaw. These local temperature differences arise due to variations in the thermal diffusivity of the bonded structure in the vicinity of the bonding irregularity as compared with the more uniform thermal properties of well-bonded regions. Bonding flaws may then be outlined on the surface with a marking device and/or the cholesteric temperature pattern photographed to obtain a permanent record. Following testing, the cholesteric materials and filler are removed by cleaning the surface with a flexible rubber scraper. The last traces of the cholesteric materials are removed by wiping with a rag containing benzene.

Cholesteric liquid crystal mixtures suitable for temperature visualization over a given range are prepared by initially purifying the constituents by recrystallization from hot ethanol or by washing with ethanol at room temperature if the raw materials are relatively pure. The necessary percentages of the various constituents are selected from graphs similar to Figs.1 through 4 to achieve light scattering at the desired temperatures. The solid compounds combined in these mixtures are weighed to 0.1% and mixed in a suitable container which is then heated to approximately 80° C. The mixture is stirred continuously for at least 10 minutes. Filler material is then added to the liquid crystals and stirring continued for an additional 10 minutes to insure intimate mixing of the filler and cholesteric materials. Upon cooling, the filled cholesteric materials are stored at approximately 0° C. or in an evacuated container at room temperature. These storage procedures are effective in stabilizing the color temperature behavior of the mixtures for several weeks.

Experimentation with the properties of cholesteric materials led to a number of combinations of chemicals which show desirable properties of viscosity, speed of response, temperature sensitivity, and reversible color-temperature behavior.

I have found that a three component composition of selected constituents will offer the sensitivity needed in cholesteric materials. The cholesteryl compositions I have found have a basic component providing sensitivity by color change at low relative temperature (approximately 0° C. to 60° C. -- a normal testing temperature range for employing cholesteryl materials) in the presence of a second component which has the function of narrowing temperature response to a small range of temperature for the occurrence of the color phenomena (red to blue transition in 1° C.) with a third component being added to adjust the actual temperature at which the color phenomena will occur.

I have found that the basic component can be selected from the group consisting of cholesteryl oleate, the second component can be selected from the group consisting of cholesteryl nonanoate, cholesteryl decanoate, cholesteryl octanoate and cholesteryl paranitrobenzoate, and the third component can be selected from the group consisting of cholesteryl acetate and cholesteryl propionate.

The amounts of the various constituents found to produce light scattering over useful temperature increments are:

	Percentage by wt.
Cholesteryl nonanoate, or decanoate, or octanoate......	0 to 70
Cholesteryl oleate......................................	24 to 91
Cholesteryl acetate, or propionate......................	2 to 21

And also:

Cholesteryl p-nitrobenzoate.............................	1 to 4
Cholesteryl oleate......................................	80 to 91
Cholesteryl acetate, or propionate......................	5 to 16

The color-temperature behavior of a series of mixtures utilizing the above-mentioned components are shown in Figs. 1 to 4. Dashed lines represent the temperatures at which red scattering commences. As the temperature is increased light is scattered successively in the orange, yellow, green, blue and violet regions of the visible spectrum. The solid lines in the figures refer to temperatures at which blue scattering is observed.

In addition to the above compositions, I have further improved their response and distinctive color patterns by making an addition of a filler material selected from the group consisting of carbon, carbon black, black pempera powder, finely divided metals, finely divided non-metals and combinations thereof. Examples of finely divided metals and non-metals which have been successfully embodied are nickel, molybdenum and silicon. Typical but not limiting particle sizes have been used from a range of 100 mesh to 500 mesh by the Tyler Screen Classification System. It has been found that an addition of an opaque filler material selected from the above group, when incorporated into a liquid cholesteric material according to the above compositions in the range of 3.0% to 30% by weight brings an improvement in their application for temperature visualization on reflective and nonreflective surfaces (e.g., metal surface and human skin respectively) and transparent materials (e.g., glass, Plexiglass and plastic). The incorporation of the filler eliminates using a black paint background, thus eliminating the problems associated with this black paint background.

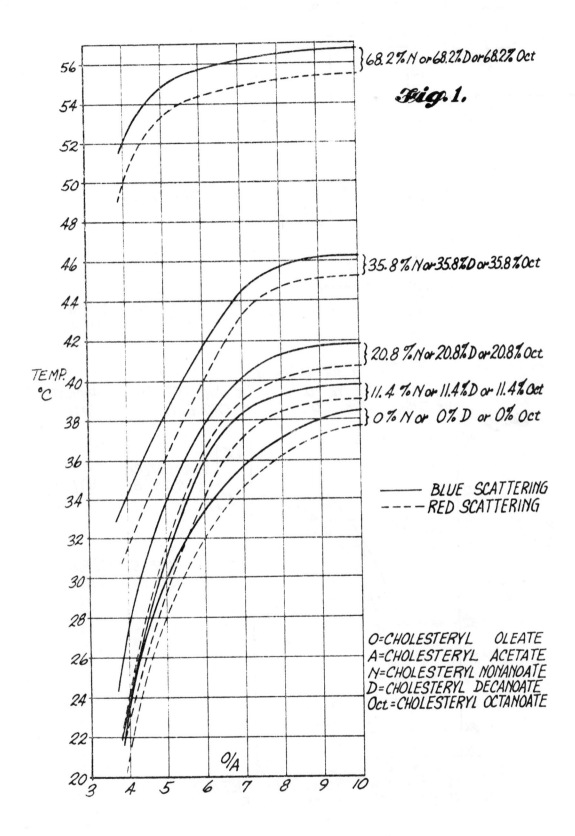

Fig. 1.

} 68.2% N or 68.2% D or 68.2% Oct

} 35.8% N or 35.8% D or 35.8% Oct

} 20.8% N or 20.8% D or 20.8% Oct

} 11.4% N or 11.4% D or 11.4% Oct

} 0% N or 0% D or 0% Oct

―――― BLUE SCATTERING
- - - - RED SCATTERING

O = CHOLESTERYL OLEATE
A = CHOLESTERYL ACETATE
N = CHOLESTERYL NONANOATE
D = CHOLESTERYL DECANOATE
Oct = CHOLESTERYL OCTANOATE

TEMP.
°C

O/A

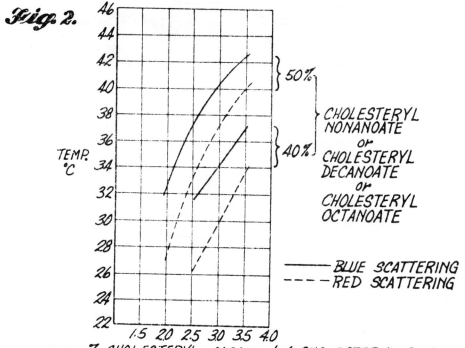

Fig. 2.

TEMP. °C

50% }
40% }

CHOLESTERYL
NONANOATE
or
CHOLESTERYL
DECANOATE
or
CHOLESTERYL
OCTANOATE

—— BLUE SCATTERING
----- RED SCATTERING

% CHOLESTERYL OLEATE / % CHOLESTERYL PROPIONATE
or % CHOLESTERYL OLEATE / % CHOLESTERYL ACETATE

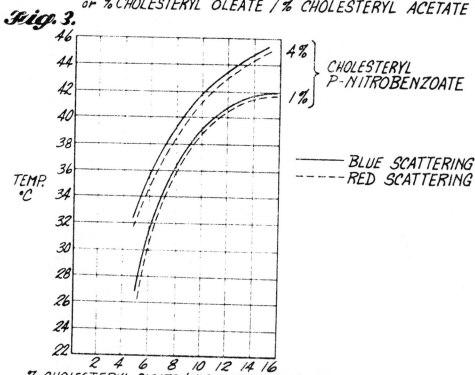

Fig. 3.

TEMP. °C

4% }
1% }

CHOLESTERYL
P-NITROBENZOATE

—— BLUE SCATTERING
----- RED SCATTERING

% CHOLESTERYL OLEATE / % CHOLESTERYL ACETATE
or % CHOLESTERYL OLEATE / % CHOLESTERYL PROPIONATE

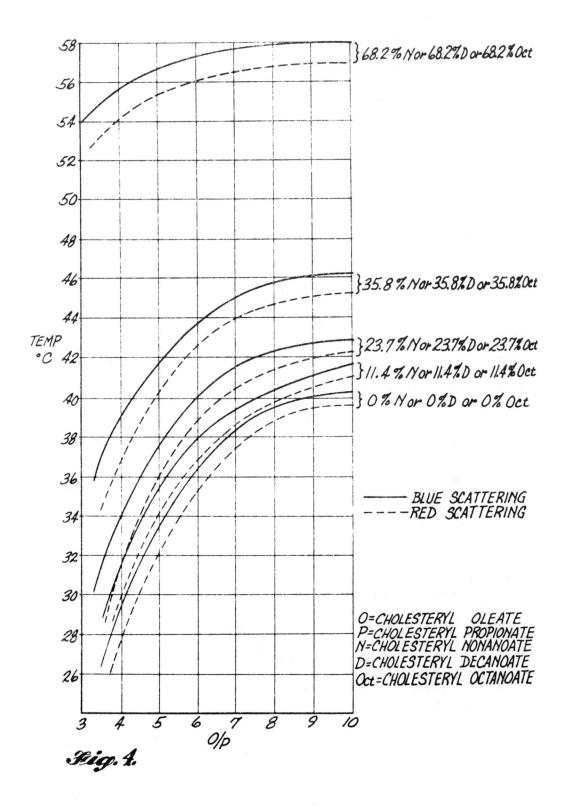

Fig. 4.

Liquid crystals, particularly with filler added, provide a rapid and very sensitive means of mapping human skin temperatures. The darkened cholesteric materials are especially useful in applications where movement of the skin, as around joints, normally sauses cracking of underlying black background paints. Several studies have been conducted in a variety of medical fields. Pediatricians are evaluating these materials as remote temperature indicators on infants in incubators. In a normal infant, the feet should be about 1° C. below the abdomen temperature. By placing liquid crystal layers on both of these areas of the infant, the respective temperatures of each area are quickly indicated. If the relative temperature difference increases beyond this, it may be an indication of an infectious disease causing vasoconstriction. If the relative temperatures are less than a degree apart, the incubator may be too warm.

The temperature indications provided by the materials set forth above reflect when vein grafts have successfully restored circulation to the extremities. The success of removal of arterial blockage is also reflected by the increase in temperature over arteries lying close to the skin. If the temperature rise does not occur, it is likely that the blood vessel has not been completely opened. The efficiency of vascular activity at sutures, skin flaps, and wounds after surgery may also be indicated by skin temperature patterns. A plastic surgeon is studying this as a means of reducing the waiting time before commencing second-stage constructive surgery.

The damage to blood vessels in areas of second and third degree burns may produce localized temperature anomalies visible by liquid crystals. To prevent infection in areas of severe burns, a common practice is to apply silver nitrate to the area. This darkens the skin and makes visual examination of the burned tissue difficult. With layers od cholesteric materials applied to small controlled areas of third degree burns in laboratory animals, we have accurately outlined the extent of severe burning due to an appreciably lower temperature indication over these areas. This would enable early removal of the tissue in the third degree areas and allow grafting to commence shortly afterwards. As above noted, these applications are not currently possible with cholesteric materials which require an opaque background.

Many applications and utilizations of the composition set forth in this invention have been found. A liquid crystal composition can be employed effectively to test adhesive bonding honeycomb structures for various faults and flaws in the fabrication of the structure. Similar inspection of electronic components can be conducted to detect flaws and failures in fabrication. Further, the attractive color patterns of very precise delineation prove useful in several areas for their decorative, intrique and colorfulness. Such areas include decorative panels for offices and aircraft interiors and toys which have psychological attractiveness to children because of their variety of color display when touched by a human hand.

To fabricate a toy or a decorative color panel, we have applied approximately 0.5 gram of any of the above compositions, with filler additions, to a sheet of clear acetate, Mylar or Plexiglass typically by spreading the cholesteryl medium by manual means. A second sheet of clear film material is placed over the clear sheet coated with the mixture. The sandwich is then placed between two metal blocks of approximately the same area as the sandwich. These blocks are heated to approximately 40-50° C. and exert a force of an order of 5 lbs. on the sandwich. The metal blocks on the sandwich are then placed in a vacuum of about 10 mm. Hg. After about one minute at this pressure, air is admitted to the chamber rapidly. The above procedure has been successful in producing a thin, uniform film of liquid crystals sandwiched between the protective layers mentioned above. To prevent slippage of the protective layers, we have investigated the following methods of sealing, any of which would be feasible with the above-mentioned materials: (a) tape, (b) adhesive, (c) ultrasonic sealing and (d) thermal sealing. Another method of sealing the toy makes use of a sandwich of vinyl materials sealed on three edges. An excess of liquid crystal material is injected into the envelope at the narrow end which remains open. The sandwich is then passed between variable pressure rolls heated to 40-50° C. This forces the air out of the envelope and spreads the liquid crystals uniformly. The open end of the envelope is then sealed thermally to close the container. This has worked quite well with small test samples and can be readily adapted to large scale productions.

Large sandwiches of compositions of the liquid crystals set forth above can be made using very thin (0.001 inch) film to permit inspection of surfaces without necessity of painting the surfaces with liquid crystal compositions. To produce these thin films, I use a vacuum frame to draw Saran wrap or Teflon film very tight and then paint the composition of liquid crystal upon the Saran wrap or Teflon film. The first Saran wrap or Teflon film is then cut to the inner dimensions of the vacuum frame and a second film is placed on the frame. When the frame is re-evacuated, the second film is pressed against the liquid crystalline composition and forms an air-free sandwich. The sandwich can then be placed on a surface to reinspect it and reuse repeatedly.

Eassentially the same process has been used in preparing larger panels of Plexiglas with the above compositions of liquid crystals deposited between the cover sheets thereof. By selectively or randomly heating portions of the panels, some very artistic effects can be gained from the color patterns exhibited by the panels.

" "

HYSTERETIC CHOLESTERIC LIQUID CRYSTALLINE COMPOSITIONS AND
RECORDING DEVICES UTILIZING SUCH COMPOSITIONS.

*James L. Fergason, and Newton N. Goldberg, assignors to Westinghouse Electric
Corporation. Prior U.S. application June 13, 1966. Also French Pat. #1,527,311.*

It has been discovered, and the present invention is in large part based
on this discovery, that certain liquid crystal cholesteric compositions may be
formulated to provide a significant color change time lag after the change from
the liquid phase to the cholesteric phase. Such hysteretic compositions may
be employed, for example, to determine not only whether a given temperature has
been exceeded but also to provide a record, for a significant time period, of
whether the temperature has been exceeded. The lag in color change will also
occur if the compositions have been exposed to high intensity electric fields
in the order of 20 volts per micron or to gas vapors, such as vapors of chloroform in concentrations in the order of 100 p.p.m. in air.

It is apparent, of course, that not all cholesterogenic materials are
hysteretic in their color transformations. Indeed, most of the heretofore
known materials rapidly change color in response to environmental changes. The
mixtures or combination of compounds of this invention return to their colored
state, from a colorless liquid phase, only after a time delay in the order of
3 to 30 minutes. Moreover, the mixtures will have bright visible colors in
the aligned cholesteric phase and will not crystallize in the range of normal
temperatures, i.e. 0° F. to 300° F. The particular substrate employed, whether
glass, polyester or some other clear plastics film, will have some effect on
the actual color change delay time for a particular composition but the time
delay phenomenon will be observed on all substrates.

The hysteretic liquid crystalline cholesteric mixtures of this invention
contain (A) from 15 to 40 percent, by weight, of at least one halide selected
from the group consisting of cholesteryl chloride, cholesteryl bromide,
cholesteryl iodide, cholestanyl chloride, cholestanyl bromide and cholestanyl
iodide and (B) at least 30 percent, by weight, of at least one compound selected from the group consisting of cholesteryl erucyl carbonate, cholestanyl
erucyl carbonate, cholesteryl oleyl carbonate, cholestanyl oleyl carbonate,
cholesteryl erucate, cholestanyl erucate, cholesteryl oleate and cholestanyl
oleate.

Referring now to Fig.1, there is illustrated as one example of the invention a simplified temperature recording or information storing device 10 that
includes a clear sheet of polyethylene terephthalate 11 having a thickness of
approximately 6 microns. A pigmented film 12 containing carbon black dispersed in a layer of polyvinyl alcohol and having a thickness of approximately
12 microns is deposited on one side of the terephthalate film 11. The film 12
is applied as an aqueous solution or suspension and dried on the film 11.
A film of the hysteretic liquid crystalline cholesteric mixture 13 having a
thickness if approximately 10 microns is deposited on the other side of the
terephthalate base 11. The film 13 is deposited by applying a 10 percent
solution of the hysteretic mixture in petroleum ether onto the film 11 and
evaporating the solvent.

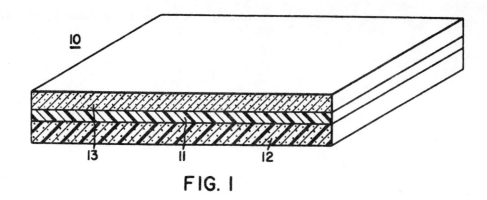

FIG. I

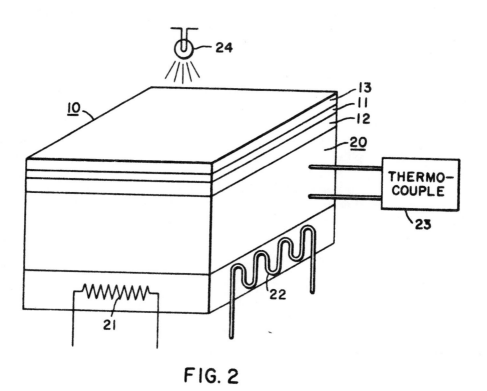

FIG. 2

As an illustration of the practice of the invention, there is shown in Fig.2, the recording device 10 placed so that film 12 is in intimate contact with an aluminum plate or block 20. The block 20 is adapted to be heated, as for example, by a resistance heater 21, and is adapted to be cooled either by lower ambient temperatures after the heating has ceased or by cooling means such as the coil 22 containing circulating cold water. A thermocouple 23 is embedded in the plate 20 so that an accurate measurement of the temperatures of the block can be made. A source of white light 24 is provided so that the color of the layer of hysteretic film in the device will be visible to the naked eye. The visible color is, of course, a known phenomenon associated with the light scattering properties of the cholesteric phase.

EXAMPLE I.

A series of simple recording devices was prepared, in the manner described hereinabove in conjunction with Fig.1, using for film 13 a variety of simple admixtures of combinations of compounds in accordance with the constituent mixtures and composition ranges set forth above for the preparation of suitable hysteretic compositions. These simple devices were then placed in contact with the aluminum plate 20 of Fig.2 and heated until there was a transformation from the cholesteric phase to the liquid phase. The phase transformation was apparent as the layer was observed to change from a vivid color to a colorless layer.

When the layer was cooled, it reverted to the cholesteric phase but the color returned only after a significant delay in time. The compositions presented in Table I hereinbelow were found to be hysteretic and their room temperature colors, i.e. the color of the cholesteric phase, and their clearing points, i.e. the melt point or liquid transition point, were as indicated. In each case, at least a three minute time lag was observed in the color change, after the layer had been cooled to a temperature where the material was in the cholesteric phase. All of the percentages in the table below and those that appear thereafter are weight percentages unless otherwise specified.

TABLE I. PROPERTIES OF HYSTERETIC MIXTURES

Example Number	Composition	Color of Cholesteric Phase	Clearing Point, °C
1	30% Cholesteryl Chloride 70% Cholesteryl Erucate	Red	37.5
2	20% Cholesteryl Chloride 80% Cholesteryl Erucate	Green	38.2
3	15% Cholesteryl Chloride 85% Cholesteryl Erucate	Blue	40
4	24% Cholesteryl Chloride 76% Cholesteryl Oleyl Carbonate	Green	45
5	20% Cholesteryl Chloride 80% Cholesteryl Oleyl Carbonate	Blue	45.4
6	30% Cholesteryl Chloride 70% Cholesteryl Oleyl Carbonate	Red	46
7	26% Cholesteryl Bromide 74% Cholesteryl Oleyl Carbonate	Green	43.8
8	26% Cholesteryl Bromide 74% Cholesteryl Oleate	Green	41.1
9	26% Cholesteryl Chloride 74% Cholesteryl Erucyl Carbonate	Green	38.6

It should be understood that the foregoing are examples and that other film thicknesses and mixtures may be employed. Glass or other clear plastics films may be employed in place of the polyethylene terephthalate film.

Other pigments e.g. gold black, may be substituted for the carbon black. The pigment may be dispersed in methyl cellulose, polyvinyl pyrrolidone or other plastics materials in place of the polyvinyl alcohol. The color of the pigment should be complementary to the color of the light beam directed onto the hysteretic cholesteric layer. When the incident light is white, the pigment should be black, and when the light is red, the pigment should be green. The cholesteric layer may be deposited from other volatile organic solvent such as chloroform, halogenated hydrocarbons and volatile hydrocarbon solvents. The cholesteric layer need only be a few microns in thickness but may be in the order of 50 microns and more. It should also be understood that cholestanyl compounds may be substituted for the foregoing cholesteryl compounds to provide similar results.

As is apparent from the data in Table I, only a small variation in the clearing point occurs with varying amounts of compounds in a given combination of compounds. It has also been discovered, however, that significant changes in clearing points may be made by the addition of certain clearing point modulating agents. Up to 35%, by weight, of (C) a clearing point elevating agent selected from the group of esters consisting of cholesteryl nonanoate, cholestanyl nonanoate, cholesteryl decanoate and cholestanyl decanoate may be included in the admixtures of compounds (A) and (B) to raise the clearing point temperature of the deposited cholesteric layer. The hysteretic effect is present in the layers even though the ester has been added to raise the clearing point. However, the total amount of materials or compounds selected from (A) and (C) should not exceed 60 percent of the weight of the total mixture. As little as 1.0 percent of the esters in the group (C) will have a noticeable and useful effect in elevating the clearing point temperature of a basic mixture (A) and (B). In general, the addition of about 5 percent of any of the esters (C) will raise the clearing point about one degree Centigrade.

EXAMPLE II.

Referring again to the devices shown in Fig.1, admixtures containing the compounds (A), (B) and the described esters (C) were employed to form the recording device 10 by depositing the admixture as a 10 micron thick layer 13 from a ten percent solution in petroleum ether onto one side of a 6 micron thick polyethylene terephthalate film 11. The other side of the film 11 had the pigmented layer 12 described hereinbefore. Recording devices, with the compositions described in Table II providing the hysteretic liquid crystalline cholesteric layers, were tested in the apparatus of Fig.2 in the manner heretofore described in conjuction with the example of Table I. Again, at least a three minute time lag was observed in the color change after the layer was cooled below its clearing point. That the esters (C) have a pronounced and predictable effect in elevating the clearing point of a basic mixture of a hysteretic cholesteric composition of (A) and (B) is apparent from the data of Table II.

It should be understood that cholestanyl nonanoate and decanoate may be substituted for the cholesteryl nonanoate and decanoate in the examples shown in Table II with similar r-sults. Some variation in the actual clearing point may occur for identical amounts of ester (C) in any hysteretic composition and the clearing points may be readily calibrated for the particular ester being employed. It should also be understood that both the cholesteryl and cholestanyl esters of the group (C) may be employed with either the cholestanyl and/or cholesteryl compounds of the groups (A) and (B).

TABLE II. ELEVATION OF CLEARING POINT

Example Number	Composition	Color of Cholesteric Phase	Clearing Point, °C
10	28% Cholesteryl Chloride 26% Cholesteryl Nonanoate 46% Cholesteryl Oleyl Carbonate	Red	51
11	28% Cholesteryl Chloride 10% Cholesteryl Nonanoate 62% Cholesteryl Oleyl Carbonate	Red	44
12	28% Cholesteryl Chloride 26% Cholesteryl Decanoate 46% Cholesteryl Oleyl Carbonate	Red	51
13	28% Cholesteryl Chloride 10% Cholesteryl Decanoate 62% Cholesteryl Oleyl Carbonate	Red	44

In order to depress the clearing point of a given mixture of (A) and (B), up to about 10 percent of another class of modulating agents (D), in this instance known as depressing agents, may be included in the mixture. Fatty compounds which dissolve the admixture (A) and (B) without crystallizing will function as clearing point depressing agents. Suitable fatty compounds for this purpose include the fatty acids, fatty esters and fatty alcohols, both saturated and unsaturated hydrocarbon acids with preferably over 8 carbon atoms, for example, oleic, stearic, palmitic, lauric, erucic, myristic and behenic acids. Suitable fatty esters are derived by reacting monohydric and polyhydric hydrocarbon alcohols, with the fatty acids, for example, methyl oleate, ethyl oleate, cetyl oleate, diolein, triolein, tributrin, tripalmitin, tristearin and mixtures thereof, particularly mixtures of trigyceryl esters of fatty acids such as the naturally occurring olive, sperm, soybean, corn and tall oils. Suitable fatty alcohols are, for example, oleyl, stearyl, cetyl and lauryl alcohols. The liquid fatty compounds are preferred but the solid compounds may be employed, if the ultimate admixture with the combination of (A) and (B) does not crystallize. Crystallization will, of course, destroy the liquid crystal cholesteric phase.

EXAMPLE III.

Again referring to Fig.1, admixtures containing the compounds (A),(B) and the fatty compounds (D) were employed to form the simple recording device 10 by depositing various admixtures as a 10 micron thick layer 13 from a ten percent solution in petroleum ether onto one side of a 6 micron thick polyethylene terephthalate film 11. The other side of the film 11 had the pigmented layer 12 described hereinabove. Recording devices, with the compositions described in Table III hereinbelow being deposited as the hysteretic liquid crystalline cholesteric layers, were tested in the apparatus of Fig.2 in the manner heretofore described. Again, at least a three minute time lag was observed in the color change after the various layers were cooled to temperatures below their clearing points. That the fatty compounds (D) have a predictable effect in depressing the clearing point of a basic mixture of a hysteretic composition of (A) and (B) is apparent from Table III.

TABLE III.   DEPRESSION OF CLEARING POINT

Example Number	Composition	Color of Cholesteric Phase	Clearing Point, °C
14	26% Cholesteryl Chloride 73% Cholesteryl Oleyl Carbonate 1% Oleic Acid	Green	36.4
15	26% Cholesteryl Chloride 72% Cholesteryl Oleyl Carbonate 2% Oleic Acid	Green	35.3
16	26% Cholesteryl Chloride 71% Cholesteryl Oleyl Carbonate 3% Oleic Acid	Green	33.4
17	26% Cholesteryl Chloride 73% Cholesteryl Oleyl Carbonate 1% Methyl Oleate	Green	36.
18	26% Cholesteryl Chloride 72% Cholesteryl Oleyl Carbonate 2% Methyl Oleate	Green	35.
19	26% Cholesteryl Chloride 71% Cholesteryl Oleyl Carbonate 3% Methyl Oleate	Green	33.
20	26% Cholesteryl Chloride 73% Cholesteryl Oleyl Carbonate 1% Triolein	Green	36.5
21	26% Cholesteryl Chloride 72% Cholesteryl Oleyl Carbonate 2% Triolein	Green	35.5
22	26% Cholesteryl Chloride 71% Cholesteryl Oleyl Carbonate 3% Triolein	Green	33.5
23	26% Cholesteryl Chloride 73% Cholesteryl Oleyl Carbonate 1% Oleyl Alcohol	Green	36.
24	26% Cholesteryl Chloride 72% Cholesteryl Oleyl Carbonate 2% Oleyl Alcohol	Green	35.
25	26% Cholesteryl Chloride 71% Cholesteryl Oleyl Carbonate 3% Oleyl Alcohol	Green	33.

Example Number	Composition	Color of Cholesteric Phase	Clearing Point, °C
26	26% Cholesteryl Chloride 73% Cholesteryl Oleyl Carbonate 1% Olive Oil	Green	36.5
27	26% Cholesteryl Chloride 72% Cholesteryl Oleyl Carbonate 2% Olive Oil	Green	35.5
28	26% Cholesteryl Chloride 71% Cholesteryl Oleyl Carbonate 3% Olive Oil	Green	33.5
29	26% Cholesteryl Chloride 73% Cholesteryl Oleyl Carbonate 1% Sperm Oil	Green	36.
30	26% Cholesteryl Chloride 72% Cholesteryl Oleyl Carbonate 2% Sperm Oil	Green	35.
31	26% Cholesteryl Chloride 71% Cholesteryl Oleyl Carbonate 3% Sperm Oil	Green	33.
32	26% Cholesteryl Chloride 73% Cholesteryl Oleyl Carbonate 1% Tributrin	Green	35.5
33	26% Cholesteryl Chloride 72% Cholesteryl Oleyl Carbonate 2% Tributrin	Green	34.5
34	26% Cholesteryl Chloride 71% Cholesteryl Oleyl Carbonate 3% Tributrin	Green	32.5

It should be understood that the depressing agents may be employed with the cholestanyl compounds as well as the cholesteryl compounds. Other fatty compounds may be substituted for those employed in the examples of Table III with equivalent results although some variations in the actual clearing point may occur. Again, calibration for the particular modulating agent being employed is recommended. The clearing point, in general, will be depressed from about 1 to 2 degrees centigrade for each weight percent of fatty compound in the admixture. As little as 0.1 percent of the fatty compound will provide a perceptible change in the clearing point of a particular admixture.

As noted heretofore, the device of Fig.1 so long as it has a layer of hysteretic cholesteric liquid crystalline material, will function as a temperature recording device for the environment contacting the device. The device may be calibrated by the selection of a proper hysteretic film composition, to determine and record whether a particular temperature has been exceeded.

All of the heretofore described hysteretic compositions may be employed as thin films in devices which will record or store information on environmental conditions other than temperature. Again referring to Fig.1, a 10 micron layer of a composition containing 28 percent cholesteryl chloride and 72 percent cholesteryl oleyl carbonate is deposited as the layer or film 13, the substrate sheet 11 and the pigmented film or layer 12 being as heretofore described in Example I. Such a device 10 will have an easily visible pronounced color at room temperature when exposed to white light. If a 200 volt per cm. field is applied across the 10 micron hysteretic cholesteric layer 13, the color will disappear and the layer will become colorless. The layer 13 will remain clear for about 3 weeks if it is not heated through its clearing point.

The same device may, instead, be employed to record the presence of contaminating vapors, for example. When exposed to air containing from 70 to 100 ppm. of either chloroform or trichloroethylene, the color will disappear. The hysteretic layer will remain colorless for about ten minutes after it is removed from the contaminating atmosphere unless heated through its clearing point.

"""""""""""""""""""""""""

A VISUAL DISPLAY DEVICE.

D. Churchill, J.V. Cartmell, R.E. Miller and P.D. Bouffard, assignors to The National Cash Register Company. Application Jan. 23, 1968; prior U.S. application Feb. 27, 1967.

This invention relates to temperature-sensitive visual display devices and, more specifically, relates to such devices in the form of a dried emulsion coating having incorporated droplets of cholesteric mesomorphic (liquid crystal) material, which material changes in iridescent characteristics where and when temperature changes occur on the coating.

In the specification of United Kingdom Patent No. 1,138,590 a display device is disclosed and claimed which includes an array of minute polymeric capsules containing cholesteric mesomorphic material and adhered to a substrate whose temperature pattern is to be displayed.

While somewhat related to the use of the above-mentioned capsule arrays, an emulsion of unencapsulated cholesteric mesomorphic material, which is part of the subject matter of this invention, is vastly different from those other disclosures in several important respects. The droplets of the material of this invention are not encapsulated but are inclusions in the continuous phase of the emulsion. The emulsion, or coating liquid, of this invention can be prepared by a simple and inexpensive, one-step, process, thereby obviating the necessity for complex capsule-manufacturing equipment and techniques with attendant high manufacturing costs. The emulsion of this invention, when dried at a coating on a body whose temperature pattern is to be displayed, provides that incident light be transmitted through only a single kind of material in order to be reflected iridescently from the unencapsulated droplets of cholesteric mesomorphic material. Due to the extremely small droplet size which can be maintained in an emulsion of unencapsulated droplets of the cholesteric mesomorphic materials, coatings prepared from an emulsion permit of a high degree of optical resolution and also have a very smooth surface.

Figure 1a is a diagrammatic edge view of a substrate sheet 10 having, on one surface, a coating of minute droplets 11 of liquid crystalline material dispersed in a matrix-like polymeric binder material 12, the liquid crystal material being shown in either the isotropic liquid state or the crystalline solid state; that is, not in the mesomorphic state.

FIG.1a.   FIG.1b.

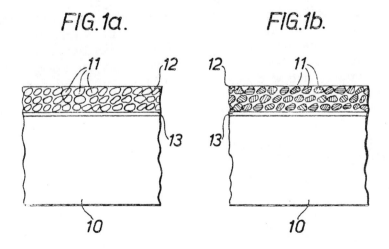

45%, by weight, cholesteryl nonanoate and had a color producing temperature, in the upward excursion, of about 33 degree Centigrade. The temperature range of color response for this mixture was from about 33 degrees Centigrade to about 35.5 degrees Centigrade. Three parts, by weight, of the above mixture of liquid crystal material were emulsified in a Waring Blendor with five parts, by weight, of a 10% by weight, aqueous solution of poly(vinyl alcohol) describe below, until a liquid crystal droplet size-range of from about five microns to about twenty microns was obtained. The poly(vinyl alcohol) used in this exampl had an average molecular weight of 88,000 and was characterized by the facts that (a) a 4%, by weight, aqueous solution of the material exhibited a viscosit of 23 to 28 centipoises at 25 degrees Centigrade, and (b) the material was 97.7% to 98.4% hydrolyzed; that is, that specified percentage of acetate chem- ical groups originally present in molecules of the subject material had been converted to hydroxyl groups.

The emulsion, once prepared, was coated by means of a draw-down applicator to a wet-film thickness of about ten mils onto a blackened substrate sheet of polyethylene terephthalate. The film was allowed to dry in air at about 25 degrees Centigrade. If the temperature of the coating was raised at a point, concentric rings representing a temperature gradient in the range of from 33 degrees Centigrade to 35.5 degrees Centigrade appeared outwardly from a central ring of blue, thence spectrally in order through red, as the temperature gradi- ent decreased. As the temperature of the point was increased or decreased, the effect was evidenced by expansion or contraction of the rings. Systems of ad- jacent expanding and contracting rings from two or more points intersected, and the resultant color of an area was a function of the temperature of that area. The dried emulsion film of this example can be stripped from its poly- ethylene terephthalate substrate and utilized as an unbacked film for displaying temperature gradient patterns. The stripped film can be blackened or opacified on one surface, or it can be used without such blackener or opacifier, as desired.

Example II.

In this example, a mixture of liquid crystal material was used which consisted of 50%, by weight, oleyl cholesteryl carbonate and 50%, by weight, cholesteryl nonanoate. Three parts of the liquid crystal mixture were emul- sified with five parts of a 1%, by weight, aqueous solution of gelatin having suitable film strength. Emulsified droplets of liquid crystal material ranged in size from about ten microns to about twenty microns.

The emulsion, once prepared, was coated, with the use of a draw-down applicator, onto a substrate sheet of polyethylene therephthalate to a wet- film thickness of about ten mils. The so-coated film was dried in air at about 25 degrees Centigrade. The resulting film exhibited temperature re- sponse characteristics similar to those of the film in Example I., and the color producing temperature was observed to be about 25 degrees Centigrade, with 25 to 30 degrees Centigrade as the temperature range for complete spectral color change.

The dried film of this example can be stripped from its substrate and used in the same manner as the film in Example I.

Figure 1b shows the coated substrate sheet 10 of Fig. 1a with the liquid crystal material 11 in the mesomorphic state. Fig.1a is intended to represent the film coating at a temperature above or below that which is required for coloration of the mesomorph-containing film material, while Fig.1b is to represent the same film coating within the temperature range of coloration. The hatching of the droplets in Fig.1b is used to depict a color change from that of Fig.1a and not to suggest particular colors, because iridescence cannot well be suggested by hatching. The coated film can be of a thickness to include only a single layer or a few layers of liquid crystal droplets, or the film can include several layers of droplets within its thickness. Droplets of liquid crystal material can range in size from about five microns to about twenty-five microns and are preferably ten to twenty microns in diameter. Depending upon conditions and requirements for use of the intended coating, several layers which include liquid crystal material of different temperature response ranges can be superimposed in direct or overlapping relation on a surface; or discrete areas of a surface can be coated with layers which include different types of liquid crystal material to obtain temperature response corresponding to the coated pattern and the material coated.

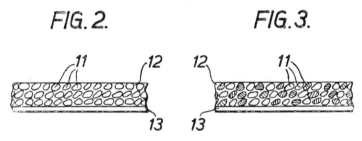

FIG. 2.   FIG. 3.

Figure 2 is a diagrammatic edge view of a self-supporting film containing minute droplets 11 of a single type of liquid crystal material dispersed in a matrix of polymeric binder material 12. Although the film is depicted as having a thickness of only a few droplets diameters, in practice the film may be of any thickness extending from slightly more than one droplet diameter at its thinnest extreme up to gross dimensions of several millimeters. The optional colored layer 13 shown in this figure as well as in Figs. 1a and 1b and in Fig.3, to follow, may be provided or not, as desired, its purpose being to color and/or opacify one surface of the film and thereby act as a background for observing the hue or to enhance the color brilliance of the display.

Figure 3 is a diagrammatic edge view of a self-supporting film containing minute droplets 11 of more than one type of liquid crystal material dispersed in a matrix of polymeric binder material 12. The figure depicts two different types of liquid crystal material contained within the film coating, a first type, for which the ambient film temperature is either above or below the temperature of its mesomorphic state, and a second type, which exists in the mesomorphic state at the film temperature of this figure. It is understood that more than just two different types of liquid crystal material may be included in a film.

Following are examples of specific embodiments of the invention...

Example I.

In this example, a mixture of the specified liquid crystal materials was used which consisted of 55%, by weight, oleyl cholesteryl carbonate and

Example III.

In this example, one part, by weight, of the same liquid crystal mixture as was used in Example II was emulsified in five parts, by weight, of a 22%, by weight, aqueous solution of poly(acrylate) polymeric material. The poly (acrylate) material was ammonium poly(acrylate) and was characterized by having a pH of 8.5 to 9.5 in a 22%, by weight, aqueous solution and by having a viscosity of 150 to 250 centipoises in a 5%, by weight, aqueous solution. Emulsification was conducted in a jacketed Waring Blendor cup equipped with a resistance-wire heater, and the temperature of the emulsified liquid was maintained at 50 degrees Centigrade. Liquid crystal droplets in the emulsion were ten to twenty microns in diameter.

The emulsion, once prepared, was coated and dried as described in Example II, and the behavior of the dried film was noted to be essentially identical to that of Example II with respect to color change according to change in temperature, since the liquid crystal mixture was the same in both example, the dried binder seemingly having little effect as to light-response. A coating was also prepared using glass as the substrate, and results were comparable to those described above.

Example IV.

This example was provided to demonstrate an embodiment of the subject invention wherein the polymeric binder material, which serves to secure droplets of liquid crystal material in dispersion in the matrix, is colored to reduce its transparency to incident light. The colored matrix-like material of this example, thereby, effectively contrasts with the iridescence of entrapped liquid crystal droplets without reliance on opaque substrates or other applied contrasting material.

Three parts, by weight, of a mixture of 85%, by weight, of cholesteryl nonanoate and 15%, by weight, oleyl cholesteryl carbonate were emulsified with five parts, by weight, of a colored binder solution, described below, in a jacketed Waring Blendor cup which was controlled to maintain the liquid temperature at about 50 degrees Centigrade. To prepare the binder solution, 10 grams of the poly(vinyl alcohol) specified in Example I was dissolved in 90 millilitres of Water, and to the solution was added 10 millilitres of fountain-pen black ink.

The emulsion, having been prepared with droplets of liquid crystal material of about 5-25 microns in size, was coated to a wet-film thickness of ten mils onto a transparent, uncolored, sheet of polyethylene terephthalate, using a draw-down applicator as in Example I, and the coating was allowed to dry in air at about 25 degrees Centigrade. The dried emulsion film could be used either as a thin self-supporting film stripped from its substrate or together with the substrate to provide durability. Change in temperature of the film in the presence of incident light resulted in the characteristic color change, which first became evident for this mixture of liquid crystal material as the temperature rose to about 55 degrees Centigrade, iridescence being caused by a variation in temperature over the film area.

Example V.

The materials used in this example were identical with those in Example IV. In this example, however, the emulsion was sprayed onto the substrate by means of a spray gun, and the resulting dried film demonstrated color-reflecting characteristics similar to those of Example IV.

Example VI.

In this example, the polymeric binder material was zein, a prolamine film-former derived from the alcohol extraction of zea mays, a grain commonly called Indian corn. The solvent system utilized in this example was a solution of nine parts, by volume, of methanol and one part by volume of water. A solution of binder material was prepared by dissolving 80 grams of zein in 400 millilitres of the solvent system.

An emulsion was prepared in a jacketed Waring Blendor cup controlled to maintain a temperature of about 50 degree Centigrade. The emulsion consisted of 50 millilitres of the binder material solution and 10 millilitres of a one-to-one mixture of oleyl cholesteryl carbonate and cholesteryl nonanoate.

The emulsion was coated as i Example II, and results were similar to those of Example II with regard to iridescent effect.

Example VII.

This example demonstrates the use of an emulsion which has two different types of liquid crystal materials separately included therein. The emulsion-coating liquid system was prepared by stirring together two emulsions which had different liquid crystal materials emulsified in separate solutions of the same kind of binder material. The two emulsions were prepared as follows:

a) 25 millilitres of 10%, by weight, aqueous poly(vinyl alcohol) solution (as used in Example I) was emulsified with 15 grams of a mixture of 65%, by weight, of oleyl cholesteryl carbonate and 35%, by weight, cholesteryl nonanoate, and
b) 25 millilitres of the 10%, by weight, aqueous poly(vinyl alcohol) was emulsified with 15 grams of a mixture of 85%, by weight, cholesteryl nonanoate and 15%, by weight, oleyl cholesteryl carbonate.

The two emulsions were then stored together carefully and by hand, it being discovered that undue agitation in combining these particular emulsions causes mixing together of the droplets of liquid crystal material.

The emulsion coating system with two different liquid crystal materials was coated onto a substrate and dried in the air at about 25 degrees Centigrade.

The visual effect of a coated dried emulsion of this example was much the same as that of the previous examples, except that color change appeared in the coating in two sequences beginning at two different temperatures. As a comparison to the visual effect described in Example I., for a coating having only one liquid crystal material, the following describes a coating with two liquid crystal materials...

In warming a test point on the film, a first sequence of concentric rings of color appeared, circling the point of heat application. When the point on the film was further warmed above the first color producing temperature but below the color producing temperature of the second emulsified material, the test point again appeared uncolored, with only a ring of color remaining, at that time, a fixed distance from the centre of the heat source, due to the static temperature gradient. Upon further warming of the test point on the film, a second set of color rings began to appear and move outwardly, but never reached the outwardly moving first rings, giving rise to a visual indication of two temperature ranges at different locations on the coated substrate. So much for point application of heat. When the coated substrate, as a whole, was heated, the film reflected changing color not in rings, but all over, colors first appearing due to one liquid crystal material and then, on further heating, the film appearing uncolored, due to the second liquid crystal material, for a time at temperatures intermediate to the different color producing temperatures. The color changes appeared in reverse order on cooling of the film.

Where, in a given small area, there are present two kinds of the liquid drops which exhibit different color reflectance at a given temperature, the effect on the eye is additive, as would be expected.

" "

ELECTRO-OPTICAL DEVICE.

George H. Heilmeier and *Louis A. Zanoni, assignors to Radio Corporation of America. Application March 27, 1968. Prior U.S. Application March 31, 1967.*

This invention relates to improved electro-optical devices useful for applications which involve the modulation of light, such as optical display devices. The invention perticularly relates to nematic liquid crystal electro-optical devices.

The devices are made possible by the discovery that layers of certain nematic liquid crystal compositions undergo or exhibit and essentially non-destructive turbulence when an electric current is caused to flow therethrough upon the application of a voltage across the layer. This turbulence which is restricted to the region of the applied voltage, causes efficient scattering of light incident on that region. The degree of light scattering can be varied by varying the magnitude of the applied voltage between the threshold value necessary to initiate turbulence and a saturation value above which there is little or no change in the degree of light scattering.

The degree of light scattering achieved when using nematic liquid crystal compositions which exhibit this effect, hereinafter called the dynamic scattering effect, is greater than that achieved when using materials as taught in the prior art in which an electric field causes rotation of domains or clusters of the nematic liquid. Display devices having this new effect have contrast ratios of up to greater than 20:1 and response speeds sufficient for commercial television applications.

Figure 1 illustrates a crossed grid optical display device 10. The device 10 is comprised of back and front transparent glass support plates 11 and 12 respectively. The two plates 11 and 12 have essentially parallel inner faces 13 and 14 respectively that are separated by a distance d, which is generally in the range of about 5 to 30 microns. The back plate 11 supports, on its inner face 13, an array of parallel spaced transparent conductive back electrode strips 15a, 15b, 15c and 15d. In this example, only four back trips are shown; but a much larger number of electrode strips may be used. The front plate 12 supports, on its inner face 14, an array of parallel spaced transparent conductive front electrode strips 16a, 16b, 16c and 16d. The front strips 16 are positioned so that their longitudinal directions are substantially perpendicular to the longitudinal direction of the conductive back strips 15. Again, only four front strips are shown, but a much larger number may be used.

The space between the back and front plate 11 and 12 is filled with a medium so as to form a film 17. The film 17 is comprised of a nematic liquid crystal composition of the type that exhibits turbulent motion upon the application of an electric field which produces an electric current in the film, for example, a film comprised of anisylidene-p-aminophenylacetate, having an excess of mobile ions therein. The film 17 is a weak electrolyte.

The device 10 includes connection means 18a to 18d and 19a to 19d for applying a voltage to the conductive back electrodes 15a to 15d and to the conductive front electrodes 16a to 16d, respectively. As used herein, said connecting means and/or said conductive strips are included in the means for applying the electric field or voltage to the liquid crystal layer.

Fig.1 also includes a schematic representation of a circuit for operating the display device 10. The circuit includes a back strip commutator switch 31 having its common contact connected to one side of a voltage source 30 and to ground 32. A plurality of commutator contacts of the switch 31 are connected to the back strip connecting means 18a to 18d through leads 33a to 33d. Also, a front strip commutator switch 35 is provided which has a plurality of commutator contacts connected to the front strip connecting means 19a to 19d through leads 36a to 36d and a common contact connected to the other side of the voltage source 30.

In a transmissive mode of operation, as shown in Fig.2, a light source 21 is positioned on one side of the device 10 so that light is directed through the device in a direction substantially normal to the major faces of the plates 11 and 12. The observer 22 is on the opposite side of the device 10 from the light source 21. At less than a threshold applied field, the observer 22 sees the entire plate area as uniformly bright. When a voltage of sufficient magnitude is applied between a back electrodestrip and a front electrode strip, such as, for example, between electrode strips 15a and 16d via the connecting means 18a and 19d respectively, the film 17 in the volume defined by the intersection of the energized electrode strips is effected by the current caused to flow across it. This voltage and current flow causes turbulence in the film in this volume and gives rise to scattering of light incident on that portion of the device. The observer sees this region of his field of view become darker than the remaining plate are due to the light scattering. The threshold voltage required to obtain this effect is generally in the range of 0.5×10^4 to 1×10^4 volts per centimeter of film thickness. Too high an applied voltage can cause unwanted dielectric breakdown of the liquid crystal medium. The applied voltage can be for example A.C., D.C. or pulsed D.C.

By sequentially energizing more than one electrode strip from each set, a plurality of predetermined areas are thus darkened. Scanning techniques known to the mural television art may be utilized to sequentially and cyclicly energize the conductive strips and to modulate the amplitude of the voltage source. In this manner various types of information may be optically displayed. Furthermore, by having a large number of closely-spaced electrode strips on eacg plate, for example electrode strips that are on the order of 1 mil wide and spaced 1/2 mil apart, a picture can be displayed on a device of this type. Also, the percent of light scattered and hence the degree of darkening for each element can be modulated by controlling the magnitude of the applied voltage above the threshold, thereby affording a grey scale. Alternatively, a display can be generated by simultaneously energizing a plurality of selected electrode strips.

In the above optical display device, operation is achieved by modulation of light transmission as illustrated in Fig.2. Alternatively, operation can be achieved by modulation of light reflection or light absorption. In an absorption. In an absorptive mode of operation, a device 10a, as illustrated in Fig.3 is used. The device 10a differs from the device 10 in that one support plate, e.g., the back plate 11, is coated with a layer of dark material 23 so that light passing through the transparent plate 12 and the nematic liquid crystal layer 17 is absorbed at the darkened plate 11. Alternatively, the back plate may itself be a dark colored composition. A light source 21 a and

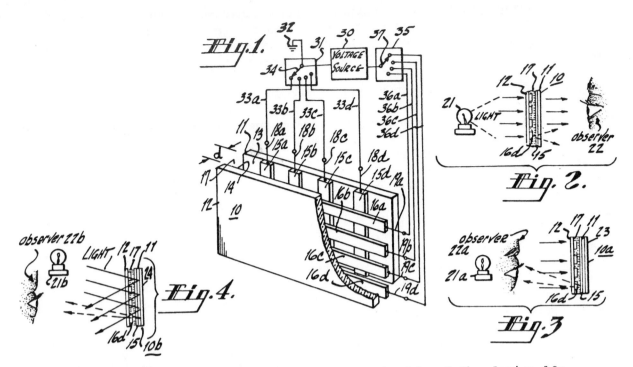

Fig. 1.

Fig. 2.

Fig. 4.

Fig. 3.

a viewer 22a are both disposed on the transparent side of the device 10a. When there is no voltage across an electrode of the group 15a through 15d and an electrode of the group 16a through 16d, the surface of the device appears dark to the viewer as essentially all of the light is absorbed by the dark plate 11 and only a small quatity of light is reflected back to the viewer. When a voltage above the threshold level is applied across any of said electrode pairs, for example electrodes 15a and 16d, some of the light at the inter-section of these electrodes is caused to be reflected by the liquid crsytal layer 17 and appears as a bright area to the viewer. In this mode of operation, the percent of light reflected is modulated by the magnitude of the applied voltage. Also, the brighter the source light or ambient the brighter the reflected image. This mode of operation is the least efficient and least desirable since about 90% of the light is forward scattered by the turbulent liquid crystal layer rather than back scattered. Hence, most of the light continues in the same general direction as prior to scattering and is absorbed on the dark surface.

The preferred mode of operation is the reflective mode and uses a device 10b as illustrated in Fig 4. Here one support plate of the device 10b, e.g., the back plate 11, is made reflective rather than absorbing, for example by a specularly reflective coating 24 on the outer face of the plate 11. In the reflective mode of operation, a light source 21b and a viewer 22b are both positioned on the transparent plate side of the device 10b. The light source 21b, preferably but not necessarily, produces a collimated beam at such an angle that the light reflected from the reflective coating 24 does not strike the viewer 22b. When a voltage is applied across the electrodes of the device as previously described, light will be scattered in the region of the electrode intersection causing some of the light to be observed by the viewer. This mode is more efficient than the absorbing mode since, here, the forward scattered light is reflected back to the viewer so as to give a brighter image.

A variety of transparent solids may be utilized for a transparent support plate, including the various types of glass, fused quartz, transparent corondum, and transparent plastics and resins. A non-transparent support plate may be made from the same materials as the transparent plate coated with a material, such as a black organic dye for absorption or a metallic film for specular reflection.

The transparent conductive strips may be made, for example, by depositing thin layers of indium oxide or stannic oxide on the desired region of the plates 11 and 12. The conductive strips on the light-absorbing or light-reflecting back support plate 11 need not be transparent and may, for example, be a film of copper, aluminum, chromium or nickel. When a D.C. field is used, it is preferable that the negative electrode be a good electron injector, such as a metal. The preferred electrode materials are films of nickel, cobalt, aluminum and transparent tin oxide, nickel and cobalt being especially useful as cathodes. The conductive strips 15a to 15d and 16a to 16d should be in contact with the liquid crystal film 17 so as to permit a current to flow therethrough. It is also possible to use conductors running through the support plates; for example, wires embedded in the support plates, or conductive plugs forming an integral part of the support plate. Alternatively, in some applications, the voltage may be applied between parallel electrodes rather than crossed electrodes.

The spacing between the support plates may be maintained in any one of several ways. For example, by means of shims, clamps, or a suitable frame-like holder.

In operation, the device is maintained at a temperature at which the nematic-liquid crystal composition is in its mesomorphic state. If heating is required, this can be done by external heaters; for example, infra-red heat lamps or heating coils in close proximity to the device. Alternatively, this can be accomplished by having transparent resistive layers on the outer faces of the support plates across which voltage is applied so that the power dissipated in these layers heats the device. It is preferable to heat the devices to temperatures somewhat above the crystal-nematic transition temperature because, when they are operated at or about the transition temperature, the response of the liquid crystal layer is slower than at higher temperatures in the mesophase. Also, the contrast ratio may be reduced at near transition temperatures due to the presence of light scattering in the absence of the field.

It was additionally discovered that in order to obtain the maximum contrast ratio of a device operated in the reflective mode and employing ambient or other non-collimated light as the light source, it is preferable to have the face of the device "look-into" a black or light absorbtive background. That is, the device should be at an angle such that most of the light striking the device which is unscattered will be reflected into a light absorbtive background. In this way the surface of the device will appear dark except in the region where scattered light is reflected back to the viewer. This region appears as a light spot having high contrast to the surrounding dark areas. Also, in order to eliminate annoying mirror-like reflections of the surrounding area, the front support plate or a separate cover plate should be made with a lightly frosted surface so as to diffuse the ambient to an extent such that the mirror-like reflections are eliminated.

Fig.5 illustrates an embodiment of a package for the device 10b employing the above arrangement. The package is comprised of a box 51 having a length of about 6-3/4 inches, a width of about 4 inches, and a depth of about 1-5/8 inches. The box 51 is completely closed except for about a 2-1/2 inch by 2-1/2 inch area cut out of the front face 52 of the box. This area is located about 1 inch from a top edge and 3/4 of an inch from each side of the front face 52. A 3 inch by 3 inch reflective display device 10b is mounted within the box 51 opposite, and in line with the opening defined by the cutout area of the front face 52. The device 10b is mounted by means of a support member 53 attached to the back portion 54 of the box 51, so that the device 10b makes an angle of about 10° with the front face 52 of the box 51. A lid 55 is pivotally mounted to the top edge of the box 51 by means of a hinge 56.

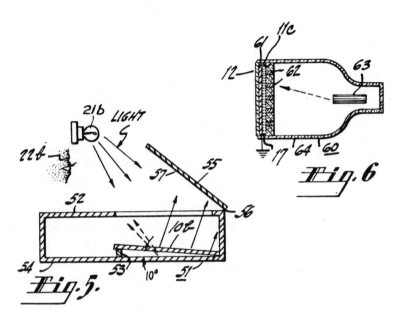

The inner face of the lid 57 is black. When the lid is raised to an appropriate position, most of the light from the ambient light source 21b, for example, strikes the reflective device 10b, and, when no voltage is applied to the device 10b, the light is reflected onto the dark inner face 57 of the lid 55, causing the device to appear dark to the viewer 22b. When a voltage is applied across a given region of the device 10b, a portion of the light incident on that region is scattered and reflected back to the observer 22b, causing that segment to appear bright as compared to the adjacent regions having no voltage thereacross.

Still another embodiment of the device is illustrated in Fig.6. Here the voltage across the film 17 is generated by the charge deposited by an electron beam which is scanned in the same manner as in a TV system. The beam supplies charge to the selective conducting area in contact with the film 17. This charge establishes the activating voltage across the film 17 in that area. The charge is drained in a frame time by injection into the liquid crystal layer where it combines with a neutral molecule to form a mobile anion. The mobile anion is discharged when it reaches the anode.

The device is comprised of a front support plate 12 having an electrically grounded transparent conductive layer 61 on one major surface thereof. A back support plate 11c is spaced from and essentially parallel to the front support plate 12. The back support plate 11c includes a plurality of holes therein and a conductor, such as conducting epoxy resin plugs 62, filling said holes. The epoxy resin plugs are preferably coated with evaporated aluminum. A film 17 as previously described fills the space between the back and front support plates and is in contact with the transparent conductive layer. The device also includes means for electron beam scanning the back support plate, such as a conventional electron beam gun 63. Instead of conductive epoxy plugs, metal wires can be embedded in the back support plate. It is also necessary to provide an evacuated envelope 64 around the back support plate 11c and the electron gun 63.

The electron gun scanning system can be made into a color system by using a backing which selectively reflects a particular primaru color. For example, the plugs may be arranged in a triad dot configuration wherein the surface of the plugs in contact with the film have a conductive layer, for example an aluminum layer thereon, and wherein said aluminum layer is treated with a dye to selectively reflect one of the primary colors, each dot in a triad reflecting a different primary color. Alternatively, a front support plate which selectively transmits a particular primary color may be used to obtain a color display. The device can then be scanned by a standard three color gun, such as the type employed in conventional shadow mask color TV tubes. The triad structure or selective transmitting support plate structure described above can also be used for producing a color display with scanning techniques other than electron beam scanning, for example, matrix scanning.

A wide variety of liquid crystal compositions are useful in the electro-optical devices which operate by the dynamic scattering mode. Preferably, the nematic liquid crystal compositions have resistivities of between about 1×10^8 ohm-centimeters and 10^{11} ohm-centimeters. The resistivity necessary for any particular device depends upon the charge density and ion concentration of the film 17. A preferred class of liquid crystal compositions that have exhibited the non-destructive turbulence effect necessary for operation of the devices are Schiff bases having oxygen atoms bonded to the furthermost para positions of the aromatic rings of the compound.

The preferred film 17 is comprised of anisylidene-p-aminophenylacetate, (hereinafter referred to as APAPA) having trace amounts of p,n-butoxybenzoic acid, (hereinafter referred to as BBA), therein. Although APAPA can be used without the BBA it is somewhat milky and causes unwanted zero field reflection which thereby reduces the contrast ratio of the device. It was found that the addition of trace amounts of BBA substantially reduces this milky appearance. Contrast ratios of greater than 20:1 have been achieved in devices having a film comprised of APAPA and BBA and operated in the reflective mode. In operation, APAPA films require voltages in the order of 10 to 100 volts across a 1/2 mil thick film with operating temperatures in the range of 65°C to 95°C. The light scattering typically has a two millisecond buildup and a 15 to 30 millisecond decay time in response to changes in electric field. The devices are operable under either A.C., D.C. or pulsed D.C. voltages. It is important for good operation and long life of the devices that the liquid crystal materials be purified at least until a reversible and constant nematic-isotropic liquid transition temperature is reached. This can generally be achieved by repeated recrystallization of the liquid crystal compounds.

The graph of Fig.7 is a plot of reflection contrast ratio versus applied D.C. voltage for a device having a 1/2 mil thick film of a mixture of p-n-anisylidene-p'-aminophenylacetate (APAPA), p-n-octoxybenzylidene-p'-amino-

148

phenylacetate, a silicon back electrode and a transparent conductive front electrode.

The change in contrast ratio with a change in applied voltage shows the grey scale control that is obtainable. A variation of contrast ratio and threshold voltage is also shown as a function of film temperature. For example, at an operating temperature of 63° C. this particular device has a contrast ratio of about 2 at a voltage of 4 volts and 19 at a voltage of 60 volts. The same device operated at 90° C. has a contrast ratio of about 1 at 4 volts and 11.5 at 60 volts.

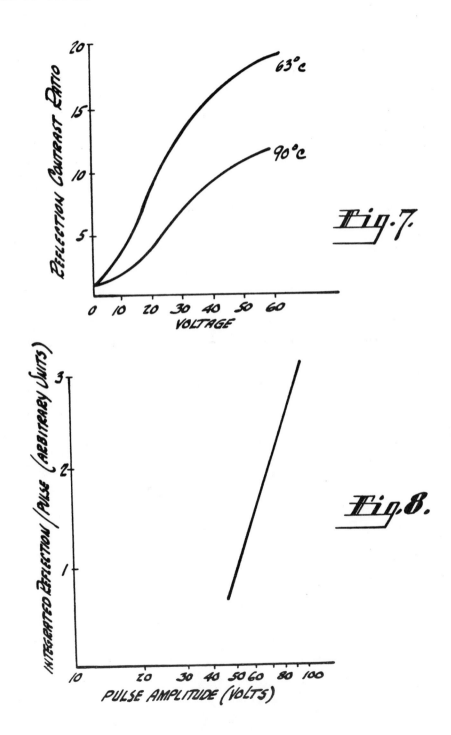

Fig. 7.

Fig. 8.

Fig. 8 is a plot of integrated reflection pulse versus the pulse amplitude of a device operated by a pulsed voltage rather than a steady D.C. voltage. The particular device was comprised of a 1/2 mil thick film composed of p-n-octoxybenzylidene-p-aminophenylacetate having a resistivity of about 1.05×10^{10} ohm-centimeters. The back electrode was chromium and the front electrode was a transparent tin oxide. Measurements were made using a 60 microsecond pulse at 15 pulses per second. The temperature of the device was 86° C. Under the above excitation a greater than threefold increase in the magnitude of the integrated reflection was achieved for a twofold increase in pulse amplitude. The pulse amplitudes used varied from about 50 volts to 100 volts.

""""""""""""""""""""""""

SCHIFF'S BASES AND ELECTRO-OPTICAL COMPOSITIONS AND DEVICES.

Joel E. Goldmacher, and Joseph A. Castellano, assignors to Radio Corporation
of America.
Prior U.S. application June 9, 1966. Also French Patent No. 1,537,000.

The invention relates to electro-optical devices comprised of a novel
nematic mesophase composition.

A device using the light-scattering effect of the novel nematic liquid
crystal compositions disclosed herein may be utilized as the light-scattering
medium in a projection television system. Nematic liquid crystal compositions
are known to have high Kerr constants when in the mesomorphic state. Hence,
the novel compositions disclosed herein may also be used in Kerr cells. The
novel nematic compositions are usable in any device employing the properties
of nematic liquid crystals presently known.

Examples of compounds included in the novel nematic liquid crystal composition are given in Table I along with their transition points.

Table II gives examples of mixtures included in the novel compositions.
The numbers representing the components given in Table II refer to the numbers
designating the novel compounds in Table I except that "11" is a known compound, namely p-(anisalamino)-phenylacetate. This compound has a crystal-
mesomorphic transition temperature of 81° C. and a mesomorphic-isotropic liquid
transition temperature of 110° C. Percent designation refers to weight percent
based on the total weight of material in the composition. The compositions
represented by the mixtures have the dual advantage of a low crystal-mesophase
transition temperature and a wide temperature range in which the mesophase is
stable. The examples given in Table II have a mesophase range of about 60 to
80 degrees. This wide range makes expensive and bulky temperature control
unnecessary.

Mixtures can be prepared, for example, by weighing the pure crystalline
components in a beaker so as to get the desired proportions. The components
are then heated with stirring above their mesophase-isotropic transitional
temperatures. The homogeneous liquid thus forming is allowed to cool to 0° C.
The resulting solid is generally a waxy homogeneous mass.

In general, the compounds included in the novel composition can be prepared, for example, by the condensation of a p-acyloxyphenylamine with the
appropriate p-alkoxybenzaldehydes. The reaction is carried out in a refluxing
benzene solution with benzenesulfonic acid or acetic acid as a catalyst and
facility for azeotropic removal of water. The compounds can be purified by
recrystallization from hexane solution. The recrystallization is repeated
until a constant mesophase-isotropic transition temperature is reached.

EXAMPLE I.

A solution of 1.51 grams of p-aminophenylacetate, 1.78 grams of p-butoxybenzaldehyde and 0.1 grams of benzenesulfonic acid in 50 ml of benzene is
refluxed for about 3 hours. A Dean-Stark trap is used to collect the water
which is azeotropically removed. After refluxing, the solvent is removed by

TABLE I

Compounds Included in the Novel Liquid Crystal Compositions

Compound Example	X	Y	Crystal-Mesomorphic Transition Temp. °C	Mesomorphic Isotropic Liq. Transition Temp. °C
1	CH$_3$CH$_2$$\overset{\overset{\text{O}}{||}}{\text{C}}$O—	—OCH$_3$	86	118
2	CH$_3$(CH$_2$)$_2$$\overset{\overset{\text{O}}{||}}{\text{C}}$O—	—OCH$_3$	86	119
3	CH$_3$(CH$_2$)$_2$$\overset{\overset{\text{O}}{||}}{\text{C}}$O—	—OC$_6$H$_{13}$	86	120
4	C$_4$H$_9$O—	—O$\overset{\overset{\text{O}}{\|\|}}{\text{C}}CH_3$	82	113
5	iso C$_5$H$_{11}$O—	—O$\overset{\overset{\text{O}}{\|\|}}{\text{C}}CH_3$	74	82
6	C$_6$H$_{13}$O—	—O$\overset{\overset{\text{O}}{\|\|}}{\text{C}}CH_3$	88	109
7	C$_8$H$_{17}$O—	—O$\overset{\overset{\text{O}}{\|\|}}{\text{C}}CH_3$	80	105.5
8	C$_9$H$_{19}$O—	—O$\overset{\overset{\text{O}}{\|\|}}{\text{C}}CH_3$	86	100
9	CH$_3$O—	—O$\overset{\overset{\text{O}}{\|\|}}{\text{C}}$(CH$_2$)$_2CH_3$	49—50	113
10	CH$_3$O—	—O$\overset{\overset{\text{O}}{\|\|}}{\text{C}}$(CH$_2$)$_3CH_3$	55	100

TABLE II

Mixtures Included in the Novel Liquid Crystal Compositions

Mixture Example	Components	Crystal-Mesormorphic Transition Temp. °C.	Mesomorphic-Isotropic Liquid Transition Temp. °C.
A	50% *11* — 50% *4*	47	108
B	35.1% *11* — 32.6% *4* — 32.3% *7*	40	103
C	25.5% *11* — 24.5% *4* — 50% *7*	45	103
D	25% each of *11, 4, 6* and *7*	39	104
E	50.1% *3* — 49.9% *2*	48	118
F	34.8% *3* — 34.6% *2* — 30.6% *1*	53	117
G	1/3 wt. ratio each of *9, 4* and *11*	22	105
H	1/3 wt. ratio each of *9, 10, 11*	25	105
I	50% *9* — 50% *10*	45	106

evaporation under reduced pressure in a rotating film evaporator. The residue is collected and recrystallized three times from hexane.

EXAMPLE II.

A solution of 1,23 g of p-anisidine, 1.78 g of p-formylphenylpropionate and 0.10 g of benzenesulfonic acid in 50 ml of benzene is refluxed for about 4 hours. The same procedure as in Example I is used to isolate and purify the product.

EXAMPLE III.

A solution of 5.4 g of p-amino-phenol, 8.9 g of p-butoxybenzaldehyde and 0.1 g of benzenesulfonic acid in 200 ml of benzene is refluxed for 4 hours. The same procedure as in Example I is used to isolate and purify the resulting yellow plates. Recrystallization of these plates from benzene results in white crystals of p-butoxybenzylidene-p-aminophenol. A mixture of 2.8 grams of this material in 10 ml of a cold (-5° C. to 10° C.) 5N sodium hydroxide solution and 100 ml of benzene is then treated with 1.4 g of propionic anhydride. This mixture is stirred for about 1 hour. The mixture is filtered with suction and its resulting two-phase filtrate is transferred to a separatory funnel. The lower aqueous phase is removed and the benzene layer is washed twice with water. The benzene solution is then dried over anhydrous sodium sulfate. The benzene is then evaporated and the residue is recrystallized from hexane to yield colorless crystals of p-butoxybenzylidene-p-aminophenylpropionate.

EXAMPLE IV.

A solution of 54.5 g of p-aminophenol, 68.0 g of anisaldehyde and 0.1 g of benzenesulfonic acid in 200 ml of benzene is refluxed for 4 hours at which time about 9.0 ml of water is collected in a Dean-Stark trap. The product is collected as in Example I and recrystallized from a 50:50 ethanol:benzene solution to give colorless crystals. A misture of 2.1 g of these crystals, 50 ml pyridine and 1.9 g of valeric anhydride is stirred at room temperature overnight. The solvent is then evaporated and the residue triturated with hexane to yield colorless crystals of p-methoxybenzylidine-p-aminophenyl-pentanoate.

EXAMPLE V.

A quantity of 100 mg of p-(anisalamino)-phenylacetate and 100 mg of p-butoxybenzylidene-p-aminophenylacetate are placed in a 5 ml beaker. The beaker is heated on a hot plate to about 120° C. and the melt is stirred so as to form a homogeneous solution. The solution is then cooled to 0° C. and the homogeneous solid mass thus formed can then be stored at room temperature. In order to form an electro-optical device using this novel composition, a support plate having electrodes thereon is heated to about 60° C. and an amount of the novel composition is placed on the surface of the support plate and allowed to flow over the surface. The front plate is then carefully placed over the fluid composition so that a continuous film essentially free of air bubbles is formed.

EXAMPLE VI.

The same procedure as described in Example V is carried out using a mixture containing 50 mg each of p(anisalamino) phenylacetate, p-butoxybenzylidene-p-aminophenylacetate, p-octoxybenzylidene-p-aminophenylacetate, and p-monoxy-benzylidene-p-aminophenylacetate.

" " " " " " " " " " " " " " " " " " " "

BIBLIOGRAPHY

Books and Conference Reports

Schenck, R., KRISTALLINISCHE FLUESSIGKEITEN AND FLUESSIGE KRISTALLE, 1905,
W. Engelman, Leipzig.

The Faraday Society, LIQUID CRYSTALS AND ANISOTROPIC MELTS, 1933,
Aberdeen University Press; also printed
in Trans Faraday Soc, v22 p881-1085 ('33)

Gray, G.W., MOLECULAR STRUCTURE AND THE PROPERTIES OF LIQUID CRYSTALS, 1962,
Academic Press, New York.

Proceedings, FIRST INTERNATIONAL CONFERENCE ON LIQUID CRYSTALS, 1965,
Kent State University, Kent, Ohio,
16-20 August 1965.
Gordon & Breach Science Publishers
New York and London.

Chistyakov, I.G., LIQUID CRYSTALS, 1966, Nauka Press, Moscow.

Baltzer, D.H., LIQUID CRYSTALS, 1967, Vari-Light Corp., Cincinnati, Ohio.

150th NATIONAL MEETING OF THE AMERICAN CHEMICAL SOCIETY, Atlantic City,
14-15 September 1965.
Published as "Advances in Chemistry
Series 63", 1967, by the American Chem-
ical Society, Washington, D.C. Porter
R.S. and Johnson, J.F., editors.

Program and Abstracts, 1969 SUMMER MEETING OF THE AMERICAN PHYSICAL SOCIETY,
Rochester, N.Y., 18-20 June 1969.

Proceedings, SECOND INTERNATIONAL LIQUID CRYSTAL CONFERENCE, 1968,
Kent State University, Kent, Ohio,
12-16 August 1968 .
Published in June 1969 by
Gordon & Breach Science Publishers,
New York and London.

Collected Abstracts, EIGHT INTERNATIONAL CONGRESS OF CRYSTALLOGRAPHY, 1969
Buffalo, Stony Brook and Upton, N.Y.
7-20 August 1969,
Abstracts produced by the American Institute of Physics.

Abstract of Papers, 158th NATIONAL MEETING OF THE AMERICAN CHEMICAL SOCIETY,
New York, 7-12 September, 1969.

Proceedings, ELECTRO-OPTICAL SYSTEMS DESIGN CONFERENCE, 1969,
New York, 16-18 September 1969,
Publisher: Industrial & Scientific
Conference Management, Inc., Chicago
(to be published in 1970)

Extended Abstracts, FALL MEETING OF THE ELECTROCHEMICAL SOCIETY, 1969,
Detroit, Mich. 5-9 October 1969.

"""""""""""""""""""""""

Articles

Adams, J., Haas, W., Wysocki, J.,
DEPENDENCE OF PITCH ON COMPOSITION IN CHOLESTERIC LIQUID CRYSTALS,
Phys Rev Letters v22 n3 p92-4 (20 Jan '69)

Adams. J., Haas, W., Wysocki, J.,
OPTICAL PROPERTIES OF CERTAIN CHOLESTERIC LIQUID CRYSTAL FILMS,
J Chem Phys v50 n6 p2458-64 (15 Mch '69)

Adams, J., Haas, W., Wysocki, J.,
STRUCTUREAL DEPENDENCE ON CONSTITUENTS IN CHOLESTERIC MIXTURES,
APS Summer Meeting; Rochester, Abstract FB2 (June '69)

Adams, J., Haas, W., Wysocki, J.,
LIGHT SCATTERING PROPERTIES OF CHOLESTERIC LIQUID CRYSTAL FILMS,
Mol Cryst Liq Cryst v8 p9-18 (Jne '69)

Adams, J., Haas, W., Wysocki, J.,
EFFECTIVE ROTARY POWER OF THE FATTY ESTERS OF CHOLESTEROL,
ACS Meeting, 158th Annual, New York, Abstract 51 (Sep '69)

Adams, J., Haas, W.,
SENSITIVITY OF CHOLESTERIC FILMS TO ULTRAVIOLET LIGHT,
Electrochem Soc, Fall Meeting, Detroit, Abstract 159, (Oct '69)

Alexandrov, V.N. Chistyakov, I.G.,
THE OPTICAL ACTIVITY OF THE MIXTURES OF p-AZOXYANISOLE AND CHOLESTERYL
PROPIONATE,
Mol Cryst Liq Cryst v8 p19-26 (Jne '69)

Allen, P.J.,
INFRARED LASER BEAM IMAGING DETECTORS USING ENCAPSULATED LIQUID CRYSTALS,
Electro-Optical Systems Design Conference, New York,(16-18 Sep '69)

Amerik, Y.B., Krentsel, B.A., Konstantinov, I.I.,
POLYMERIZATION OF VINYL OLEATE IN THE LIQUID CRYSTALLINE STATE,
Dokl Akad Nauk SSSR v165 n5 p1097-100 ('65)

Amerik, Y.B., Krentsel, B.A.,
POLYMERIZATION OF CERTAIN VINYL MONOMERS IN LIQUID CRYSTALS,
J Pol-m Sci Pt.C v16 p1383-93 ('67)

Amerik, Y.B., Konstantinov, I.I., Krentsel, B.A., Malakhaev, E.M.,
POLYMERIZATION OF p-METHYLACRYLOYLOXYBENZOIC ACID IN THE LIQUID
CRYSTALLINE STATE,
Vysokomol, Soedin, Ser.A v9 p2591-7 ('67)

Anon,
LIQUID CRYSTALS' SPECTRA SHOW FINE STRUCTURE,
Chem & Eng N v42 p42-4+ (16 Mch '64)

LIQUID CRYSTALS: LIKE A CHAMELEON,
Product Eng v35 p56-7 (21 Dec '64)

STUDY OF LASER BEAM AIDED BY LIQUID CRYSTAL SENSORS,
Laser Focus p12 (15 Jan '65)

LIQUID CRYSTAL I.R. PATTERN VIEWER,
Laser Focus p9-10 (1 Mch '65)

LASERS AND LIQUID CRYSTALS,
Mech Eng v87 p68 (Mch '65)

N.M.R. HAS ROLE IN STUDY OF LIQUID CRYSTALS,
Chem & Eng N v43 p25 (23 Aug '65)

LIQUID CRYSTALS DEMONSTRATE RESEARCH UTILITY,
Chem & Eng N v43 p52-3 (30 Aug '65)

DEFECTS SHOWN IN COLOR,
Iron Age v196 p85 (16 Sep '65)

LIQUID CRYSTAL FINDS FLAWS VIA COLOR IN NONDESTRUCTIVE TESTING,
Steel v157 p65 (20 Sep '65)

COLOR BY CHOLESTEROL,
Electronics v38 p46 (18 Oct '65)

COLOR COAT ON SKIN DETECTS DISEASE,
Product Eng v37 p35 (6 Jne '66)

DISCUSSION OF NOMENCLATURE OF LIQUID CRYSTALS,
Mol Cryst v2 n1 p189-93 (Dec '66)

LIQUID CRYSTALS FIND ADHESIONS IN PLASTICS,
Product Eng v38 p124 (20 Nov '67)

NEW T.V. SYSTEM; VOLTAGE CONTROLS COLOR,
Machine Design v40 p12 (28 Mch '68)

FROM PHOSPHORS TO LIQUID CRYSTALS,
Iron Age v201 p27 (4 Apr '68)

HOLOGRAMS, LIQUID CRYSTALS FIND FLAWS IN HONEYCOMB,
Materials Eng v67 p94 (May '68)

NEW TYPE OF ELECTRONIC DISPLAY UTIZES LIQUID CRYSTALS,
Computer Design v7 p18 (Jly '68)

NEW THIN-SCREEN DISPLAYS UTILIZE LIQUID CRYSTAL EFFECT,
IEEE Spectrum v5 p129 (Jly '68)

LIQUID CRYSTAL APPLICATIONS,
Wireless World v74 p222 (Jly '68)

LIQUID CRYSTALS MAKE BRIGHT EFFICIENT DISPLAYS,
Machine Design v40 p16 (4 Jly '68)

LIQUID CRYSTALS: A STEP CLOSER TO LOW-VOLTAGE DISPLAYS,
Electronic Eng v27 p17 (Aug '68)

TAKE A LOOK AT WHAT'S NEW IN DISPLAYS,
Instrumentation Tech v15 p10-1 (Aug '68)

LIQUID CRYSTALS: NEW TYPE OF ELECTRONIC DISPLAY,
Glass Ind v49 p423-5 (Aug '68)

LIQUID CRYSTAL DISPLAYS,
Radio-Electronics v39 p4 (Aug '68)

COLOR OF LIGHT SWITCHED,
Chem & Eng N v46 p12-3 (19 Aug '68)

LIQUID CRYSTAL WORK CUTS TIME TO LARGE-SCALE ELECTRONIC USES,
Chem & Eng N v46 p32-3 (30 Sep '68)

MORE LIQUID CRYSTALS MEAN BETTER DISPLAYS,
Electronic Eng v27 p15 (Nov '68)

NEW LIQUID CRYSTALS USED FOR DISPLAYS,
Materials Eng v69 p81 (May '69)

LIQUID CRYSTALS CONFERENCE REPORT,
(Woolwich Polytechnic, June, 1969)
Nature v223 n5204 p350-1 (26 Jly '69)

Armstrong, J.A., Bloembergen, N., Ducuing, J., Pershan, P.S.,
INTERACTIONS BETWEEN LIGHT WAVES IN A NONLINEAR DIELECTRIC,
Phys Rev v127 n6 p1918-39 (15 Sep '62)

Arnold, H., Roedinger, P.,
CALORIMETRY OF CRYSTALLINE LIQUID COMPOUNDS. Di-ETHYL AZOXYBENZOATE AND
ETHYETHOXY-BENZOLAMINOCINNAMATE,
Z Phys Chem (Leipzig) v231 n5-6 p407-15 ('66)

Arnold, H.,
HEAT CAPACITY AND ENTHALPHY OF TRANSITION OF AROMATIC LIQUID CRYSTALS,
Mol Cryst v2 n1 p63-70 (Dec '66)

Arnold, H., Roedinger, P.,
CALORIMETRY OF CRYSTALLINE-LIQUID SUBSTANCES. CHOLESTERYL ESTERS,
Z Phys Chem (Leipzig) v239 n5-6 p283-8 ('68)

Arnold, H., Jacobs, J., Sonntag, O.,
CALORIMETRY OF CRYSTALLINE LIQUIDS. REACTIONS OF SMECTIC PHASES,
Z Phys Chem (Leipzig) v240 n3-4 p177-84 ('69)

Arnold, H., Demus, D., Kock, A.J., Nelles, A., Sackmann, H.,
CALORIMETRY OF CRYSTALLINE LIQUIDS. HEATS OF REACTIONS AND CRYSTALLINE
LIQUIDS SYSTEMATICS.
Z Phys Chem (Leipzig) v240 n3-4 p185-95 ('69)

Arora, S.L., Taylor, T.R., Fergason, J.L., Saupe, A.,
LIQUID CRYSTAL PLYMORPHISM IN BIS-(4'-n-ALKOXYBENZAL)-1,4-PHENYLENDIAMINES,
Am Chem Soc J v91 p3671 ('69)

Arora, S.L., Taylor, T.R., Fergason, J.L.,
POLYMORPHISM OF SMECTIC PHASES WITH SMECTIC A MORPHOLOGY,
A.C.S. Meeting, 158th Annual, New York, Abstract 77 (Sep '69)

Arora, S.L., Taylor, T.R., Fergason, J.L.,
MESOMORPHIC PROPERTIES OF ALKOXY BENZYLIDENE-AMINOACETOPHENONES,
J Org Chem (in press)

Arora, S.L., Fergason, J.L., Saupe, A.,
TWO LIQUID CRYSTAL PHASES WITH NEMATIC MORPHOLOGY,
Mol Cryst Liq Cryst (in Press)

Augustine, C.F.,
FIELD DETECTOR WORKS IN REAL TIME,
Electronics v41 p118-22 (24 Jne '68)

Augsutine, C.F., Kock, W.E.,
MICROWAVE HOLOGRAMS USING LIQUID CRYSTAL DISPLAYS,
IEEE Proc v57 n3 p354-5 (Mch '69)

Augustine, C.F., Deutsch, C., Fritzler, D., Marom, M.,
MICROWAVE HOLOGRAPHY USING LIQUID CRYSTAL AREA DETECTORS,
IEEE Proc v57 n7 p1333-4 (Jly '69)

Axmann, A.,
DIELECTRIC INVESTIGATION OF THE LIQUID CRYSTAL PHASES IN THE MICROWAVE
RANGE. II. MEASUREMENTS ON SOME 4,4'-Di-n-ALKOXYAZOBENZOLES,
Z Naturforsch v21A n5 p615-20 ('66)

Axmann, A.,
DIELECTRIC STUDY OF CRYSTALLINE LIQUID PHASES IN THE MICROWAVE RANGE. I.
MEASUREMENTS ON TWO AZOPHENOL ETHERS.
Z Naturforsch v21A n3 p290-5 ('66)

Axmann, A.,
BERECHNUNG DER MOLEKULAREN HAUPTPOLARISIERBARKEITEN VON EINIGEN 4,4'-Di-n-
ALKOXY-AZOBENZOLEN UND EINIGEN 4,4'-Di-n-ALKOXY-AZOXYBENZOLEN AUS DEN HAUPT-
DIELEKTRIZITAETSKONSTANTEN DER NEMATISCHEN SCHICHTEN,
Mol Cryst v3 n4 p471-8 (May '68)

Bacon, W.E., Brown, G.H.,
LIQUID CRYSTAL SOLVENTS AS REACTION MEDIA FOR THE CLAISEN REARRANGEMENT,
Mol Cryst Liq Cryst v6 n1 p155-9 (Aug '69)

Baessler, H., Labes, M.M.,
RELATIONSHIP BETWEEN ELECTRIC FIELD STRENGTH AND HELIX PITCH IN
INDUCED CHOLESTERIC-NEMATIC PHASE TRANSITIONS,
Phys Rev Letters v21 n27 p1791-3 (30 Dec '68)

Baessler, H., Labes, M.M.,
ELECTRIC FIELD EFFECTS ON THE DIELECTRIC PROPERTIES AND MOLECULAR
ARRANGEMENTS OF CHOLESTERIC LIQUID CRYSTALS,
J Chem Phys v51 n5 p1846-52 ('69)

Baessler, H., Laronge, T.M., Labes, M.M.,
ELECTRIC FIELD EFFECTS ON THE OPTICAL ROTATORY POWER OF A COMPENSATED
CHOLESTERIC LIQUID CRYSTAL,
ACS Meeting, 158th Annual, New York, Abstract 52 (Sep '69)

Balmbra, R.R., Clunie, J.S., Goodman, J.F.,
STRUCTURE OF MESOMORPHIC PHASES BY ELECTRON MICROSCOPY,
Proc Roy Soc (London) serA v285 n1403-4 p534-41 ('65)

Balmbra, R.R., Clunie, J.S., Goodman, J.F.,
THE STRUCTURE OF NEAT MESOMORPHIC PHASE,
Mol Cryst v3 n2 p281-91 (Nov '67)

Balmbra, R.R., Clunie, J.S., Goodman, J.F.,
CUBIC MESOMORPHIC PHASES,
Nature v222 n5199 p1159-60 (21 Jne '69)

Baranov, V.G., Volkov, T.I., Frenkel, S.Y.,
POLARIZATION DIFFRACTOMETRIC INVESTIGATION OF THE FORMATION OF A SUPER-
MOLECULAR STRUCTURE IN A SOLUTION OF A SPIRAL POLYPEPTIDE.
Dokl Akad Nauk SSSR v162 n4 p836-8 ('65)

Barrall, E.M.,II, Porter, R.S., Johnson, J.F.,
HEATS OF TRANSITION FOR NEMATIC MESOPHASES,
J Phys Chem v68 p2810 ('64)

Barrall, E.M.II., Porter, R.S., Johnson, J.F.,
TEMPERATURES OF LIQUID CRYSTAL TRANSITIONS IN CHOLESTERYL ESTERS
BY DIFFERENTIAL THERMAL ANALYSIS,
J Phys Chem v70 p385 ('66)

160

Barrall, E.M.II., Porter, R.S., Johnson, J.F.,
GAS CHROMATOGRAPHY USING CHOLESTERYL ESTER LIQUID PHASES,
J Chromatog v21 p392 ('66)

Barrall, E.M.II., Porter, R.S., Johnson, J.F.,
HEATS OF TRANSITION OF SOME CHOLESTERYL ESTERS BY DIFFERENTIAL
SCANNING CALORIMETRY,
J Phys Chem v71 p1224 ('67)

Barrall, E.M.II., Porter, R.S., Johnson, J.F.,
THE POLYMORPHISM OF CHOLESTERYL ESTERS: DIFFERENTIAL THERMAL, DEPOLARIZED
LIGHT, AND MICROSCOPIC MEASUREMENTS ON CHOLESTERYL MYRISTATE,
Mol Cryst v3 p103 ('67)

Barrall, E.M.II., Porter, R.S., Johnson, J.F.,
SPECIFIC HEATS OF NEMATIC, SMECTIC AND CHOLESTERIC LIQUID CRYSTALS
BY DIFFERENTIAL SCANNING CALORIMETRY,
J Phys Chem v71 p895 ('67)

Barrall, E.M.II., Porter, R.S., Johnson, J.F.,
HEATS AND TEMPERATURES OF TRANSITION OF SOME AROMATIC LIQUID CRYSTAL-
FORMING MATERIALS,
Mol Cryst v3 p299 ('68)

Barrall, E.M.II., Sweeney, M.A.,
DEPOLARIZED LIGHT INTENSITY AND OPTICAL MICROSCOPY OF SOME
MESOPHASE-FORMING MATERIALS,
Molec Cryst v5 n3 p257-71 (Feb '69)

Barrall, E.M.II., Porter, R.S., Johnson, J.F.,
THE HOMOLOGOUS SERIES OF ALIPHATIC ESTERS OF CHOLESTEROL:
THERMODYNAMIC PROPERTIES,
In "Thermal Analysis," R.F. Schwenker and P.D. Garn, eds.,
Volume I. p555-65 ('69)

Barrall, E.M.II., Johnson, J.F., Porter, R.S.,
SCANNING CALORIMETRY OF AROMATIC, DIFUNCTIONAL, UNSATURATED, AND
SUBSTITUTED ACID ESTERS OF CHOLESTEROL,
Mol Cryst Liq Cryst v8 p27-44 (Jne '69)

Barrall, E.M.II., Vogel, M.J.,
THE EFFECT OF PURITY ON THE THERMODYNAMIC PROPERTIES OF
CHOLESTERYL HEPTADECANOATE,
Thermochemica Acta (in press)

Basarov, I.P.,
THEORY OF THE CRYSTAL-LIQUID PHASE TRANSITION
Acta Chim Acad Sci Hung v57 n3 p255-60 ('67)

Bernheim, R.A., Krugh, T.R.,
CHEMICAL SHIFT ANISOTROPIES FROM N.M.R. STUDIES IN LIQUID CRYSTALS,
Am Chem Soc J v89 p6784-5 (6 Dec '67)

Bernheim, R.A., Lavery, B.J.,
N.M.R. OF MOLECULES ORIENTED BY LIQUID CRYSTALS,
J Colliod Interface Sci v26 n3 p291-6 ('68)

Billard, J.,
EXPERIMENTAL INVESTIGATION OF THE PROPAGATION OF PLANE ELECTROMAGNETIC
WAVES IN A NEMATIC HELICOIDAL FOIL,
Compt Rend v261 n4,5,6 p939-42 ('65)

Billard, J., Cerne, R.,
RECHERCHE D'UNE PHASE NEMATIQUE A LA TEMPERATURE AMBIANTE
Mol Cryst v2 n1 p27-44 (Dec '66)

Billard, J.,
DES ONDES ELECTROMAGNETIQUES QUI NE SATISFONT PAS AUX CONDITIONS D'AIRY
PEUVENT SE PROPAGER DANS LES LAMES NEMATIQUES HELICOIDALES
Mol Cryst v3 n2 p227-40 (Nov '67)

Billard, J., Meunier, J.P.,
SURFACES OF A SMECTIC PHASE OF DIETHYLENE GLYCOL LAURATE,
Compt Rend serC v266 p937-9 ('68)

Bishop, D.E.,
A PROCEDURE FOR APPLYING A PROTECTED LAYER OF LIQUID CRYSTALS,
C.F.S.T.I. PB-183 838 (Nov '68)

Black, P.J., Lawson, K.D., Flautt, T.J.,
PROTON MAGNETIC RESONANCE SPECTRUM OF BENZENE ORIENTED IN A
LYOTROPIC MESOPHASE,
J Chem Phys v50 n1 p542-3 (1 Jan '69)

Black, P.J., Lawson, K.D., Flautt, T.J.,
N.M.R. SPECTRA OF MOLECULES ORIENTED IN A LYOTROPIC MESOPHASE,
Mol Cryst Liq Cryst v7 p201-13 (Jne '69)

Blinc, R., O'Reilly, D.E., Peterson, E.M., Lahajnar, G., Levstek, I.,
PROTON SPIN-LATTICE RELAXATION STUDY OF THE LIQUID CRYSTAL TRANSITION
IN p-ANISALDEHYDE AZINE,
Solid State Commun v6 n12 p839-41 ('68)

Blylum, G.Z., Danielova, G.T., Efanove, L.N.,
LIQUID CRYSTAL PHASE EQUILIBRIUM IN THE TRI-CHLOROSILANE--
CARBONTETRACHLORIDE SYSTEM,
Zh Fiz Khim v40 n2 p407-10 ('66)

Bobovich, Y.S., Belyaevskaya, N.M.,
RAMAN SPECTRA OF A-BENZENE AZO(ANISAL-A/-NAPHTHYLAMINE) IN CRYSTALLINE
AND VITRIFIED LIQUID CRYSTALLINE STATES,
Zh Prikl Spektrosk v8 p1018-20 ('68)

Bourdon, J.,
LIQUID CRYSTALS,
Mes Regul Automat v32 p174-80 ('67)

Bravo, N., Doane, J.W., Arora, S.L., Fergason, J.L.,
N.M.R. STUDY OF MOLECULAR CONFIGURATION AND ORDER IN A FLUORINATED
LIQUID CRYSTAL SHIFF BASE,
J Chem Phys v50 n3 p1398-403 (1 Feb '69)

Brown, G.H., Shaw, W.G.,
THE MESOMORPHIC STATE. LIQUID CRYSTALS,
Chem Rev v57 n6 p1049-1157 (Dec '57) [contains 475 references]

Brown, G.H.,
PROPERTIES OF LIQUID CRYSTALS,
Abstracts, 8th Int'l Congr Crystallography p143 (Aug '69)

Brown, G.H.,
REVIEW OF THE STRUCTURE AND PROPERTIES OF LIQUID CRYSTALS,
Electrochem Soc, Fall Meeting, Detroit, Abstract 154 (Oct '69)

Brown, S.P.,
CHOLESTERIC CRYSTALS FOR NONDESTRUCTIVE TESTING,
Mater Eval v26 n8 p163-6 (Aug '68)

Brown, S.P.,
DETECTION OF FLAWS IN METAL-HONEYCOMB STRUCTURES BY MEANS OF LIQUID CRYSTALS,
Rpt. No. RS-TR-67-5, U.S. Army Missile Command, Redstone Arsenal, Ala. ('67)

Brown, S.P.,
DETECTION OF FLAWS IN METAL-HONEYCOMB STRUCTURES BY MEANS OF LIQUID CRYSTALS,
C.F.S.T.I. AD-816 482 ('69)

Buckingham, A.D., Burnell, E.E.,
CHEMICAL SHIFT ANISOTROPIES FROM N.M.R. STUDIES OF ORIENTED MOLECULES,
Am Chem Soc J v89 p3341 ('67)

Buckingham, A.D., Burnell, E.E., DeLange, C.A.,
N.M.R. SPECTRA OF HYDROGEN IN A NEMATIC PHASE,
Chem Commun n22 p1408-9 ('68)

Buckingham, A.D., Burnell, E.E., DeLange, C.A., Rest, A.J.,
N.M.R. STUDIES OF 3,3,3-TRIFLUOROPROPYNE DISSOLVED IN DIFFERENT NEMATIC
LIQUID CRYSTALS,
Mol Phys v14 n2 p105-9 ('68)

Buckingham, A.D., Burnell, E.E., De Lange, C.A.,
DETERMINATION OF NUCLEAR MAGNETIC SHIELDING ANISOTROPIES OF SOLUTES
IN LIQUID CRYSTAL SOLVENTS,
Am Chem Soc J v90 p2972-4 (22 May '68)

Buckingham, A.D., Burnell, E.E., DeLange, C.A.,
N.M.R. STUDY OF ETHYL FLUORIDE DISSOLVED IN A NEMATIC LIQUID CRYSTAL,
Mol Phys v16 n2 p191-4 ('69)

Buckingham, A.D., Burnell, E.E., De Lange, C.A.,
N.M.R. STUDIES OF 1.1-DIFLUOROETHYLENE IN NEMATIC SOLVENTS,
Mol Phys v16 n3 p299-302 ('69)

Bucknall, D.A.B., Clunie, J.S., Goodman, J.F.,
ELECTRON MICROSCOPY OF LYOTROPIC MESOMORPHIC PHASES,
Mol Cryst Liq Cryst v7 p215-33 (Jne '69)

Bulkin, B.J., Grunbaum, D., Santoro, A.,
VIBRATIONAL SPECTRA OF LIQUID CRYSTALS. I. CHANGES IN THE INFRARED SPECTRUM
AT THE CRYSTAL-NEMATIC TRANSITION,
J Chem Phys v51 n4 p1602-6 (15 Aug '69)

Bulkin, B.J., Grunbaum, D.,
INFRARED SPECTROSCOPIC MEASUREMENTS ON THE CRYSTAL-NEMATIC TRANSITION,
ACS Meeting, 158th Annual, New York, Abstract 74 (Sep '69)

Bulthuis, J., Gerritsen, J., Hilbers, C.W., MacLean, C.,
N.M.R. SPECTRA OF SUBSTITUTED BENZENES WITH d(24) SYMMETRY IN A
NEMATIC SOLVENT,
Recl Trav Chim Pays-Bas v87 p417-42 ('68)

Burnell, E.E., DeLange, C.A.,
N.M.R. STUDIES OF PYRIDAZINE AND PYRIDINE ORIENTED IN A NEMATIC PHASE,
Mol Phys v16 n1 p95-7 ('69)

Byron, D.J., Gray, G.W., Worrall, B.M.,
MESOMORPHISM AND CHEMICAL CONSTITUTION. Di, Tri, AND tetra-SUBSTITUTED
4,4/-di-(p-n ALKOXYBENZYLIDENEAMINO) BIPHENYLS,
J Chem Soc p3706-15 (Jne '65)

Caesar, G.P., Gray, H.B.,
POLARIZED ELECTRONIC SPECTROSCOPY OF MOLECULES ORIENTED BY
A NEMATIC LIQUID CRYSTAL,
Am Chem Soc J v91 n1 p191-3 (1 Jan '69)

Caesar, G.P., Yannoni, C.S., Dailey, B.P.,
STUDIES OF CHEMICAL-SHIFT ANISOTROPY IN LIQUID CRYSTAL SOLVENTS. I.
EXPERIMENTAL RESULTS FOR THE METHYL HALIDES,
J Chem Phys v50 n1 p373-9 (1 Jan '69)

Caesar, G.P., Levenson, R.A., Gray, H.B.,
POLARIZED INFRARED SPECTROSCOPY OF MOLECULES ORIENTED IN A
NEMATIC LIQUID CRYSTAL,
Am Chem Soc J v91 n3 p772-4 (29 Jan '69)

Cameron, L.M.,
THE DEPOLARIZATION OF LIGHT SCATTERED FROM LIQUID CRYSTALS,
Mol Cryst Liq Cryst v7 p235-52 (Jne '69)

Cano, R., Chatelain, P.,
SUR LES VARIATIONS DE L'EQUIDISTANCE DES PLANS DE FRANDJEAN AVEC LE TITRE
DES MELANGES DE p-CYANOBENZALAMINOCINNAMATE D'AMYLE ACTIF ET INACTIF,
Compt Rend v253 n17 p1815-7 (23 Oct '61)

Cano, R., Chatelain, P.,
ESSAI DE VERIFICATION D'UNE THEORIE SUR LE POUVOIR ROTATOIRE
DES CORPS CHOLESTERIQUE,
Compt Rend v259 n2 p352-5 (15 Jly '64)

Cano, R.,
OPTICAL ROTATORY POWER OF CHOLESTEROL LIQUID CRYSTALS,
Bull Soc Fr Mineral Cristallogr v90 n3 p333-51 ('67)

Carlisle, C.H., Smith, C.H.,
THE STRUCTURES OF p-AZOXYANISOLE AND p-AZOXYPHENETOLE,
Abstracts, 8th Int'l Congress of Crystallography, p47 (Aug '69)

Caroli, C., Dubois-Violette, E.,
ENERGY OF A DISINCLINATION LINE IN AN ANISOTROPIC CHOLESTERIC LIQUID CRYSTAL,
Solid State Commun v7 n11 p799-802 (Jne '69)

Carr, E.F., Spence, R.D.,
INFLUENCE OF A MAGNETIC FIELD ON THE MICROWAVE DIELECTRIC CONSTANT
OF A LIQUID CRYSTAL,
J Chem Phys v22 p1481-5 ('54)

Carr, E.F.,
MICROWAVE DIELECTRIC MEASUREMENTS IN LIQUID CRYSTALS,
J Chem Phys v26 p420-2 ('57)

Carr, E.F.,
MICROWAVE DIELECTRIC MEASUREMENTS IN THE LIQUID CRYSTAL
ETHYL p-AZOXYBENZOATE,
J Chem Phys Notes Section v30 p600 ('59)

Carr, E.F.,
MICROWAVE DIELECTRIC MEASUREMENTS IN A LIQUID THAT SHOWS POLYMESOMORPHISM,
J Chem Phys Notes Section v32 p620 ('60)

Carr, E.F.,
DIELECTRIC LOSS IN THE LIQUID CRYSTAL p-AZOXYANISOLE,
J Chem Phys v37 p104-6 ('62)

Carr, E.F.,
INFLUENCE OF ELECTRIC AND MAGNETIC FIELDS ON THE DIELECTRIC CONSTANT
AND LOSS OF THE LIQUID CRYSTAL ANISALDAZINE,
J Chem Phys v38 p1536-40 ('63)

Carr, E.F.,
INFLUENCE OF AN ELECTRIC FIELD ON THE DIELECTRIC LOSS OF THE
LIQUID CRYSTAL p-AZOXYANISOLE,
J Chem Phys v39 p1979-83 ('63)

Carr, E.F.,
INFLUENCE OF ELECTRIC AND MAGNETIC FIELDS ON THE DIELECTRIC CONSTANT
OF A LIQUID CRYSTAL WITH A POSITIVE DIELECTRIC ANISOTROPY,
J Chem Phys v42 p738-42 ('65)

Carr, E.F.,
INFLUENCE OF ELECTRIC AND MAGNETIC FIELDS ON THE MOLECULAR ALIGNMENT
IN THE LIQUID CRYSTAL ANISAL-p-AMINOAZOBENZENE,
J Chem Phys v43 p3905-10 ('65)

Carr, E.F.,
ORDERING IN LIQUID CRYSTALS OWING TO ELECTRIC AND MAGNETIC FIELDS,
Adv Chem Ser No. 63 p76-88 ('67)

Carr, E.F.,
INFLUENCE OF ELECTRIC FIELDS ON THE MOLECULAR ALIGNMENT IN THE
LIQUID CRYSTAL p-AZOXYANISOLE,
J Chem Phys v46 p2765-8 ('67)

Carr, E.F., Hoar, E.A., MacDonald, W.T.,
INFLUENCE OF ELECTRIC FIELDS ON THE N.M.R. SPECTRA OF THE LIQUID
CRYSTAL p-(ANISALAMINO)-PHENYL ACETATE,
J Chem Phys v48 p2822-3 ('68)

Carr, E.F.,
INFLUENCE OF ELECTRIC FIELDS ON THE MOLECULAR ALIGNMENT IN THE
LIQUID CRYSTAL p-(ANISALAMINO)-PHENYL ACETATE,
Mol Cryst Liq Cryst v7 p253-68 (Jne '69)

Carr, E.F., Parker, J.H., McLemore, D.P.,
EFFECTS OF ELECTRIC FIELDS ON MIXTURES OF NEMATIC AND CHOLESTERIC
LIQUID CRYSTALS,
ACS Meeting, 158th Annual, New York, Abstract 57 (Sep '69)

Carrington, A., Luckhurst, G.R.,
THE ELECTRON (SPIN) RESONANCE SPECTRA OF FREE RADICALS DISSOLVED
IN LIQUID CRYSTALS,
Mol Phys v8 n4 p401-2 ('64)

Caspary, W.J., Millett, F., Reichbach, M., Dailey, B.P.,
N.M.R. DETERMINATION OF DEUTERIUM QUADRUPOLE COUPLING CONSTANTS
IN NEMATIC SOLUTIONS,
J Chem Phys v51 n2 p623-7 (15 Jly '69)

Castano, F.,
SPECTROSCOPIC BEHAVIOR OF CHOLESTERIC MESOPHASES,
Am Fis v65 n1-2 p45-54 ('69)

Castano, F.,
STRUCTURAL MECHANISM OF THE TRANSDUCTION OF THE MESOMORPHIC AGGREGATE
BETWEEN DEOXY-CHOLIC ACID AND PI SYSTEMS,
Am Fis v65 n1-2 p55-61 ('69)

Castellano, J.A., Goldmacher, J.E., Barton, L.A., Kane, J.S.,
LIQUID CRYSTALS. II. EFFECTS OF TERMINAL GROUP SUBSTITUTION ON THE
MESOMORPHIC BEHAVIOR OF SOME BENZYLIDENEANILINES,
J Org Chem v33 n9 p3501-4 (Sep '68)

Castellano, J.A., McCaffrey, M.T.,
ELECTRO-OPTIC EFFECTS IN p-ALKOXYBENZYLIDENE-p'-AMINOALKYL-PHENONES
AND RELATED COMPOUNDS,
ACS Meeting, 158th Annual, New York, Abstract 72 (Sep '69)

Chaikovskii, V., Chistyakov, I.C.,
APPARATUS FOR X-RAY DIFFRACTION STUDIES OF LIQUID CRYSTALS IN
MAGNETIC FIELDS,
Kristallografiya v13 n1 p158-62 ('68)

Chandrasekhar, S., Krishnamurti, D.,
VIBRATIONAL SPECTRUM OF LIQUID CRYSTALLINE METHYL STEREATE,
Nature v212 n5063 p746B-7 ('66)

Chandrasekhar, S.,
SURFACE TENSION OF LIQUID CRYSTALS,
Mol Cryst v2 n1 p71-81 (Dec '66)

Chandrasekhar, S., Krishnamurti, D., Madhusudana, N.V.,
THEORY OF BIREFRINGENCE OF NEMATIC LIQUID CRYSTALS,
Mol Cryst Liq Cryst v8 p45-69 (Jne '69)

Chapman, D.,
LIQUID CRYSTALS,
Sci J v1 n8 p32-8 (Oct '65)

Chapman, D., Byrne, P., Shipley, G.G.,
PHYSICAL PROPERTIES OF PHOSPHOR LIPIDS.SOLID STATE AND MESOMORPHIC
PROPERTIES OF SOME 2,3-DI-ACYL-DL-PHOSPHATIDYL ETHANOL AMINES,
Proc Roy Soc (A) v290 n1420 p115-42 ('66)

Chapman, D.,
LIQUID CRYSTALS AND CELL MEMBRANES,
Ann NY Acad Sci v137 n2 p745-54 ('66)

Chapman, D.,
LIQUID CRYSTALLINE NATURE OF PHOSPHOLIPIDS,
Adv Chem Ser #63 p157-66 ('67)

Chapman, D., Williams, R.M., Ladbrooke, B.D.,
PHYSICAL STUDIES OF PHOSPHOLIPIDS. VI. THERMOTROPIC AND LYOTROPIC
MESOMORPHISM OF SOME 1,2-DIACYLPHOSPHATIDYLCHOLINES (LECITHINS),
Chem Phys Lipids v1 p445 ('67)

Chatelain, P., Germain, M.,
INDICES DES MELANGES DE PARAAZOXYANISOLE ET DE PARA-AZOXYPHENETOLE
DANS L'ETAT NEMATIQUE,
Compt Rend v259 n1 p127-30 (6 Jly '64)

Chatelain, P., Brunet-Germain, M.,
MESURES DU POUVOIR ROTATOIRE DE MELANGES DE p-AZOXYANISOL ET DE BENZOATE
DE CHOLESTEROL, ET ESSAI DE VERIFICATION DE LA THEORIE DE VRIES,
Compt Rend v268 serC p205-8 (20 Jan '69)

Chatelain, P., Martin, J.-C.,
SEPARATION DE DEUX VIBRATOIRES CIRCULAIRES SE PROPAGEANT DANS
UN CRISTAL-LIQUIDE CHOLESTERIQUE,
Compt Rend v268 serC p758-60 (3 Mch '69)

Chatelain, P., Martin, J.-C.,
CALCULTHEORIQUE DES INDECES POUR LES VIBRATIONS CIRCULAIRES SE PROPAGEANT
DANS UN CRISTAL-LIQUIDE CHOLESTERIQUE ET COMPARAISON AVEC L'EXPERIENCE,
Compt Rend v268 serC p898-90 (lo Mch '69)

Chatelain, P., Brunet-Germain, M.,
NOUVEAUX TYPES DE DISCONTINUITES DE GRANDJEAN-CANO DANS UNE STRUCTURE
CHOLESTERIQUE ET INTERPRETATION HYPOTHETIQUE,
Compt Rend v268 serC p1016-8 (17 Mch '69)

Chatelain, P., Brunet, M., Cano, J.,
OPTICAL PROPERTIES OF NEMATIC AND CHOLESTERIC LIQUID CRYSTALS (Motion picture),
APS 1969 Winter Meeting, UCLA, Los Angeles (29-31 Dec '69)

Chen, D.H., Luckhurst, G.R.,
ELECTRON RESONANCE STUDY OF THE PERTURBATION OF THE ORDER IN A NEMATIC
MESOPHASE BY A SECOND COMPONENT,
Trans Faraday Soc v65 Pt 3 p656-64 ('69)

Chen, D.H., James, P.G., Luckhurst, G.R.,
ORDER IN THE NEMATIC MESOPHASE,
Mol Cryst Liq Cryst v8 p71-83 (Jne '69)

Chistyakov, I.G.,
LIQUID CRYSTALS. INTRODUCTION - BASIC KNOWLEDGE AND TERMINOLOGY,
Vsp Fiz Nauk v89 n4 p563-602 ('66)

Chistyakov, I.G.,
LIQUID CRYSTALS,
Soviet Physics: Uspekhi v9 n3 p551-73 (Jan-Feb '67)

Chistyakov, I.G., Chaikovskii, V.M.,
STRUCTURE OF NEMATIC p-AZOXYANISOLE IN MAGNETIC FIELDS,
Kristallografiya v12 n5 p883-7 ('67)

Chistyakov, I.G., Vainshtein, B.K.,
STRUCTURE OF α-BENZENEAZO-(ANISAL-α'-NAPHTHYLAMINE) IN VITRIFIED
LIQUID CRYSTALLINE STATE,
Soviet Phys Cryst v8 n4 p458-63 ('64)

Chistyakov, I.G., Gusakova, L.A.,
TEXTURES OF CHOLESTERIC LIQUID CRYSTALS,
Kristallografiya v14 n1 p153-7 ('69)

Chistyakov, I.G., Chaikovskii, V.M.,
THE STRUCTURE OF p-AZOXYBENZENES IN MAGNETIC FIELDS,
Mol Cryst Liq Cryst v7 p269-77 (Jne '69)

Chistyakov, I.G., Schabishev, L.S., Jarenov, R.I., Gusakova, L.A.,
THE POLYMORPHISM OF THE SMECTIC LIQUID CRYSTAL,
Mol Cryst Liq Cryst v7 p279-84 (Jne '69)

Chow, L.C., Martire, D.E.,
THERMODYNAMICS OF SOLUTIONS WITH LIQUID CRYSTAL SOLVENTS,
J Phys Chem v73 n4 p1127-32 ('69)

Churchill, D., Bailey, L.W.,
SURFACE TENSION OF CHOLESTERIC LIQUID CRYSTALS: CHOLESTERYL MYRISTATE,
Mol Cryst Liq Cryst v7 p285-93 (Jne '69)

Ciampelli, F., Cambini, M., Lachi, M.P.,
INFRARED STUDY OF THE CRYSTALLINITY OF POLYMERS,
J Polymer Sci (C) v7 p213-8 ('64)

Clunie, J.S., Corkill, S.M., Goodman, J.F.,
STRUCTURE OF LYOTROPIC MESOMORPHIC PHASES,
Proc Roy Soc (London) serA v285 n1403-4 p520-33 ('65)

Cocivera, M.,
ANALYSIS OF PROTON N.M.R. OF S-TRIOXANE DISSOLVED IN A NEMATIC SOLVENT,
J Chem Phys v47 n8 p3061-7 ('67)

Cole, G.D.,
POSITRON LIFETIMES IN LIQUID CRYSTALLINE COMPOUNDS,
Dissertation, Univ. Microfilms #64-9117

Cole, G.D., Walker, W.W.,
POSITRON ANNIHILATION IN LIQUID CRYSTALS,
J Chem Phys v42 n5 p1692-4 ('65)

Cole, G.D., Merrit, W.G., Walker, W.W.,
POSITRON LIFETIMES IN CHOLESTERL PROPIONATE,
J Chem Phys v49 n4 p1980-1 ('68)

Conners, G.H.,
ELECTROMAGNETIC WAVE PROPAGATION IN CHOLESTERIC MATERIALS,
Opt Soc Am J v58 n7 p875-9 (Jly '68)

Cook, B.D., Werchan, R.,
MAPPING OF ULTRASONIC FIELDS USING LIQUID CRYSTALS,
78th Meeting, Acoustical Society of America, San Diego, Paper-SC9 (4-7 Nov '69)

Coombes, G.E., Grady, J.M., Reid, S.T.,
PHOTOCHEMICAL TRANSFORMATIONS. PHOTOCHEMISTRY OF 6-NITRO CHOLESTERYL
ACETATE AND RELATED COMPOUNDS,
Tetrahedron v23 n3 p1341-6 ('67)

Cole, F.W.,
SOLID STATE MECHANISM IN ION TRANSPORT IN BIOLOGICAL SYSTEMS,
Mol Cryst v2 n1 p45-54 (Dec '66)

Cotter, M.A., Martire, D.E.,
A QUASI-CHEMICAL LATTICE TREATMENT OF ROD-LIKE MOLECULES.
APPLICATIONS TO THE NEMATIC-ISOTROPIC TRANSITION,
Mol Cryst Liq Cryst v7 p295-323 (Jne '69)

Crissey, J.T., Gordy, E., Fergason, J.L., Lyman, R.B.,
A NEW TECHNIQUE FOR THE DEMONSTRATION OF SKIN TEMPERATURE PATTERNS,
J Invest Dermatol v43 p89 ('65)

Crissey, J.T., Fergason, J.L., Bettenhausen, J.M.,
CUTANEOUS THERMOGRAPHY WITH LIQUID CRYSTALS,
J Invest Dermatol v45 n5 p329-33 ('65)

Cristol, S.J., Barbour, R.V.,
ELECTRON TRANSFER REACTION OF RADICAL ANIONS WITH CHOLESTERYL
AND CYCLO-CHOLESTANYL CHLORIDES,
Am Chem Soc J v88 n18 p4262 ('66)

Cutler, D.,
SPIN LATTICE RELAXATION TIME MEASUREMENTS ON CHOLESTEROL DERIVATIVES,
Mol Cryst Liq Cryst v8 p85-92 (Jne '69)

Dave, J.S., Dewar, M.J.S.,
MIXED LIQUID CRYSTALS,
J Chem Soc p4616-21 ('54)

Dave, J.S., Lohar, J.M.,
EFFECT OF STRUCTURE ON MIXED MESOMORPHISM. MESOMORPHIC CHARACTERISTICS
OF BINARY SYSTEMS CONTAINING p-METHOXYCINNAMIC ACID, p-AZOXYANISOLE
AND SCHIFF'S BASES,
Indian J Chem v4 n9 p389-90 ('66)

Dave, J.S., Patel, P.R., Vasanth, K.L.,
INFLUENCE OF MOLECULAR STRUCTURE ON LIQUID CRYSTALLINE PROPERTIES AND
PHASE TRANSITIONS IN MIXED LIQUID CRYSTALS IN SMECTIC PHASE,
Indian J Chem v4 n12 p505-8 ('66)

Dave, J.S., Patel, P.R.,
INFLUENCE OF MOLECULAR STRUCTURE ON LIQUID CRYSTALLINE PROPERTIES AND
PHASE TRANSITIONS IN THESE STRUCTURES, Pt.I.,
Mol Cryst v2 n1 p103-14 (Dec '66)

Dave, J.S., Patel, P.R.,
...see above title, Pt. II.,
Mol Cryst v2 n1 p115-123 (Dec '66)

Dave, J.S., Vasanth, K.L.,
INFLUENCE OF MOLECULAR STRUCTURE ON LIQUID CRYSTALLINE PROPERTIES
AND PHASE TRANSITION IN MIXED LIQUID CRYSTALS,
Mol Cryst v2 n1 p125-33 (Dec '66)

Dave, J.S., Lohar, J.M.,
MIXED LIQUID CRYSTALS. ADDITIVE EFFECTS OF TERMINAL POLAR GROUPS
IN SCHIFF BASES,
J Chem Soc p1473-7 ('67)

Dave, J.S., Patel, P.R., Vasanth, K.L.,
MIXED MESOMORPHISM IN BINARY SYSTEMS FORMING SMECTIC-NEMATIC PHASES,
Mol Cryst Liq Cryst v8 p93-100 (Jne '69)

Davis, F.,
LIQUID CRYSTALS; A NEW TOOL FOR NONDESTRUCTIVE TESTING,
Res/Dev v18 n6 p24-7 (Jne '67)

170

Davis, F., Lauriente, M.,
LIQUID CRYSTAL THERMAL MAPPING FOR SEMICONDUCTORS AND RELATED HARDWARE,
1968 IEEE Int'l Conv Digest p97

Davis, F., Partain, B.,
A MEMORY-TYPE LIQUID CRYSTAL FOR PERMANENT IMAGE FLAW DETECTION,
ASNT 1968 Fall Conf, Detroit (14-17 Oct '68)
Materials Eval v26 n9 p40A (Sep '68)

Davis, G.J., Porter, R.S.,
EVALUATION OF THERMAL TRANSITIONS IN SOME CHOLESTERYL ESTERS OF SATURATED
ALIPHATIC ACIDS BY DIFFERENTIAL SCANNING CALORIMETRY,
ACS Meeting, 158th Annual, New York, Abstract 91 (Sep'69)

Davis, G.J., Porter, R.S., Barrall, E.M.II.,
EVALUATION OF THERMAL TRANSITIONS IN SOME CHOLESTERYL ESTERS OF
SATURATED ALIPHATIC ACIDS,
Mol Cryst Liq Cryst (to be published)

Davison, L.,
LINEAR THEORY OF HEAT CONDUCTION AND DISSIPATION IN LIQUID CRYSTALS
OF THE NEMATIC TYPE,
Phys Rev v180 n1 p232-7 ('69)

Davison, L., Amos, D.E.,
DISSIPATION IN LIQUID CRYSTALS,
Phys Rev v183 n1 p288-90 (Jly '69)

Day, G.W., Gaddy, O.L.,
ELECTRIC-FIELD-INDUCED OPTICAL ROTATION IN CHOLESTERIC LIQUID CRYSTALS,
C.F.S.T.I. AD-677 507, see also IEEE Proc v56 n6 p1113-4 (Jne '68)

Defermos, C.M.,
STABILITY OF ORIENTATION PATTERNS OF LIQUID CRYSTALS SUBJECT TO
MAGNETIC FIELDS,
SIAM J Appl Math v16 p1305-18 (Nov '68)

De Gennes, P.-G.,
FLUCTUATIONS D'ORIENTATION ET DIFFUSION RAYLEIGH DANS UN CRISTAL NEMATIQUE,
Compt Rend v266 serB p15-7 (3 Jan '68)

De Gennes, P.-G.,
DISTORTION OF THE CHOLESTERIC LIQUID CRYSTAL STRUCTURE BY A MAGNETIC FIELD,
Solid State Commun v6 p163 ('68)

De Gennes, P.-G.,
STRUCTURE DES CLOISONS DE GRANDJEAN-CANO,
Compt Rend v266 serB p571-3 (26 Feb '68)

De Gennes, P.-G.,
POSSIBILITES OFFERTES PAR LA RETICULATION DE POLYMERES EN PRESENCE
D'UN CRISTAL LIQUIDE,
Phys Letters v28A n11 p725-6 (10 Mch '69)

De Gennes, P.-G.,
LONG RANGE ORDER AND THERMAL FLUCTUATION IN LIQUID CRYSTALS,
Mol Cryst Liq Cryst v7 p325-45 (Jne '69)

De Gennes, P.-G.,
DEPOLARISATION DE LA LUMIERE DIFFUSEE LORS D'UNE TRANSITION HELICE-
PELOTE STATISTIQUE,
Compt Rend v269 SerB n15 p705-7 (13 Oct '69)

Delord, P., Falguerettes, J.,
X-RAY DIFFRACTION BY A LIQUID SINGLE CRYSTAL OF p-AZOXYANISOLE.
CYLINDRICAL DISTRIBUTION OF ATOMS AND MOLECULAR AXES,
Compt Rend v267 SerC n22 p1437-40 ('68)

Delord, P., Falguerettes, J.,
STRUCTURE OF p-AZOXYANISOLE IN THE NEMATIC STATE,
Compt Rend v267 serC n23 p1528-31 ('68)

Demus, D.,
NEMATIC LIQUIDS STABLE AT LOW TEMPERATURES,
Z. Naturforsch (A) v22 n2 p285-6 ('67)

Demus, D., Kunicke, G., Neelsen, J., Sackmann, H.,
ISOMORPHIC RELATIONS BETWEEN CRYSTALLINE-LIQUID PHASES. POLYMORPHISM
OF CRYSTALLINE LIQUID MODIFICATIONS IN THE HOMOLOGOUS SERIES OF
4'-n-ALKOXY-3'-NITRODIPHENYL CARBOXYLIC ACIDS,
Z. Naturforsch (A) v23 n1 p84-90 ('68)

Demus, D., Sackmann, H., Kunicke, G., Pelz, G., Salffner, R.,
ISOMORPHIC RELATIONS BETWEEN CRYSTALLINE-LIQUID PHASES. POLYMORPHISM IN
LIQUID CRYSTALLINE SUBSTANCES. SMECTIC TRIMORPHISM,
Z. Naturforsch (A) v23 n1 p76-83 ('68)

Denbich, K.G., White, E.T.,
LIQUID INCLUSIONS IN CRYSTALS,
Chem Enh Sci v21 n9 p739-54 ('66)

Dervichian, D.G.,
CONDITIONS GOVERNING THE FORMATION OF LYOTROPIC LIQUID CRYSTALS BY
MOLECULAR ASSOCIATION,
Mol Cryst v2 n1 p55-62 (Dec '66)

Deutsch, Ch., Keating, P.N.,
SCATTERING OF COHERENT LIGHT FROM NEMATIC LIQUID CRYSTALS IN THE
DYNAMIC SCATTERING MODE,
J Appl Phys v40 n10 p4049-54 (Sep '69)

De Vries, A.,
X-RAY PHOTOGRAPHIC STUDIES OF LIQUID CRYSTALS,
Abstracts, 8th Int'l Congress of Crystallography p135 (Aug '69)

De Vries, J.J., Berendsen, H.J.C.,
NUCLEAR MAGNETIC RESONANCE MEASUREMENTS ON A MACROSCOPICALLY ORDERED
SMECTIC LIQUID CRYSTALLINE PHASE,
Nature v221 n5186 p1139-40 (22 Mch '69)

Dewar, M.J.S., Schroeder, J.P.,
LIQUID CRYSTALS AS SOLVENTS. I. THE USE OF NEMATIC AND SMECTIC
PHASES IN GAS-LIQUID CHROMATOGRAPHY,
Am Chem Soc J v86 n23 p5235-9 ('64)

Dewar, M.J.S., Schroeder, J.P.,
P-ALKOXY AND p-CARBALKOXY BENZOATES OF DIPHENOLS. SERIES OF
LIQUID CRYSTALLINE COMPOUNDS,
J Org Chem v30 n7 p2296-300 ('65)

Dewar, M.J.S., Schroeder, J.P.,
LIQUID CRYSTALS AS SOLVENTS. LIQUID CRYSTALS AS STATIONARY PHASES
IN GAS-LIQUID CHROMATOGRAPHY,
J Org Chem v30 n10 p3485-90 ('65)

Dewar, M.J.S., Schroeder, J.P., Schroeder, D.C.,
MOLECULAR ORDER IN THE NEMATIC MESOPHASES OF 4,4'-Di-n-HEXYLOZYAZOXY
BENZENE AND ITS MIXTURES WITH 4,4'-DIMETHYLOXYAZOXY-BENZENE,
J Org Chem v32 n5 p1692 ('67)

Diehl, P.,
N.M.R. SPECTRA OF SYMMETRICAL ORTHO DISUBSTITUTED BENZENES
DISSOLVED IN THE NEMATIC PHASE,
Mol Cryst v15 n2 p201-4 ('68)

Diehl, P., Khetrapal, C.L., Kellerhals, H.P.,
N.M.R. SPECTRUM OF PYRIDINE ORIENTED IN THE NEMATIC PHASE,
Mol Phys v15 p333-7 ('68)

Diehl, P., Khetrapal, C.L.,
N.M.R. SPECTRA OF PYRAZINE AND p-BENZOQUINONE ORIENTED
IN A NEMATIC PHASE,
Mol Phys v14 p327-31 ('68)

Diehl, P., Khetrapal, C.L., Kellerhals, H.P.,
PROTON N.M.R. SPECTRUM OF ORIENTED FURAN IN A NEMATIC-CRYSTALLINE SOLUTION,
Helv Chim Acta v51 p529-32 ('68)

Diehl, P., Khetrapal, C.L.,
N.M.R. SPECTRA OF SYMMETRICAL META DISUBSTITUTED BENZENES IN A NEMATIC
PHASE AT ROOM TEMPERATURE,
Mol Phys v15 n6 p633-7 ('68)

Diehl, P., Khetrapal, C.L.,
STUDY OF ISOTROPIC EFFECTS AND DETERMINATION OF THE QUADRUPOLE COUPLING
CONSTANT FROM THE N.M.R. SPECTRA OF MONO DUTERIO BENZENE IN THE NEMATIC PHASE,
Can J Chem v47 n8 p1411-16 ('69)

Dintenfass, L.,
THE INTERNAL VISCOSITY OF THE RED CELL AND THE STRUCTURE OF THE RED CELL
MEMBRANE. CONSIDERATIONS OF THE LIQUID CRYSTALLINE STRUCTURE OF THE RED CELL
INTERIOR AND MEMBRANE FOR RHEOLOGICAL DATA,
Mol Cryst Liq Cryst v8 p101-139 (Jne '69)

Dixon, G.D., Scala, L.C.,
THERMAL HYSTERESIS IN CHOLESTERIC LIQUID CRYSTALS,
Electrochem Soc, Fall Meeting, Detroit, Abstract 156   (Oct '69)

Douy, A., Rossi, J., Gallot, B.,
AMORPHOUS SEQUENCE ORDERED CO-POLYMERS. EFFECT OF SOLVENT ON THE STRUCTURAL
PARAMETERS OF MESOMORPHIC GELS,
Compt Rend v267 serC n21 p1392-5 ('68)

Douy, A., Mayer, R., Rossi, J., Gallot, B.,
STRUCTURE OF LIQUID CRYSTALLINE PHASES FROM AMORPHOUS BLOCK COPOLYMERS,
Mol Cryst Liq Cryst v7 p103-126 (Jne '69)

Dowley, M.W., Peticolas, W.L.,
THE STUDY OF LASER-INDUCED ABSORPTION OF A SECONDARY LIGHT BEAM IN
MOLECULAR LIQUIDS AND SOLUTIONS,
IBM J Res & Dev v12 n1 p188+ (Jan '68)

Dreyer, J.F.,
THE FIXING OF MOLECULAR ORIENTATION,
J Phys Colloid Chem v52 n5 p808-10 ('48)

Dreyer, J.F.,
THE ALIGNMENT OF MOLECULES IN THE NEMATIC LIQUID CRYSTAL STATE,
ACS Meeting, 158th Annual, New York, Abstract 75 (Sep '69)

Dreyer, J.F.,
THE ALIGNMENT OF MOLECULES IN THE NEMATIC LIQUID CRYSTAL STATE,
Am Chem Soc J (to be published)

Dreyer, J.F.,
LIGHT POLARIZATION FROM FILMS OF LYOTROPIC NEMATIC LIQUID CRYSTALS,
Journal Physique (to be published)

Ducuing, J., Bloembergen, N.,
OBSERVATION OF REFLECTED LIGHT HARMONICS AT THE BOUNDARY
OF PIEZOELECTRIC CRYSTALS,
Phys Rev Letters v10 n11 p474-6 (1 Jne '63)

Ducuing, J., Bloembergen, N.,
STATISTICAL FLUCTUATIONS IN NON-LINEAR OPTICAL PROCESSES,
Phys Rev v133A n6 p1493-1502 (15 Mch '64)

Durand, G.,
DIFFRACTION DE LA LUMIERE ET INVERSION DU PAS DE LA MESOPHASE CHOLESTERIQUE
DE TROIS CRISTAUX LIQUIDES,
Compt Rend v264 serB n17 p1251-3 (24 Apr '67)

Durand, G., Narasimha Rao, D.V.L.G.,
BRILLOUIN SCATTERING OF LIGHT IN LIQUID CRYSTALS,
Bull Am Phys Soc v12 n7 p1054 ('67)

Durand, G., Lee, C.H.,
SUR L'ORIGINE DE LA GENERATION D'HARMONIQUE LUMINEUX DANS UN CRISTAL LIQUIDE,
Compt Rend v264 serB n20 p1397-9 (17 May '67)

Durand, G., Narasimha, R.,
BRILLOUIN SCATTERING OF LIGHT IN A LIQUID CRYSTAL,
Phys Letters v27A n7 p455-6 (26 Aug '68)

Durand, G., Lee, C.H.,
ON THE ORIGIN OF SECOND HARMONIC GENERATION OF LIGHT IN LIQUID CRYSTALS,
Mol Cryst v5 n2 p171-83 (Oct '68)

Durand, G., Leger, L., Rondelez, F., Veyssie, M.,
MAGNETICALLY INDUCED CHOLESTERIC-TO-NEMATIC PHASE TRANSITION
IN LIQUID CRYSTALS,
Phys Rev Letters v22 n6 p227-8 ('69)

Durand, G., Leger, L., Rondelez, F., Veyssie, M.,
QUASI-ELASTIC RAYLEIGH SCATTERING IN NEMATIC LIQUID CRYSTALS,
Phys Rev Letters v22 n25 p1361-3 ('69)

Dyro, J.F., Edmonds, P.D.,
ULTRASONIC ABSORPTION AND DISPERSION AT PHASE TRANSITION IN LIQUID
CRYSTALLINE SYSTEMS: N-OCTYLAMINE-WATER,
Mol Cryst Liq Cryst v8 p141-55 (Jne '69)

Edmonds, P.D., Orr, D.A.,
ULTRASONIC ABSORPTION AND DISPERSION AT PHASE TRANSITIONS IN LIQUID
CRYSTALLINE COMPOUNDS,
Mol Cryst v2 n1 p135-66 (Dec '66)

Ekwall, P., Mandell, L., Fontell, K.,
LAMELLAR MESOPHASE WITH SINGLE AMIPHILE LAYERS,
Acta Chem Scand v22 p365-7 ('68)

Ekwall, P., Mandell, L., Fontell, K.,
LYOTROPIC MESOPHASES WITH "NORMAL" AND "REVERSED" AND TWO-DIMENSIONAL
HEXAGONAL STRUCTURE,
Acta Chem Scand v22 p373-5 ('68)

Ekwall, P., Mandell, L.,
MINIMUM WATER CONTENT OF A NUMBER OF "REVERSED" MICELLAR AND
MESOMORPHOUS STRUCTURES,
Acta Chem Scand v22 p699-702 ('68)

Ekwall, P., Mandell, L., Fontell, K.,
SOLUBILIZATION IN MICELLES AND MESOPHASES AND THE TRANSITION FROM
"NORMAL" TO "REVERSED" STRUCTURES,
Mol Cryst Liq Cryst v8 p157-213 (Jne '69)

Elefante, G., Mark, H.F., Mark, J.E.,
INVESTIGATION OF THE INFLUENCE OF POLYMER SURFACES ON THE TEXTURES
OF THE CHOLESTERIC MESOPHASE,
C.F.S.T.I. AD-805 577 (Apr '66)

Elliott, G., Gibson, J.G.,
DOMAIN STRUCTURES IN LIQUID CRYSTALS, INDUCED BY ELECTRIC FIELDS,
Nature v205 n4975 p995-6 (6 Mch '65)

Elliott, G.F., Rome, E.M.,
LIQUID-CRYSTALLINE ASPECTS OF MUSCLE FIBERS,
Mol Cryst Liq Cryst v8 p215-8 (Jne '69)

Elser, W.,
THE MESOMORPHIC BEHAVIOR OF CHOLESTERYL n-ALKYL CARBONATES,
Mol Cryst v2 n1 p1-13 (Dec '66)

Elser, W.,
THE MESOMORPHIC BEHAVIOR OF SULFUR CONTAINING STEROID DERIVATIVES,
Mol Cryst Liq Cryst v8 p219-32 (Jne '69)

Elson, B.M.,
EXPERIMENTAL DISPLAY DEVICES USE FILMS OF LIQUID CRYSTALS,
Aviation W v89 p71-2 (8 Jly '68)

Englert, G., Saupe, A.,
MOLECULAR GEOMETRY OF ACETONITRILE, DETERMINED BY PROTON MAGNETIC
RESONANCE IN NEMATIC SOLUTIONS,
Mol Cryst Liq Cryst v8 p233-45 (Jne '69)

Ennulat, R.D.,
REMARKS ABOUT THE PHASE IDENTIFICATION OF MESOMORPHIC STATES,
Mol Cryst v3 n4 p405-22 (May '68)

Ennulat, R.D.,
MESOMORPHISM OF HOMOLOGOUS SERIES,
Mol Cryst Liq Cryst v8 p247-65 (Jne '69)

Ergun, S., Bayer, J., Van Buren, W.,
NORMALIZATION AND ABSORPTION CORRECTION OF ARBITRARY X-RAY SCATTERING
INTENSITIES OF PARACRYSTALLINE SUBSTANCES,
J Appl Phys v38 p3540-4 ('67)

Ericksen, J.L.,
ANISOTROPIC FLUIDS,
Arch Rat'l Mech Anal v4 p231-7 ('60)

Ericksen, J.L.,
THEORY OF ANISOTROPIC FLUIDS,
Trans Soc Rheol v4 p29-39 ('60)

Ericksen, J.L.,
TRANSVERSELY ISOTROPIC FLUIDS,
Koll Zeitschr. v173 p117-22 ('60)

Ericksen, J.L.,
A VORTICITY EFFECT IN ANISOTROPIC FLUIDS,
J Poly Sci v47 p327-31 ('60)

Ericksen, J.L.,
POISENILLE FLOW OF CERTAIN ANISOTROPIC FLUIDS,
Arch Rat'l Mech Anal v8 p1-8 ('61)

Ericksen, J.L.,
CONSERVATION LAWS FOR LIQUID CRYSTALS,
Trans Soc Rheol v5 p23-34 ('61)

Ericksen, J.L.,
HYDROSTATIC THEORY OF LIQUID CRYSTALS,
Arch Rat'l Mech Anal v9 p371-8 ('62)

Ericksen, J.L.,
NILPOTENT ENERGIES IN LIQUID CRYSTAL THEORY
Arch Rat'l Mech Anal v10 p189-96 ('62)

Ericksen, J.L.,
SINGULAR SURFACES IN ANISOTROPIC FLUIDS,
Int'l J Engr Sci v1 p157-61 ('63)

Ericksen, J.L.,
INEQUALITIES IN LIQUID CRYSTAL THEORY,
Phys Fluids v9 p1205-7 ('66)

Ericksen, J.L.,
SOME MAGNETOHYDRODYNAMIC EFFECTS IN LIQUID CRYSTALS,
Arch Rat'l Mech Anal v23 p266-75 ('66)

Ericksen, J.L.,
INSTABILITY IN COUETTE FLOW OF ANISOTROPIC FLUIDS,
Quart J Mech Appl Math v19 p455-9 ('66)

Ericksen, J.L.,
TWISTING OF LIQUID CRYSTALS,
J Fluid Mech v27 p59-64 ('67)

Ericksen, J.L.,
GENERAL SOLUTIONS IN THE HYDROSTATIC THEORY OF LIQUID CRYSTALS,
Trans Soc Rheol v11 p5-14 ('67)

Ericksen, J.L.,
CONTINUUM THEORY OF LIQUID CRYSTALS,
AMR v20 p1029-32 ('67)

Ericksen, J.L.,
TWISTING OF PARTIALLY ORIENTED LIQUID CRYSTALS,
Quart Appl Math v25 p474-9 ('68)

Ericksen, J.L.,
PROPAGATION OF WEAK WAVES IN LIQUID CRYSTALS OF NEMATIC TYPE,
Ac Soc Am J v44 n2 p444-6 (Aug '68)

Ericksen, J.L.,
TWIST WAVES IN LIQUID CRYSTALS,
Quart J Mech Appl Math v21 p463-5 ('68)

Ericksen, J.L.,
A BOUNDARY LAYER EFFECT IN VISCOMETRY OF LIQUID CRYSTALS,
Trans Soc Rheol v13 p9-15 ('69)

Ericksen, J.L.,
CONTINUUM THEORY OF LIQUID CRYSTALS OF NEMATIC TYPE,
Mol Cryst Liq Cryst v7 p153-164 (Jne '69)

Ericksen, J.L.,
TWISTING OF LIQUID CRYSTALS BY MAGNETIC FIELDS,
ZAMP v20 p383-8 ('69)

Ericksen, J.L.,
SINGULAR SOLUTIONS IN LIQUID CRYSTAL THEORY,
ACS Meeting, 158th Annual, New York, Abstract 54 (Sep '69)

Ewing, A.,
CHAMELEON COMPOUNDS,
Sci News v94 p321-5 (Sep '68)

Falle, H.R., Luckhurst, G.R., Lemaire, H., Marechal, Y., Rasat, A., Rey, P.,
THE ELECTRON RESONANCE OF GROUND STATE TRIPLETS IN LIQUID CRYSTAL SOLUTIONS,
Mol Phys v11 n1 p49-56 ('66)

Falle, H.R., Luckhurst, G.R.,
LINE WIDTH VARIATIONS IN THE ELECTRON RESONANCE SPECTRA OF RADICALS
DISSOLVED IN NEMATIC LIQUID CRYSTALS,
Mol Phys v12 p493-6 ('67)

Feeney, J.,
HIGH RESOLUTION N.M.R. SPECTROSCOPY,
Annu Rep Progr Chem 1968 (publ. in '69) 65 (sect.A) p63-81

Fergason, J.L.,
LIQUID CRYSTALS,
Sci Amer v211 p76-82+ (Aug '64)

Fergason, J.L., Goldberg, N.N., Jones, C.H., et al,
DETECTION OF LIQUID CRYSTAL GASES (REACTIVE MATERIALS)
AD-62- 940, Defense Documentation Center, Defense Supply Agency (Aug '65)

Fergason, J.L.,
CHOLESTERIC STRUCTURE. I. OPTICAL PROPERTIES,
Mol Cryst v1 n2 p293-307 (Apr '66)

Fergason, J.L., Goldberg, N.N., Nadalin, R.J.,
CHOLESTERIC STRUCTURE. II. CHEMICAL SIGNIFICANCE,
Mol Cryst v1 n2 p309-23 (Apr '66)

Fergason, J.L., CHOLESTERIC STRUCTURE. III. THERMAL MAPPING,
Trans N.Y. Acad Sci v21 n1 p26-9 ('66)

Fergason, J.L., Brown, G.H.,
LIQUID CRYSTALS AND LIVING SYSTEMS,
Am Oil Chem Soc J v45 p120-7 (Mch '68)

Fergason, J.L.,
LIQUID CRYSTALS IN NON-DESTRUCTIVE TESTING,
Appl Opt v7 n9 p1729-37 (Sep '68)

Fergason, J.L.,
LIQUID CRYSTALS AS DETECTORS,
2nd Int'l Symp on Acoustical Holography, Huntington Beach (6-7 Mch '69)

Fergason, J.L.,
CHOLESTERIC LIQUID CRYSTALS AND THEIR APPLICATIONS,
Electrochem Soc, Fall Meeting, Detroit, Abstract 155 (Oct '69)

Fergason, J.L.,
EXPERIMENTS WITH CHOLESTERIC LIQUID CRYSTALS,
Amer J Phys (in press)

Fischer, D.W., Baun, W.L.,
EFFECT OF CHEMICAL COMBINATION OF THE SOFT X-RAY "L" EMISSION SPECTRA
OF POTASSIUM CHLORINE, AND SULFUR USING A STEREATE SOAP FILM CRYSTAL,
Anal Chem v37 n7 p902-6 ('65)

Fisher, J., Fredrickson, A.G.,
INTERFACIAL EFFECTS ON THE VISCOSITY OF A NEMATIC MESOPHASE,
Mol Cryst Liq Cryst v8 p267-84 (Jne '69)

Fisher, J., Fredrickson, A.G.,
TRANSPORT PROCESS IN ANISOTROPIC FLUIDS. II. COUPLING OF MOMENTUM
AND ENERGY TRANSPORT IN A NEMATIC MESOPHASE,
Mol Cryst Liq Cryst v6 n2 p255-71 (Oct '69)

Flautt, T.J., Lawson, K.D.,
CHARACTERIZATION OF MESOMORPHIC PHASES BY NUCLEAR MAGNETIC RESONANCE
SPECTROSCOPY,
Adv Chem Ser #63 p26-50 ('67)

Fontell, K., Nandell, L., Ekwall, P.,
ISOTROPIC MASEOPHASES IN SYSTEMS CONTAINING AMPHIPHILIC COMPOUNDS,
Acta Chem Scand v22 n10 p3209-23 ('68)

Foote, H.W.,
LIQUID CRYSTALS,
Int'l Critical Tables p314-20 ('26)

Francis, P.D., Luckhurst, G.R.,
ELECTRON RESONANCE IN THE SMECTIC MESOPHASE,
Chem Phys Letters v3 n4 p213-15 (Apr '69)

Francois, J., Skoulios, A.,
ETUDE DE L'INFLUENCE DE LA TEXTURE DES GELS MESOMORPHES DES SYSTEMES
SAVON-EAU SUR LEUR CONDUCTIVITE ELECTRIQUE,
Compt Rend v268 serC p61-4 (16 Jly '69)

Freeman, N.K., Lampo, E., Windsor, A.A.,
SEMI AUTOMATIC ANALYSIS OF SERUM TRIGLYCERIDES AND CHOLESTERYL
ESTERS BY INFRARED ABSORPTION,
J Amer Oil Chem Soc v44 n1 p1-4 ('67)

Freiser, M.J., Joenk, R.J.,
ENHENCEMENT OF SELF-TRAPPING BY COOPERATIVE PHENOMENA. APPLICATION TO
LIQUID CRYSTALS,
Phys Letters v24A n12 p683-4 ('66)

Freund, I., Rentzepis, P.M.,
SECOND-HARMONIC GENERATION IN LIQUID CRYSTALS,
Phys Rev Letters v18 n11 p393-4 (13 Mch '67)

Friberg, S., Mandell, L., Larsson, M.,
MESOMORPHOUS PHASES, A FACTOR OF IMPORTANCE FOR THE PROPERTY OF EMULSIONS,
J Colloid Interface Sci v29 n1 p155-6 ('69)

Friedel, G.,
LES ETATS MESOMORPHES DE LA MATIERE,
Annales de Physique v18 p273-474 ('22)

Friedel, G.,
SUR LES CORPS CHOLESTERIQUES,
Compt Rend v176 n8 p475-8 (17 Feb '23)

Friedel, J., De Gennes, P.-G.,
BOUCLES DE DISCLINATION DANS LES CRYSTAUX LIQUIDES,
Compt Rend v268 serB p257-9 (20 Jan '69)

Friedman, H.L.,
MAGNETO-OPTIC SHUTTER,
I.B.M. Tech Discl Bull v8 n1 p120 (Jne '65)

Gardner, A.R.,
MEASURING TEMPERATURE WITHOUT COMPLEX SYSTEMS,
Product Eng v38 p110-3 (25 Sep '67)

Garn, P.D.,
PRESSURE-INDUCED SHIFTS OF MESOMORPHIC PHASE TRANSITION TEMPERATURES,
Am Chem Soc J v91 n19 p5382 ('69)

Gilg, B., Francois, J., Skoulios, A.,
ELECTRIC INTERACTIONS IN THE MESOMORPHIC PHASES IN WATER AMPHIPHIL SYSTEMS.
ROLE OF THE POLARITY OF THE MEDIUM,
Kolloid Z, Z Polymer v205 n2 p139-45 ('65)

Gilchrist, C.A., Rogers, J., Steel, G., Vaal, E.G., Winsor, P.A.,
CONSTITUTION OF AQUEOUS LIQUID CRYSTALLINE SOLUTIONS OF AMPHILES,
J Colloid Interface Sci v25 p409-20 ('67)

Giordmaine, J.A.,
MIXING LIGHT BEAMS IN CRYSTALS,
Phy Rev Letters v8 n1 p19-20 (1 Jan '62)

Glarum, S.H., Marshall, J.H.,
PARAMAGNETIC RELAXATION IN LIQUID CRYSTAL SOLVENTS,
J Chem Phys v46 n1 p55-62 ('67)

Goldberg, L.S., Schnur, J.M.,
OPTICAL SECOND- AND THIRD-HARMONIC GENERATION IN CHOLESTERYL
NONANOATE LIQUID CRYSTALS,
Appl Phys Letters v14 n10 p306-7 (15 May '69)

Goldmacher, J.E., Barton, L.A.,
LIQUID CRYSTALS. I. FLUORINATED ANILS,
J Org Chem v32 n2 p476-7 ('67)

Goldmacher, J.E., McCaffrey, M.T.,
NEMATIC MESOMORPHISM IN BENZYLIDENE ANILS CONTAINING A TERMINAL ALCOHOL GROUP,
ACS Meeting, 158th Annual, New York, Abstract 92 (Sep '69)

Goncharenko, A.M., Sotskii, B.A., Federov, F.I.,
SLEF-EXCITATION IN PLANE-PARALLEL ANISOTROPIC LAYERS,
Kristallografiya v8 nl p47-50 ('63)

Gopalakrishna, C.V.S.S.V., Haranadh, C., Murty, C.R.K.,
DIPOLE MOMENTS OF SOME CHOLESTERYL COMPOUNDS,
Trans Faraday Soc v63 p1953-8 ('67)

Gopalakrishna, C.V.S.S.V., Avadhanulu, M.N., Sarma, V.V.S., Murty, C.R.K.,
DIELECTRIC PROPERTIES OF CHOLESTERYL LIQUID CRYSTALS,
Indian J Pure Appl Phys v5 p579 ('68)

Gopalakrishna, C.V.S.S.V., Haranadh, C., Murty, C.R.K.,
TEMPERATURE VARIATION OF STATIC DIELECTRIC CONSTANT IN LIQUID
CRYSTALS: CHOLESTERYL ESTERS,
Indian J Pre Appl Phys v6 n7 p375-6 ('68)

Gopalakrishna, C.V.S.S.V., Avadhanulu, M.N., Murty, C.R.K.,
INFLUENCE OF MAGNETIC AND ELECTRIC FIELDS ON THE DIELECTRIC CONSTANT OF THE
LIQUID CRYSTAL PHASE OF ANISYLIDENE-p-AMINO-AZONBENZENE,
Indian J Pure Appl Phys v6 n12 p713-4 ('68)

Grall, Y., Tricoire, J.,
CUTANEOUS THERMOGRAPHY BY LIQUID CRYSTALS OF CHOLESTEROL ESTERS,
C.R. Soc Biol v16 n6 p1309-12 ('67)

Gravatt, C.C., Brady, G.W.,
SMALL ANGLE X-RAY STUDIES OF LIQUID CRYSTAL PHASE TRANSITIONS:
p-AZOXYANISOLE,
Mol Cryst Liq Cryst v7 p355-69 (Jne '69)

Gravatt, C.C., Brady, G.W.,
SMALL ANGLE X-RAY STUDIES OF LIQUID CRYSTAL PHASE TRANSITIONS,
Abstracts, 8th Int'l Congr of Crystallography, p20 (Aug'69)

Gravatt, C.C., Brady, G.W.,
SMALL ANGLE X-RAY STUDIES IN LIQUID CRYSTAL PHASE TRANSITIONS,
ACS Meeting, 158th Annual, New York, Abstract 86 (Sep '69)

Gray, G.W.,
THE INFLUENCE OF MOLECULAR STRUCTURE ON LIQUID CRYSTALLINE PROPERTIES,
Mol Cryst v1 n2 p333-49 (Apr '66)

Gray, G.W.,
ADVANCES IN SYNTHESIS AND THE ROLE OF MOLECULAR GEOMETRY IN LIQUID CRYSTALLINITY
Mol Cryst Liq Cryst v7 p127-51 (Jne '69)

Gross, M.J., Porter, J.E.,
ELECTRICALLY INDUCED CONVECTION IN DIELECTRIC LIQUIDS,
Nature v212 p1343-5 ('66)

Gulik-Krzywicki, T., Tardieu, A., Luzzati, V.,
THE SMECTIC PHASE OF LIPID-WATER SYSTEMS: PROPERTIES RELATED TO THE NATURE
OF THE LIPID AND TO THE PRESENCE OF NET ELECTRICAL CHARGES,
Mol Cryst Liq Cryst v8 p285-91 (Jne '69)

Gulrich, L.W., Brown, G.H.,
AN X-RAY DIFFRACTION STUDY OF NEMATIC LIQUID CRYSTALLINE AND LIQUID
p-METHOXYBENZYLIDENE-p'-CYANOANILINE,
Mol Cryst v3 n4 p493-506 (May '68)

Gupta, D.N., Schilling, G., Just, G.,
STEROIDS. SOLVOLYSIS OF 4,4-DIETHYL CHOLESTERYL METHANE SULFONATE,
Can J Chem v43 n4 p792-9 ('65)

Gusakove, L.A., Chistyakov, I.G.,
STRUCTURE AND PROPERTIES OF LIQUID CRYSTALLINE MIXTURES OF
p-ISOALKOXY BENZAL-1-amino NAPHTALENE-4-AZOBENZENES,
Kristallografiya v13 p545-9 ('68)

Haas, W., Adams, J.,
ELECTROPHOTOGRAPHIC IMAGING WITH CHOLESTERIC LIQUID CRYSTALS,
Appl Opt v7 n6 p1203-6 (Jne '68)

Haas, W.,
NEW DEVELOPMENTS IN LIQUID CRYSTALS,
1969 SPSE Annual Conference, Preprints: p158-9 (12-16 May '69)

Haas, W., Adams, J., Wysocki, J.,
INTERACTION BETWEEN U.V. RADIATION AND CHOLESTERIC LIQUID CRYSTALS,
Mol Cryst Liq Cryst v7 p371-9 (Jne '69)

Haas, W., Adams, J., Wysocki, J.,
IMAGEWISE DEFORMATION AND COLOR CHANGE OF LIQUID CRYSTALS IN ELECTRIC FIELDS,
Appl Opt Suppl #3, Electrophotography 1969 p196-8 ('69)

Haas, W., Adams, J., Wysocki, J.,
DYNAMICS OF THE CHOLESTERIC-NEMATIC PHASE TRANSITION,
ACS Meeting, 158th Annual, New York, Abstract 73 (Sep '69)

Haas, W., Adams, J.,
ELECTRIC FIELD EFFECTS ON THE SYSTEM OLEYL CHOLESTERYL CARBONATE -
CHOLESTERYL CHLORIDE,
Electrochem Soc, Fall Meeting, Detroit, Abstract 157 (Oct '69)

Haller, I.,Cox, R.J.,
EFFECT OF END-CHAIN POLARITY ON THE MESOPHASE STABILITY OF SOME SUBSTITUTED
SCHIFF BASES, ACS Meeting, 158th Annual, New York, Abstract 94 (Sep '69)

Hansen, J.R., Fergason, J.L., Okaya, A.,
DISPLAY OF INFRARED LASER PATTERNS BY A LIQUID CRYSTAL VIEWER,
Appl Opt v3 p987 (Aug '64)

Hansen, J.R., Schneeberger, R.J.,
LIQUID CRYSTAL MEDIA FOR ELECTRON BEAM RECORDING,
IEEE Trans Electron Devices vED-15 n11 p896-906 (Nov '68)

Hansen, T.S.,
LIQUID CRYSTAL AS A SOLVENT IN INFRARED SPECTROSCOPY,
Z. Naturforsch (A) v24 n5 p866-7 ('69)

Hardy, G., Fedorova, N., Kovacs, G., Boros-Gyevi, J.,
RADIATION POLYMERIZATION BEHAVIOR IN THE SUPERCOOLED LIQUID
AND MESOMORPHOUS PHASE,
J Polym Sci Pt.C v16 p2675-80 ('67)

Harper, W.J.,
VOLTAGE EFFECT IN CHOLESTERIC LIQUID CRYSTALS,
Mol Cryst v1 n2 p325-32 (Apr '66)

Havlice, J.F.,
VISUALIZATION OF ACOUSTIC BEAMS USING LIQUID CRYSTALS,
Electronics Letters v5 n20 p477 (2 Oct '69)

Heilmeier, G.H.,
POSSIBLE FERROELECTRIC BEHAVIOR IN p-AZOXYANISOLE AND RELATED LIQUIDS,
1965 Liquid Crystal Conference, Kent State University (Aug '65)

Heilmeier, G.H.,
TRANSIENT BEHAVIOR OF DOMAINS IN LIQUID CRYSTALS,
1965 Liquid Crystal Conference, Kent State University (Aug '65)

Heilmeier, G.H.,
TRANSIENT BEHAVIOR OF DOMAINS IN LIQUID CRYSTALS,
J Chem Phys v44 n2 p644-7 (15 Jan '66)

Heilmeier, G.H., Heyman, P.M.,
NOTE ON TRANSIENT CURRENT MEASUREMENTS IN LIQUID CRYSTALS AND RELATED SYSTEMS,
Phys Rev Letters v18 n15 p583-5 (10 Apr '67)

Heilmeier, G.H.,
SOME COOPERATIVE EFFECTS IN BUTYL p-ANISYLIDENE-p'-AMINOCINNAMATE,
Adv Chem Ser #63 p68-71 ('67)

Heilmeier, G.H.,
DYNAMIC SCATTERING IN LIQUID CRYSTALS,
Appliance Eng v2 p21 ('68)

Heilmeier, G.H.,
LIQUID CRYSTAL DISPLAYS,
Northern New Jersey IEEE; also Pittsburgh IEEE ('68)

Heilmeier, G.H.,
DYNAMIC SCATTERING. A NEW ELECTRO-OPTIC EFFECT IN CERTAIN CLASSES
OF NEMATIC LIQUID CRYSTALS,
SSDRC -CEDR, Boulder, Colo. (Jne '68)

Heilmeier, G.H., Zanoni, L.A., Barton, L.A.,
DYNAMIC SCATTERING: A NEW ELECTROOPTIC EFFECT IN CERTAIN CLASSES OF
NEMATIC LIQUID CRYSTALS,
IEEE Proc v56 n7 p1162-71 (Jly '68)

Heilmeier, G.H., Zanoni, L.A., Barton, L.A.,
DYNAMIC SCATTERING IN NEMATIC LIQUID CRYSTALS,
Appl Phys Letters v13 n1 p46-7 (1 Jly '68)

Heilmeier, G.H.,
GUEST-HOST INTERACTIONS IN NEMATIC LIQUID CRYSTALS,
Liq Cryst Conf, Kent State University (Aug '68)

Heilmeier, G.H.,
APPLICATIONS OF LIQUID CRYSTALS,
Liq Cryst Conf, Kent State University (Aug '68)

Heilmeier, G.H. Zanoni, L.A.,
QUEST-HOST INTERACTIONS IN NEMATIC LIQUID CRYSTALS. A NEW ELECTRO-OPTIC EFFECT,
Appl Phys Letters v13 n3 p91-2 (1 Aug '68)

Heilmeier, G.H., Goldmacher, J.E.,
A NEW ELECTRIC-FIELD-CONTROLLED REFLECTIVE OPTICAL STORAGE EFFECT
IN MIXED-LIQUID CRYSTAL SYSTEMS,
Appl Phys Letters v13 n4 p132-3 (15 Aug '68)

Heilmeier, G.H.,
A NEW ELECTRIC FIELD CONTROLLED OPTICAL STORAGE EFFECT,
PGED, Washington, D.C. (Oct '68)

Heilmeier, G.H.,
DYNAMIC SCATTERING IN LIQUID CRYSTALS,
Appliance Eng v2 n4 p21-5 (Nov '68)

Heilmeier, G.H., Goldmacher, J.E.,
A NEW ELECTRIC FIELD CONTROLLED REFLECTIVE OPTICAL STORAGE EFFECT IN
MIXED LIQUID CRYSTAL SYSTEMS,
IEEE Proc v57 p34-8 (Jan '69)

Heilmeier, G.H.,
DYNAMIC SCATTERING AND RELATED ELECTRO-OPTIC EFFECTS IN LIQUID CRYSTALS,
CCNY Seminar (Apr '69)

Heilmeier, G.H.,
DYNAMIC SCATTERING AND RELATED ELECTRO-OPTIC EFFECTS IN LIQUID CRYSTALS,
IEEE Albuquerque, Seminar on Electro-optics (Apr '69)

Heilmeier, G.H. Castellano, J.A., Zanoni, L.A.,
GUEST-HOST INTERACTIONS IN NEMATIC LIQUID CRYSTALS,
Mol Cryst Liq Cryst v8 p293-304 (Jne '69)

Heilmeier, G.H.,
LIQUID CRYSTALS -- THE FIRST ELECTRONIC METHOD FOR CONTROLLING
THE REFLECTION OF LIGHT,
RCA Engineer v15 n1 p14-8 (Jne/Jly '69)

Heilmeier, G.H., Goldmacher, J.E.,
ELECTRIC-FIELD-INDUCED CHOLESTERIC-NEMATIC PHASE CHANGE IN LIQUID CRYSTALS,
J Chem Phys v51 n3 p1258-60 (1 Aug '69)

Heilmeier, G.H., Zanoni, L.A., Goldmacher, J.E.,
SOME EXPERIMENTS ON ELECTRIC FIELD INDUCED STRUCTURAL CHANGES IN
MIXED LIQUID CRYSTAL SYSTEMS,
ACS Meeting, 158th Annual, New York, Abstract 58 (Sep '69)

Heilmeier, G.H., Helfrich, W.,
ORIENTATIONAL OSCILLATIONS IN NEMATIC LIQUID CRYSTALS,
Appl Phys Letters (to be published)

Heilmeier, G.H.,
DISPLAY APPLICATIONS OF NEMATIC LIQUID CRYSTALS,
Science (to be published)

Heilmeier, G.H.,
ELECTRO-OPTIC EFFECTS IN NEMATIC LIQUID CRYSTALS AND THEIR APPLICATIONS,
Scientific American (to be published)

Helfrich, W.,
ALIGNMENT-INVERSION WALLS IN NEMATIC LIQUID CRYSTALS
IN THE PRESENCE OF A MAGNETIC FIELD,
Phys Rev Letters v21 n22 p1518-21 ('68)

Helfrich, W.,
MOLECULAR THEORY OF FLOW ALIGNMENT OF NEMATIC LIQUID CRYSTALS,
J Chem Phys v50 n1 p100-6 (1 Jan '69)

Helfrich, W.,
CAPILLARY FLOW OF CHOLESTERIC AND SMECTIC LIQUID CRYSTALS,
Phys Rev Letters v 23 p372-4 (18 Aug '69)

Helfrich, W.,
CAPILLARY VISCOMETRY OF CHOLESTERIC AND SMECTIC LIQUID CRYSTALS,
ACS Meeting, 158th Annual, New York, Abstract 61 (Sep '69)

Helfrich, W.,
ORIENTATION PATTERN OF DOMAINS IN NEMATIC p-AZOXYANISOLE,
J Chem Phys v51 n6 p2755-6 (15 Sep '69)

Helfrich, W.,
ELECTROOPTIC EFFECTS IN NEMATIC CRYSTALS,
Electrochem Soc, Fall Meeting, Detroit Abstract 158 (Oct '69)

Helfrich, W.,
CONDUCTION-INDUCED ALIGNMENT OF NEMATIC LIQUID CRYSTALS: BASIC
MODEL AND STABILITY CONSIDERATIONS,
J Chem Phys v51 n9 p4092-105 (Nov '69)

Hofstein, S.R.,
IMPROVED LIQUID CRYSTAL DISPLAY CELL,
RCA Tech Notes No. 824   (31 Mch '69)

Holzman, G.R.,
LIQUID CRYSTAL LIGHT MODULATOR AND SCANNER,
IBM Tech Discl Bull   v8   nl   p151-2   (Jne '65)

Hosemann, R., Lemm, K., Wilke, W.,
THE PARA CRYSTAL AS A MODEL FOR LIQUID CRYSTALS,
Mol Cryst   v2   n4   p333-62   ('67)

Hoyer, W.A., Nolle, A.W.,
BEHAVIOR OF LIQUID CRYSTAL COMPOUNDS NEAR THE ISOTROPIC-
ANISOTROPIC TRANSITION,
J Chem Phys   v24   n4   p803-11   (Apr '56)

Hudson, K.C.,
TEMPERATURE CONTROL CIRCUIT,
RCA Tech Notes No. 806   (11 Dec '68)

Irvin, B.W.,
GEL FORMATION AND SPERULITE PRODUCTION IN THE MESOMORPHIC
MELTS OF CHOLESTEROL ESTERS,
J Colloid Interface Sci   v23   n2   p221-9   ('67)

Johnson, J.F., Porter, R.S., Barrall, E.M.II.,
THERMODYNAMICS OF MESOPHASE TRANSITIONS FROM CALORIMETRIC MEASUREMENTS,
Mol Cryst Liq Cryst   v8   p1-7   (Jne '69)

Jones, C.H., Fergason, J.L., Asars, J.A., et al,
INVESTIGATION OF LARGE-AREA DISPLAY SCREEN USING LIQUID CRYSTALS,
Westinghouse Tech Rept   RADC-TR-65-274   (Dec '65)

Kallmeyer, B.,
PURITY CONTROL BY THERMAL ANALYSIS. DETERMINATION OF THE CRYSTAL-LIQUID
DISTRIBUTION COEFFICIENT S FOR IMPURIFIED BENZENE,
Z Phys Chem (Frankfurt)   v46   n5-6   p353-8   ('65)

Kapustin, A.P., Zvereva, G.E.,
STUDY OF PHASE TRANSITION IN POLYMESOMORPHIC LIQUID CRYSTALS
BY ULTRASONIC METHODS,
Kristallografiya   v10   n5   p723-6   ('65)

Kapustin, A.P., Bykova, N.T.,
PHASE CHANGES IN LIQUID CRYSTALS,
Kristallografiya   v11   n2   p297-8   ('66)

Kapustin, A.P., Bykova, N.T.,
PHASE TRANSITION IN LIQUID CRYSTALS,
Kristallografiya   v11   n2   p330-2   ('66)

Kapustin, A.P.,
SOME PROPERTIES OF LIQUID CRYSTALS,
Izv Vyssh Ucheb Zaved   v10   n11   p55-61   ('67)

Kapustin, A.P.,
EFFECT OF TEMPERATURE ON LIGHT SCATTERING BY LIQUID CRYSTALS
OF THE CHOLESTERYL TYPE,
Kristallografiya v12 n3 p516A ('67)

Kapustin, A.P.,Bykova, N.T.,
PHASE TRANSITIONS IN LIQUID CRYSTALS OF THE POLYMESOMORPHIC TYPE,
Kristallografiya v13 p345-8 ('68)

Kassubek, P., Meier, G.,
OPTICAL STUDIES ON GRANDJEAN PLANES IN CHOLESTERIC LIQUID CRYSTALS,
Mol Cryst Liq Cryst v8 p305-14 (Jne '69)

Keating, P.N.,
A THEORY OF THE CHOLESTERIC MESOPHASE,
Mol Cryst Liq Cryst v8 p315-26 (Jne '69)

Keating, P.N., Deutsch, Ch.,
THE SCETTERING OF COHERENT LIGHT FROM NEMATIC LIQUID CRYSTS
IN THE DYNAMIC SCATTERING MODE,
ACS Meeting, 158th Annual, New York, Abstract 56 (Sep '69)

Kelker, H., Winterscheidt, H.,
BEHAVIOR OF CRYSTALLINE LIQUIDS AS SOLVENTS IN GAS-LIQUID CHROMATOGRAPHY.
CHOLESTERIC MESOPHASE AND ITS MIXTURES WITH 4,4/-ETHOXYAZOBENZENE,
Z Anal Chem v219 n5 p1-8 ('66)

Kelker, H., Scheurle, B.,
LIQUID CRYSTALLINE BEHAVIOR AND CONSTITUTIONAL ANALYSIS OF
1,5-DIMETHOXYNAPHTHALENE DICARBOXYLIC ACID DERIVATIVES,
Mol Cryst Liq Cryst v7 p381-94 (Jne '69)

Kessler, J.O., Longley-Cook, M., Pasmussen, W.O.,
LOW FREQUENCY ELECTRICAL PROPERTIES OF NEMATIC p,p'-AZOXYANISOLE,
Mol Cryst Liq Cryst v8 p327-37 (Jne '69)

Kessler, J.O.,
MAGNETIC ALIGNMENT OF NEMATIC LIQUID CRYSTALS,
ACS Meeting, 158th Annual, New York, Abstract 88 (Sep '69)

Klein, E.J., Margozzi, A.P.,
MEASUREMENT OF SKIN FRICTION BY MEANS OF LIQUID CRYSTALS,
Israel J Technol v7 n1-2 p173-80 ('69)

Klein, M.P.,
E.P.R. OF FREE RADICALS IN NEMATIC SOLVENTS,
APS 1969 Winter Meeting, UCLA, Los Angeles (29-31 Dec '69)

Knapp, F.F., Nicholas, H.J.,
24-METHYL-9,19-CYCLOLANSTAN-3β-γl PALMITATE. NEW LIQUID CRYSTAL,
J Org Chem v33 p3995 ('68)

Knapp, F.F., Nicholas, H.J.,
STRUCTURAL STUDIES OF THE CHOLESTERIC MESOPHASE,
ACS Meeting, 158th Annual, New York, Abstract 49 (Sep '69)

Kolke, A., Demus, D.,
H-D ISOTOPE EFFECT IN CRYSTALLINE LIQUID ALKOXYBENZOIC ACIDS,
Z Naturforsch v23a n8 p1237 ('68)

Koller, K., Lorenzen, K., Schwab, G.M.,
QUASI CRYSTALLINE LIQUID (p-n-BUTYLOXYBENZOIC ACID), BY RAMAN SPECTROSCOPY,
Z Phys Chem (Frankfurt) v44 n1-2 p101-11 ('65)

Kopf, L.,
REFRACTIVE INDICES OF LIQUID CRYSTAL CHOLESTERYL 2-(2-ETHOXYETHOXY)
ETHYL CARBONATE,
Opt Soc Am J v58 p269 (Feb '68)

Kosterin, E.A., Chistyakov, I.G.,
STRUCTURE OF LIQUID CRYSTALLINE p-AZOXYANISOLE IN CONSTANT ELECTRIC FIELD,
Kristallografiya v13 p295 ('68)

Kotsev, N., Shopov, D.,
DETERMINATION OF THE STABILITY CONSTANTS OF AN OLEFIN LIQUID CRYSTAL
SYSTEM BY MEANS OF GAS-LIQUID CHROMATOGRAPHY,
Dokl Bolg Akad Nauk v21 n9 p889 ('68)

Kreutzer, C.,
KALORIMETRISCHE MESSUNGEN BEIM UEBERGANG VON DER ANISOTROPEN ZUR
ISOTROPEN FLUESSIGEN PHASE,
Ann Physik (5th ser) v33 p192-209 ('38)

Krishnamurty, D., Krishnamurty, K.S., Shashidhar, R.,
THERMAL, OPTICAL, X-RAY, INFRARED AND N.M.R. STUDIES ON THE
α-PHASE OF SOME SATURATED ALIPHATIC ESTERS,
Mol Cryst Liq Cryst v8 p339-66 (Jne '69)

Kusabayashi, S., Labes, M.M.,
CONDUCTIVITY IN LIQUID CRYSTALS,
Mol Cryst Liq Cryst v7 p395-405 (Jne '69)

Kusakov, M.M., Shishkina, M.V.M Kohodzhaeva, V.L.,
LIQUID-CRYSTAL STATE OF p-(n-ALKOXY) BENZOIC ACIDS,
Dokl Akad Nauk SSSR v186 n2 p366-8 ('69)

Kusakov, M.V., Khodzhaeva, V.L., Shishkina, M.V., Konstantinov, I.I.,
STUDY OF LIQUID CRYSTALS OF p-ALKOXYBENZOIC ACID BY INFRARED DICHROISM,
Kristallografiya v14 n3 p485-90 ('69)

Larsson, K.,
STRUCTURE OF MESOMORPHIC PHASES AND MICELLES IN AQUEOUS GLYCERIDE SYSTEMS,
Z Phys Chem (Frankfurt) v56 n3-4 p173-98 ('67)

Lauriente, M., Fergason, J.L.,
LIQUID CRYSTALS PLOT THE HOT SPOTS,
Electronic Design v19 p71-9 (13 Sep '67)

Lauriente, M., Farhood, J.F.,
HIGH RESOLUTION THERMAL MAPPING WITH LIQUID CRYSTALS,
ASNT 1968 Fall Conference, Detroit (14-17 Oct '68); Mater Eval v26 n9 p40A ('68)

Lavery, B.J.,
N.M.R. SPECTRA OF FLUOROMETHANE MOLECULES IN A LIQUID CRYSTAL SOLVENT,
Dissertation, University Microfilms #68-8718 ('68)

Lawrence, A.S.C.,
LYOTROPIC MESOMORPHISM IN LIPID-WATER SYSTEMS,
Mol Cryst Liq Cryst v7 p1-57 (Jne '69)

Lawson, K.D., Flautt, T.J.,
MAGNETICALLY ORIENTED LYOTROPIC LIQUID CRYSTALLINE PHASES,
Am Chem Soc J v89 p5489-91 (11 Oct '67)

Lechner, B.J., Marlowe, F.J., Nester, E.O., Tults, J.,
LIQUID CRYSTAL MATRIX DISPLAYS,
1969 IEEE Int'l Solid-State Circuits Conf, University of Pennsylvania,
                                        (19-21 Feb '69)

Leclerq, M., Billard, J., Jacques, S.,
APPLICATION OF DIFFERENTIAL MICRO ANALYSIS TO MESOMORPHIC SUBSTANCES,
Compt Rend v264 serC p1789-91 ('67)

Leclerq, M., Billard, J., Jaques, J.,
COMPOSES CHOLESTERIQUES PAR DEDOUBLEMENT DE RECAMIQUES NEMATIQUES,
Comp Rend v266 serC p654-6 (4 Mch '68)

Leclerq, M., Billard, J., Jacques, J.,
SEPARATION DE RECAMIQUES NEMATIQUES EN DEUX ANTIPODES CHOLESTERIQUES,
Mol Cryst Liq Cryst v8 p367-87 (Jne '69)

Leffre, H.,
UEBER ADDITIONSVERBINDUNGEN UND MISCHKRYSTALLE IN DER STERIN-REIHE,
Annalen   v495 p41-60 ('32)

Leslie, F.M.,
THERMAL EFFECTS IN CHOLESTERIC LIQUID CRYSTALS,
Proc Roy Soc v397 serA p359 ('68)

Leslie, F.M.,
CONTINUUM THEORY OF CHOLESTERIC LIQUID CRYSTALS,
Mol Cryst Liq Cryst v7 p407-20 (Jne '69)

Longuet-Higgins, H.C., Luckhurst, G.R.,
COMPOSITION OF THE NEMATIC MESOPHASE OF p-AZOXYANISOLE,
Mol Cryst v8 n6 p613-5 ('64)

Luckhurst, G.R.,
LIQUID CRYSTALS AS SOLVENTS IN N.M.R. SPECTROSCOPY,
Oesterr Chem Ztg v68 n4 p113-21 ('67)

Luckhurst, G.R.,
THE EQUIVALENCE OF THE TWO THEORIES OF THE NEMATIC MESOPHASE
WHEN APPLIED TO MAGNETIC RESONANCE EXPERIMENTS,
Mol Cryst v2 n4 p363-71 ('67)

Luckhurst, G.R.,
LIQUID CRYSTALS AS SOLVENTS IN N.M.R.,
Quart Rev (London) v22 p179-98 ('68)

Lukianoff, G.V.,
INFORMATION CONTENT AND RESOLUTION ASPECTS IN THERMAL MAPPINGS USING
CHOLESTERIC COMPOUNDS,
Mol Cryst Liq Cryst v8 p389-401 (Jne '69)

Lvova, A.S., Sabirov, L.M., Arefyev, I.M., Sushinsky,
STUDY OF THE 100 cm^{-1} ABSORPTION BAND OF p-AZOXYPHENETOL IN THE SOLID,
LIQUID-CRYSTALLINE, AND LIQUID STATES,
Opt Spektrosk v24 p613-4 ('68)

Magne, M., Pinard, P., Thome, P., Chretien, N.,
APPLICATION OF LIQUID CRYSTAL PROPERTIES IN NONDESTRUCTIVE TESTING,
Bull Inform Sci Tech (Paris) n136 p45-54 ('69)

Maker, P.D., Terhune, R.W., Nisenoff, M., Savage, C.M.,
EFFECTS OF DISPERSION AND FOCUSING ON THE PRODUCTION OF OPTICAL HARMONICS,
Phys Rev Letters v8 n1 p21-2 (1 Jan '62)

Malim, T.H.,
TESTING BLOSSOMS OUT IN COLOR,
Iron Age v197 p69-74 (27 Jan '66)

Mandell, L., Fontell, K., Ekwall, P.,
OCCURRENCE OF DIFFERENT MESOMORPHOUS PHASES IN TERNARY SYSTEMS OF
AMPHIPHILIC SUBSTANCES AND WATER,
Adv Chem Ser #63 p89-127 ('67)

Mann, J.A.,Jr., Hohl, H.-R., Sborov, M.J.,
DYNAMIC RESPONSE OF LIPID-CHOLESTEROL MEMBRANES TO MECHANICAL OSCILLATIONS,
Nature v222 n5192 p471-2 (3 May '69)

Mannschreck, A.,
CRYSTALLINE LIQUIDS, NEW STATE OF AGGREGATIONS,
Chem Ztg, Chem App v92 p69 ('68)

Marks, A.M.,
ELECTROOPTICAL CHARACTERISTICS OF DIPOLE SUSPENSIONS,
Appl Opt v8 n7 p1397-1412 (Jly '69)

Martire, D.E., Blasco, P.A., Carone, P.F., Chow, L.C., Vicini, H.,
THERMODYNAMICS OF SOLUTIONS WITH LIQUID CRYSTAL SOLVENTS. GAS -LIQUID
CHROMATOGRAPHIC STUDY OF CHOLESTERYL MYRISTATE,
J Phys Chem v72 p3489 ('68)

Massen, C.H., Poulis, J.A., Spence, R.D.,
THE FIELD DEPENDENCE OF THE MAGNETIC SUSCEPTIBILITY OF LIQUID CRYSTALS,
Bull Soc Belge Phys v6 p395-8 ('65)

Massen, C.H., Poulis, J.A., Spence, R.D.,
FIELD DEPENDENCE OF THE MAGNETIC SUSCEPTIBILITY OF THE LIQUID
CRYSTAL PHASE OF p-AZOXYANISOLE, Adv Chem Ser #63 p72-5 ('67)

McCoy, J.B., Kowalczyk, L.S.,
THERMAL CONDUCTIVITY OF SOME MESOMORPHIC COMPOUNDS,
Chem Eng Prog Symp Ser #30 v56 p11-4 ('60)

McDonald, M.P.,
MOLECULAR ASSOCIATION IN MONO- AND DIHYDRIC ALCOHOL AND ALCOHOL-WATER SYSTEMS,
Adv Chem Ser #63 p125-40 ('67)

Meiboom, S., Snyder, L.C.,
STRUCTURE OF CYCLOPROPANE AND CYCLOBUTANE FROM PROTON N.M.R. IN A NEMATIC SOLVENT,
Am Chem Soc J v89 n4 p1038-9 ('67)

Meiboom, S., Snyder, L.C.,
N.M.R. IN LIQUID CRYSTALS,
Science v162 n3860 p1337-45 (20 Dec '68)

Meier, G., Saupe, A.,
AVERAGE ORIENTATION OF SOLUTE MOLECULES IN NEMATIC LIQUID CRYSTALS BY PROTON
MAGNETIC RESONANCE MEASUREMENTS AND ORIENTATION-DEPENDENT INTERMOLECULAR FORCES,
Mol Cryst v1 n4 p527-40 ('66)

Meier, G., Saupe, A.,
DIELECTRIC RELAXATION IN NEMATIC LIQUID CRYSTALS,
Mol Cryst v1 n4 p515-25 (Sep '66)

Meunier, J.P., Billard, J.,
FACIES D'UNE STASE SMECTIQUE,
Mol Cryst Liq Cryst v7 p421-31 (Jan '69)

Meyer, R.B.,
EFFECTS OF ELECTRIC AND MAGNETIC FIELDS IN THE STRUCTURE OF CHOLESTERIC
LIQUID CRYSTALS,
Appl Phys Letters v12 n9 p281-2 (1 May '68)

Meyer, R.B.,
EFFECTS OF A MAGNETIC FIELD ON THE STRUCTURE OF A CHOLESTERIC LIQUID CRYSTAL,
Bull of APS ser11 v14 n1 p73A (Jan '69)

Meyer, R.B.,
DISTRIBUTION OF A CHOLESTERIC STRUCTURE BY A MAGNETIC FIELD,
Appl Phys Letters v14 n7 p208-9 (1 Apr '69)

Meyer, R.B.,
EFFECTS OF ELECTRIC AND MAGNETIC FIELDS ON THE STRUCTURE OF LIQUID CRYSTALS,
APS 1969 Winter Meeting, UCLA, Los Angeles, 29-31 Dec '69

Mock, J.A.,
LIQUID CRYSTALS TRACK FLAWS IN A COLORFUL WAY,
Materials Eng v69 p66-7 (Feb '69)

Moebius, K., Haustein, H., Plato, M.,
HIGH RESOLUTION ELECTRIC PARAMAGNETIC RESONANCE SPECTROSCOPY OF ORGANIC
RADICALS IN LIQUID CRYSTALS WITH NEMATIC MESOPHASE,
Z Naturforsch (A) v23 n10 p1626-38 ('68)

Moriarty, R.M., D'Silva, R.S.D.,
EFFECT OF REMOTE SUBSTITUENTS UPON THE COURSE AND REACTIVITY OF HOMO ALLYLIC
SYSTEMS. SOLVOLYSIS OF 19-SUBSTITUTED CHOLESTERYL p-TOLUENE
SULFONATE ESTERS,
Tetrahedron v21 n3 p547-58 ('65)

Muller, J.H.,
ELECTRIC FIELD EFFECTS IN CHOLESTERIC LIQUID CRYSTALS,
Z Naturforsch v20a n6 p849-51 (Jne '65)

Muller, J.H.,
EFFECTS OF ELECTRIC FIELDS ON CHOLESTEROL NONANOATE LIQUID CRYSTALS,
Mol Cryst v2 n1 p167-88 (Dec '66)

Musher, J.I.,
EQUIVALENCE OF NUCLEAR SPINS,
J Chem Phys v46 p1537 ('67)

Naggiar, V.,
PRODUCTION DES FILS ET DES TOURBILLONS DANS LES LIQUIDES NEMATIQUE,
Compt Rend v200 p903-5 ('35)

Neff, V.D., Gulrich, L.W., Brown, G.H.,
DETERMINATION OF THE DEGREE OF ORIENTATION IN THIN FILMS OF NEMATIC LIQUID
CRYSTALS FROM INFRARED DICHROIC MEASUREMENTS IN A HOMOGENEOUS ELECTRIC FIELD,
Mol Cryst v1 n2 p225-39 (Apr '66)

Nehring, J., Saupe, A.,
ORIENTATION STUDIES ON FLUOROBENZENES IN NEMATIC LIQUID CRYSTALS BY N.M.R.,
Mol Cryst Liq Cryst v8 p403-15 (Jne '69)

Noguchi, S., Nishina, T.,
X-RAY SPECTROMETRIC STUDY OF THE ODD-NUMBERED FATTY SOAPS,
Nippon Nogei Kagaku Kaishi v38 n4 p207-12 ('64)

Nordland, W.A.,
PRELIMINARY INVESTIGATION OF BRILLOUIN SCATTERING IN A LIQUID CRYSTAL,
J Appl Phys v39 n11 p5033-6 ('68)

Orsay Liquid Crystal Group,
EXISTENCE AND MAGNETIC UNSTABILITY OF DOUBLE OF DOUBLE DISCLINATION LINES
IN CHOLESTERIC LIQUID CRYSTALS,
Phys Letters v28A n10 p687-8 (24 Feb '69)

Orsay Liquid Crystal Group,
DYNAMICS OF FLUCTUATIONS IN NEMATIC LIQUID CRYSTALS,
J Chem Phys v51 n2 p816-22 (15 Jly '69)

Orsay Liquid Crystal Group,
INELASTIC SCATTERING OF LIGHT BY NEMATICS,
ACS Meeting, 158th Annual, New York, Abstract 55 (Sep '69)

Orsay Liquid Crystal Group
RECENT EXPERIMENTAL INVESTIGATIONS IN NEMATIC AND CHOLESTERIC MESOPHASES,
ACS Meeting, 158th Annual, New York, Abstract 62 (Sep '69)

Paleos, C.M., Laronge, T.M., Labes, M.M.,
LIQUID CRYSTAL MONOMERS. n-(p-ALKOXYBENZYLIDENE)-p-AMINOSTYRENES,
Chem Commun p1115-6 ('68)

Papahadjopoulos, D., Miller, N.,
PHOSPHOLIPID MODEL MEMBRANES. STRUCTURAL CHARACTERISTICS OF
HYDRATED LIQUID CRYSTALS,
Biochim Biophys Acta v135 n4 p624-38 ('67)

Papahadjopoulos, D., Watkins, J.C.,
PHOSPHOLIPID MODEL MEMBRANES. PERMEABILITY PROPERTIES OF HYDRATED
LIQUID CRYSTALS,
Biochim Biophys Acta v135 n4 p639-52 ('67)

Papoular, M.,
STRUCTURE AND DISPERSION OF SURFACE WAVES OF A NEMATIC LIQUID,
J Phys v30 n5-6 p406-12 (May '69)

Papoular, M.,
ON THE BEHAVIOR OF VISCOSITY AT THE NEMATIC-ISOTROPIC TRANSITION,
Phys Letters, v30 n1 p5-6 (8 Sep '69)

Parisi, A.J.,
COLOR IMAGING BRIGHTENS ENGINEERING ANALYSIS,
Product Eng v39 p18-25 (29 Jly '68)

Parry, D.A.D., Elliott, A.,
X-RAY DIFFRACTION PATTERNS OF LIQUID CRYSTALLINE SOLUTIONS OF
POLYGAMMA-BENZYL-1-GLUTAMATE,
Nature v206 n4983-4 p616B-17 ('65)
Parsegian, V.A.,
THEORY OF LIQUID CRYSTAL PHASE TRANSITIONS IN LIQUID + WATER SYSTEMS,
Trans Faraday Soc v62 n4 p848-60 ('66)

Pelzl, G., Demus, D., Sackmann, H.,
ISOMORPHIC RELATIONS BETWEEN CRYSTALLINE-LIQUID PHASES. CRYSTALLINE-LIQUID
PHASES IN THE HOMOLOGOUS SERIES DI-n-ALKYL-p,p'-AZOXYCINNAMATE AND
THEIR MISCIBILITY WITH p,p'-AZOXYBENZAL BIS(m-TOLUDINE),
Z Phys Chem (leipzig) v238 p22-32 ('68)

Phiney, J.T., Rizzardo, J.E.,
PHOTOCHEMISTRY OF 6-NITRO CHOLESTERYL ACETATE,
Chem Commun v15 p362-4 ('65)

Picot, J.J.C., Fredrickson, A.G.,
INTERFACTIAL AND ELECTRICAL EFFECTS ON THERMAL CONDUCTIVITY
OF NEMATIC LIQUID CRYSTALS,
Ind & Eng Chem Fundamentals v7 p84-9 (Feb '68)

Picot, J.J.C., Fredrickson, A.G.,
INTERFACIAL AND ELECTRICAL EFFECTS ON THE THERMAL CONDUCTIVITY
OF NEMATIC LIQUID CRYSTALS,
Ind & Eng Chem Fundamentals v8 n1 p176 ('69)

Pincus, P.A.,
RAYLEIGH SCATTERING IN A LIQUID CHOLESTEROL CRYSTAL,
Compt Rend serB v267 n23 p1290-2 ('68)

Pincus, P.,
NUCLEAR RELAXATION IN A NEMATIC LIQUID CRYSTAL,
Solid State Commun v7 n4 p415-7 ('69)

Pincus, P.,
FLUCTUATIONS IN LIQUID CRYSTALS,
APS 1969 Winter Meeting, UCLA, Los Angeles, 29-31 Dec '69)

Pohlmann, J.L.W.,
THE MESOMORPHIC BEHAVIOR OF STIGMASTERYL CARBONATE,
Mol Cryst v2 nl p15-26 (Dec '66)

Pohlmann, J.L.W.,
STRUCTURE DEPENDENCE OF CHOLESTERIC MESOPHASES,
Mol Cryst :iq Cryst v8 p417-25 (Jne '69)

Pohlmann, J.L.W., Elser, W.,
REMARKS ON THE SYNTHESIS OF PURE MESOMORPHIC COMPOUNDS,
Mol Cryst Liq Cryst v8 p427-441 (Jne '69)

Porter, R.S., Johnson, J.F.,
ORIENTATION OF NEMATIC MESOPHASES,
J Phys Chem v66 p1826 ('62)

Porter, R.S., Johnson, J.F.,
ORDER AND FLOW OF LIQUID CRYSTALS; NEMATIC MESOPHASE,
J Appl Phys v34 p51-4 (Jan '63)

Porter, R.S., Johnson, J.F.,
ORDER AND FLOW OF LIQUID CRYSTALS; CHOLESTERIC MESOPHASE,
J Appl Phys v34 p55-9 (Jan '63)

Porter, R.S., Barrall, E.M.II., Johnson, J.F.,
SOME FLOW CHARACTERISTICS OF MESOPHASE TYPES,
J Chem Phys v45 p1452 ('66)

Porter, R.S., Johnson, J.F.,
RHEOLOGY OF LIQUID CRYSTALS.
A Chapter in "Rheology. IV.", F. Eirich, editor; John Wiley, N.Y., p317-45 ('68)

Porter, R.S., Barrall, E.M.II., Johnson, J.F.,
AN INTERPRETATION OF MESOPHASE TRANSITIONS,
J Chem Phys p3897 ('68)

Porter, R.S., Barrall, E.M.II., Johnson, J.F.,
THERMODYNAMIC ORDER IN MESOPHASES,
Accounts Chem Res v2 n2 p53-9 ('69)

Porter, R.S., Barrall, E.M.II., Johnson, J.F.,
MESOPHASE TRANSITION THERMODYNAMICS FOR SEVERAL HOMOLOGOUS SERIES,
In "THERMAL ANALYSIS," R.F. Schwenker, P.D. Garn, eds., Vol.I., Academic Press,
N.Y., p597-613 ('69)

Powers, J.C.,
THE AGGREGATION OF poly-γ-BENZYL-L-GLUTAMATE IN MIXED SOLVENT SYSTEMS,
ACS Meeting, 158th Annual, New York, Abstract 90 (Sep '69)

Rabin, H., Bey, P.P.,
PHASE MATCHING IN HARMONIC GENERATION EMPLOYING OPTICAL ROTATORY DISPERSION,
Phys Rev v156 n3 p1010-6 (15 Apr '67)

Raggatt, P.R., Dean, P.D.G., Whitehouse, M.W.,
METABOLIC PROPERTIES OF CHOLESTERYL 3B-SULFATE AND CHOLEST-4-en-3-one,
Biochem J v96 n2 p26 ('65)

Rapini, A., Papoular, M., Pincus, P.,
DISTORTION OF THE STRUCTURE OF A NEMATIC FILM UNDER THE EFFECT OF A MAGNETIC
FIELD,
Compt Rend serB v267 n22 p1230-3 ('68)

Rhodes, M.B., Stein, R.S.,
SCATTERING OF LIGHT FROM ASSEMBLIES OF ORIENTED RODS,
J Polymer Sci v7 Pt.A-2 n9 p1539-58 (Sep '69)

Robinder, R.C., Poirier, J.C.,
MONOTROPIC CRYSTALLINE PHASES OF p-AZOXYANISOLE FROM THE NEMATIC MELT,
Am Chem Soc J v90 p4760-1 ('68)

Robinson, C.,
THE CHOLESTERIC PHASE IN PLYPEPTIDE SOLUTIONS AND BIOLOGICAL STRUCTURES,
Mol Cryst v1 n4 p467-94 ('66)

Rogers, J., Winsor, P.A.,
OPTICALLY POSITIVE, ISOTROPIC, AND NEGATIVE LAMELLAR
LIQUID CRYSTALLINE SOLUTIONS,
Nature, v216 n5114 p477-9 ('67)

Rosenheim, O.,
A SPECIFIC COLOUR REACTION FOR ERGOSTEROL,
Biochem J v23 p47-53 ('29)

Rosenheim, O., Callow, R.K.,
COLOR REACTIONS OF STEROLS WITH NITRIC ACID,
Biochem J v25 p74-8 ('31)

Rosevear, F.B.,
LIQUID CRYSTALS. MESOMORPHIC PHASES OF SURFACTANT COMPOSITIONS,
J Soc Cosmet Chem v19 n9 p581-94 ('69)

Rovesti, P., Massera, A.,
USE OF CHOLESTERYL OLEATE IN COSMETICS,
Parfum Cosmet, Savono v11 n2 p71-3 ('68)

Rowell, J.C., Phillips, W.D., Melby, L.R., Panar, M.,
N.M.R. STUDIES OF SOME LIQUID CRYSTAL SYSTEMS,
J Chem Phys v43 n10 p3442-54 ('65)

Ryumtsev, E.I., Tsvetkov, V.N.,
ELECTROOPTICAL PROPERTIES OF THE AMORPHOUS PHASE OF SOME LIQUID CRYSTALS,
Opt Spektrosk v26 n4 p607-12 ('69)

Sackmann, E., Meiboom, S., Snyder, L.C.,
THE RELATION OF NEMATIC TO CHOLESTERIC MESOPHASES,
Am Chem Soc J v89 n23 p5981-2 ('67)

Sackmann, E., Meiboom, S., Snyder, L.C., Meixner, A.E., Dietz, R.E.,
STRUCTURE OF THE LIQUID CRYSTALLINE STATE OF CHOLESTEROL DERIVATIVES,
Am Chem Soc J v90 p3567-9 ('68)

Sackmann, E., Meiboom, S., Snyder, L.C.,
N.M.R. SPECTRA OF ENANTIOMERS IN OPTICALLY ACTIVE LIQUID CRYSTALS,
Am Chem Soc J v90 p2183-4 (10 Apr '68)

Sackmann, E.,
ELECTRON FIELD INDUCED ORIENTATION OF LIQUID CRYSTALS AND OPTICAL
ABSORPTION EXPERIMENTS,
Chem Phys Letters v3 n4 p253-4 (Apr '69)

Sackmann, H., Demus, D.,
RELATION OF ISOMORPHISM BETWEEN CRYSTALLINE-LIQUID PHASES.
CRYSTALLINE-LIQUID INTERMEDIARY PHASE,
Z Phys Chem (Leipzig) v230 n5-6 p285-302 ('65)

Sackmann, H., Demus, D.,
THE POLYMORPHISM OF LIQUID CRYSTALS,
Mol Cryst v2 n1 p81-102 (Dec '66)

Sackmann, H., Diele, S., Brand, P.,
X-RAY DIFFRACTION AND POLYMORPHISM OF LIQUID CRYSTALS,
Abstracts, 8th In'l Congress of Crystallography, p37 (Aug '69)

Sakamoto, K., Porter, R.S., Johnson, J.F.,
THE VISCOSITY OF MESOPHASES FORMED BY CHOLESTERYL MYSRISTATE,
Mol Cryst Liq Cryst v8 p443-55 (Jne '69)

Sakevich, N.M.,
TEMPERATURE DEPENDENCE OF THE SPECIFIC VOLUME OF SOME LIQUID CRYSTALS IN THE
REGION OF AN ISOTROPIC LIQUID PHASE TRANSITION IN THE LIQUID
CRYSTALLINE PHASE,
Zh Fiz Khim v42 n11 p2930-2 ('68)

Samulski, E.T., Tobolsky, A.V.,
SOLID "LIQUID CRYSTAL" FILMS OF POLY-GAMMA-BENZYL-L-GLUTAMATE,
Nature v216 n5119 p997A ('67)

Samulski, E.T., Tobolsky, A.V.,
THE LIQUID CRYSTAL PHASE OF POLY-GAMMA-BENZYL-L-GLUTAMATE IN
SOLUTION AND IN THE SOLID STATE,
Mol Cryst Liq Cryst v7 p433-42 (Jne '69)

Santoro, A.V., Spielhoetz, G.I.,
HEATS OF TRANSITIONS AND KINETIC STUDY OF LIQUID CRYSTALS
BY DIFFERENTIAL THERMAL ANALYSIS,
Anal Chim Acta v42 n3 p537-9 ('68)

Saupe, A.,
N.M.R. IN LIQUID CRYSTALS AND LIQUID CRYSTAL SOLUTIONS,
Z Naturforsch v19a p161-71 ('64)

Saupe, A.,
PROTON MAGNETIC RESONANCE SPECTRUM OF BENZENE ORIENTED IN NEMATIC SOLUTIONS,
Z Naturforsch Pt.A v20 n4 p572-80 ('65)

Saupe, A.,
THE AVERAGE ORIENTATION OF SOLUTE MOLECULES IN NEMATIC LIQUID CRYSTALS,
Mol Cryst v1 n4 p527-40 (Sep '66)

Saupe, A., Englert, G., Povh, A.,
DETERMINATION OF BOND ANGLE OF CH_3 GROUPS BY PROTON MAGNETIC RESONANCE
IN NEMATIC LIQUID CRYSTALLINE SOLUTIONS,
Adv Chem Ser #63 p51-60 ('67)

Saupe, A.,
RECENT RESULTS IN THE FIELD OF LIQUID CRYSTALS,
Angew Chem Int'l Ed v7 n2 p97-112 ('68)

Saupe, A.,
ON MOLECULAR STRUCTURE AND PHYSICAL PROPERTIES OF THERMOTROPIC LIQUID CRYSTALS,
Mol Cryst Liq Cryst v7 p59-74 (Jne '69)

Scala, L.C., Dixon, G.D.,
LONG TERM STABILITY OF CHOLESTERIC LIQUID CRYSTAL SYSTEMS,
Mol Cryst Liq Cryst v7 p443-55 (Jne '69)

Scala, L.C., Dixon, G.D.,
LONG TERM STABILITY OF CHOLESTERIC LIQUID CRYSTALS. II.,
ACS Meeting, 158th Annual, New York, Abstract 76 (Sep '69)

Schmitt, A., Varoqui, R., Skoulios, A.,
OBTENTION DE PHASES MESOMORPHES DANS LES SOLUTIONS ACQUEUSES
CONCENTREES D'UN POLYELECTROLYTE AMPHIPATHIQUE,
Comp Rend v268 serC p1469-72 (28 Apr '69)

Schmidt, E., Leidenfrost, W.,
DIE EINFLUSS ELEKTRISCHER FELDER AUF DEN WAERMETRANSPORT IN
FLUESSIGEN ELEKTRISCHEN NICHTLEITERN,
Forsch Ing v19 p65-80 ('53)

Schroeder, J.P., Schroeder, D.C.,
LIQUID CRYSTALS. STABLE SMECTIC MIXTURES OF 4,4'-Di-n-HEXYLOXAZOXYBENZENE
AND p-NITRO SUBSTITUTED AROMATIC COMPOUNDS,
J Org Chem v33 p591-7 ('68)

Schroeder, J.P., Schroeder, D.C., Katsikas, M.,
NEMATIC MIXTURES AS STATIONARY LIQUID PHASES IN GAS-LIQUID CHROMATOGRAPHY,

ACS Meeting, 158th Annual, New York, Abstract 53 (Sep '69)

Schubert, H., Koch, R., Weinbercher, C.,
CRYSTALLINE-LIQUID TRANS-DIBENZOYL ETHYLENES,
Z Chem v6 n12 p467A ('66)

Schubert, H., Eissfeldt, I., Lange, R., Trefflich, F.,
SYNTHESIS OF CRYSTALLINE LIQUID COMPOUNDS. n-ALKYL AND n-ALKOXY DERIVATIVES
OF 3-HYDROXY-2,5-DIPHENYL PYRAZINE,
J Prakt Chem v33 n5-6 p265-76 ('66)

Schubert, H., Hacker, R., Kindermann, K.,
SYNTHESIS OF CRYSTALLINE-LIQUID COMPOUNDS. n-ALKYL AND n-ALKOXY DERIVATIVES
OF 2,5 DIPHENYLPYRAZINE,
J Prakt Chem v37 p12-20 ('68)

Segerman, E.,
STRUCTURE MODELS AND TRANSFORMATION MECHANISMS IN MESOMORPHIC LIPID PHASES,
Abstracts, 8th Int'l Congress of Crystallography, p181 (Aug '69)

Selawry, O.S., Selawry, H.S., Holland, J.F.,
THE USE OF LIQUID CHOLESTERIC CRYSTALS FOR THERMOGRAPHIC
MEASUREMENT OF SKIN TEMPERATURE IN MAN,
Mol Cryst v1 n4 p495-501 (Sep '66)

Semechenko, V.K., Kuznetskova, N.V.,
THERMODYNAMICS OF LIQUID CRYSTALLS,
Kolloid Zh v30 p279-83 ('68)

Shore, B.,
OP ELECTRONICS,
Ind Phot v18 p30-2+ (Feb '69)

Silverman, D.N., Dailey, B.P.,
STUDIES OF CHEMICAL-SHIFT ANISOTROPY IN LIQUID CRYSTAL SOLVENTS. III.
THE N.M.R. SPECTRA OF NEMATIC SOLUTIONS OF ETHANE AND 1,1,1-TRIFLUOROETHANE,
J Chem Phys v51 n2 p655-63 (15 Jly '69)

Small, D.M., Bourges, M.,
LYOTROPIC PARACRYSTALLINE PHASES OBTAINED WITH TERNARY AND QUATERNARY
SYSTEMS OF AMPHIPHILIC SUBSTANCES IN WATER: STUDIES ON AGREOUS SYSTEMS
OF LECITHIN, BILE SALT AND CHOLESTEROL,
Mol Cryst v1 n4 p541-61 (Sep '66)

Smith, G.W.,
LIQUID LIKE SOLIDS,
Int'l Sci & Tech p72-80 (Jne '67)

Snart, R.S.,
LIQUID CRYSTALLINE BEHAVIOR IN MIXTURES OF CHOLESTEROL WITH STEROID HORMONES,
Nature v215 p957-8 ('67)

Snyder, L.C., Anderson, E.W.,
ANALYSIS OF THE PROTON N.M.R. SPECTRUM OF BENZENE IN A NEMATIC LIQUID CRYSTAL,
Am Chem Soc J v86 p5023-4 (20 Nov '64)

Snyder, L.C., Anderson, E.W.,
ANALYSYS OF THE FLUORINE N.M.R. SPECTRUM OF HEXAFLUOROBENZENE
IN A NEMATIC LIQUID CRYSTAL,
J Chem Phys v42 n9-10 p3336-7 ('65)

Snyder, L.C.,
ANALYSIS OF N.M.R. SPECTRA OF MOLECULES IN LIQUID CRYSTAL SOLVENTS,
J Chem Phys v43 n11 p4041-50 ('65)

Snyder, L.C., Meiboom, S.,
N.M.R. OF TETRAHEDRAL MOLECULES IN A NEMATIC SOLVENT,
J Chem Phys v44 n10 p4057-8 ('66)

Snyder, L.C., Meiboom, S.,
N.M.R. IN LIQUID CRYSTAL SOLVENTS,
Mol Cryst Liq Cryst v7 p181-200 (Jne '69)

Snyder, L.C., Meiboom, S.,
MOLECULAR STRUCTURE OF CYCLOBUTANE FROM ITS PROTON N.M.R. IN A
NEMATIC SOLVENT,
ACS Meeting, 158th Annual, New York, Abstract 87 (Sep '69)

Sobijama, S.,
N.M.R. STUDIES ON ORIENTATION OF LIQUID CRYSTALS OF POLY-GAMMA-BENZYL-
L-GLUTAMATE IN MAGNETIC FIELDS,
Phys Soc Japan J v23 n5 p1070-8 ('67)

Sousa, R.M.D.E., Moriarty, R.M.,
SOLVOLYSIS OF 4A- and 4B-METHYL CHOLESTEROL p-TOLUENE SULFONATES.
KINETIC STUDY,
J Org Chem v30 n5 p1509-12 ('65)

Spier, H.L., Van-Senden, K.G.,
PHASE TRANSITION OF CHOLESTEROL,
Steroids v6 n6 p871-3 ('65)

Spiesecke, H., Bellion-Jourdan, J.,
LOW MELTING NEMATIC PHASES FOR RECORDING N.M.R. SPECTRA OF ORIENTED MOLECULES,
Angew Chem v79 n10 p475-6 ('67)

Sprow, E.,
LIQUID CRYSTALS: A FILM IN YOUR FUTURE?
Machine Design v41 p34-7 (6 Feb '69)

Squire, I.M., Elliott, A.,
LIQUID CRYSTALLINE PHASES OF POLY-GAMMA-BENZYL-GLUTAMATE IN SOLUTION,
Mol Cryst Liq Cryst v7 p457-68 (Jne '69)

Stahl, K.,
INFRARED-DETEKTOREN,
Optik v27 n1 p11-30 (Feb '68)

Stein, R.S., Rhodes, M.B., Porter, R.S.,
LIGHT SCATTERING BY LIQUID CRYSTALS,
J Colloid Interface Sci v27 p336 ('68)

Stein, R.S.,
THE SPECIFICATION OF ORDER IN MESOPHASES,
Mol Cryst Liq Cryst v6 n1 p125-54 (Aug '69)

Stewart, G.T.,
LIQUID CRYSTALS IN BIOLOGICAL SYSTEMS,
Mol Cryst v1 n4 p563-80 (Sep '66)

Stewart, G.T.,
LIQUID CRYSTALS AS ORDERED COMPONENTS OF LIVING SUBSTANCE,
Adv Chem Ser #63 p141-56 ('67)

Stewart, G.T.,
CHANGE OF PHASE AND CHANGE OF STATE IN BIOLOGICAL SYSTEMS,
Mol Cryst Liq Cryst v7 p75-102 (Jne '69)

Stewart, G.W., Holland, D.O., Reynolds, L.M.,
ORIENTATION OF LIQUID CRYSTALS BY HEAT CONDUCTION,
Phys Rev v58 p174-6 ('40)

Stewart, G.W.,
HEAT CONDUCTION EFFECTS WITH LIQUID CRYSTALS AND SUSPENDED PARTICLES,
Phys Rev v69 p51 ('45)

Stockman, H.E., Zarwyn, B.,
OPTICAL FILM SENSORS FOR R.F. HOLOGRAPHY,
IEEE Proc v56 p763 (Apr '68)

Stockman, H.E.,
SEEING IN THE DARK IS AIM OF R.F. HOLOGRAPHY,
Electronics v42 n24 p110-4 (24 Nov '69)

Strebel, E.,
AN ELECTRON-OPTICAL DEVICE EMPLOYING LIQUID CRYSTALS,
Electro-optical Systems Design Conference, New York (16-18 Sep '69)

Sukharevskii, B.J.,
BINARY SOLID SOLUTIONS OF SUBSTITUTION BETWEEN MESOMORPHIC CRYSTALS,
Dokl Akad Nauk SSSR v167 n5 p1046-9 ('66)

Sullivan, J.T.,
TRANSPORT PHENOMENA IN LIQUID CRYSTALS,
Ph.D. Thesis, 1966, N68-19920; Available: University Microfilm No. 67-7792

Tanner, E.C., Hansen, J.R., Schneeberger, R.J.,
MEDICAL THERMOGRAPHY USING LIQUID CRYSTALS EQUIPMENT, DEVELOPMENT
AND APPLICATION,
Westinghouse Research report, 6-30-64.

Terhune, R.W., Maker, P.D., Savage, C.M.,
MEASUREMENT OF NON-LINEAR LIGHT SCATTERING,
Phys Rev Letters v14 n17 p681-4 (26 Apr '65)

Tomkiewicz, Y., Weinreb, A.,
DECAY TIME OF PYRENE IN A LIQUID CRYSTAL,
Chem Phys Letters v3 n4 p229-30 ('69)

Torgalkar, Anil, Porter, R.S., Barrall, E.M.II., Johnson, J.F.,
INTERPRETATION OF MESOPHASE TRANSITIONS,
J Chem Phys v48 p3897 ('68)

Toriyama, K., Nomura, S.,
LIQUID CRYSTALS AND THEIR APPLICATIONS TO ELECTRONICS,
Oyo Buturi v38 n7 p698-703 (Jly '69)

Trzebowski, N., Langholf, E.,
CHANGES OF I.R. SPECTRA IN THE CRYSTALLINE AND LIQUID CRYSTALLINE
TRANSITIONS OF SODIUM STEATE,
Z Chem v7 p282-3 ('67)

Tsvetkov, V.N.,
LIQUID CRYSTALS,
In the Encyclopaedic Directory of Physics, Pergamon Press, New York,
Vol. 2, p14 ('63)

Tsvetkov, V.N., Ryumtsev, E.I.,
ORIENTATION FLUCTUATIONS IN THE AMORPHOUS PHASE OF LIQUID CRYSTAL
SUBSTANCES AND THEIR ELECTRO OPTICAL PROPERTIES,
Dokl Akad Nauk SSSR v176 n2 p382-4 ('67)

Tsvetkov, V.N., Ryumtsev, E.I.,
PRETRANSITION PHENOMENA AND ELECTROOPTICAL PROPERTIES OF LIQUID CRYSTALS,
Kristallografiya v13 p290-4 ('68)

Tsvetkov, V.N.,
HINDERED ROTATIONAL MOTION OF MOLECULES, AND DIELECTRIC ANISOTROPY
OF NEMATIC LIQUID CRYSTALS,
Kristallografiya v14 n4 p681-6 ('69)

Twitchell, R.P., Carr, E.F.,
INFLUENCE OF ELECTRIC FIELDS ON THE MOLECULAR ALIGNMENT IN THE
LIQUID CRYSTAL PARA-AZOXY ANISOLE,
J Chem Phys v46 n7 p2765-8 ('67)

Usol'tseva, V.A., Chistyakov, I.G.,
CHEMICAL CHARACTERISTICS, STRUCTURE, AND PROPERTIES OF LIQUID CRYSTALS,
Russian Chemical Reviews v32 n9 p495-509 ('63)

Vainshtein, B.K., Christyzkov, I.G., Kosterin, E.A., Chaikovskii, V.M.,
X-RAY DIFFRACTION STUDY USING DISTRIBUTION FUNCTIONS OF NEMATIC LIQUID CRYSTALS
IN ELECTRIC AND MAGNETIC FIELDS,
Dokl Akad Nauk SSSR v174 n2 p341-4 ('67)

Van Raalte, J.A.,
REFLECTIVE LIQUID CRYSTAL TELEVISION DISPLAY,
IEEE Proc v56 n12 p2146-9 (Dec '68)

Vazina, A.A., Lemazhikhin, B.K., Frank, G.M.,
LIQUID CRYSTALLINE STRUCTURE IN UNORIENTED GELS AND SOLUTIONS OF F-ACTIN,
Biofizika v10 n3 p420-3 ('65)

Vistin, L.K., Kapustin, A.P.,
DOMAINS IN SMECTIC TYPE LIQUID CRYSTALS,
Kristallografiya v13 p349-52 ('68)

Vistin, L.K., Kapustin, A.P.,
DOMAIN STRUCTURE OF LIQUID CRYSTALS,
Kristallografiya v14 n4 p740-3 ('69)

Vainsh tein, B.K., Chistyakov, I.G., Kosterin, E.A., Chaikovskii, V.M.,
STRUCTURE OF NEMATIC p-AZOXYANISOLE IN ELECTRIC AND MAGNETIC FIELDS,
Mol Cryst Liq Cryst v8 p457-70 (Jne '69)

Vanzo, E.,
ORDERED STRUCTURES OF STYRENE BUTADIENE BLOCK COPOLYMERS,
Rubber Chem & Tech v40 p1526-8 (Dec '67)

Vogel, M.J., Barrall, E.M.II., Mignosa, S.P.,
EFFECT OF SOLVENT TYPE ON THE THERMODYNAMIC PROPERTIES OF NORMAL ALIPHATIC
CHOLESTERYL ESTER,
ACS Meeting, 158th Annual, New York, Abstract 78 (Sep '69)

Wang, C.C.,
MATNEMATICS. SYMMETRIES OF CERTAIN HYPER ELASTIC SIMPLE LIQUID CRYSTALS,
Proc Nat'l Acad Sci v55 n3 p468-71 ('66)

Weise, H., Axmann, A.,
PRINCIPAL DIELECTRIC CONSTANTS OF HOMOGENEOUSLY ORIENTED, CRYSTALLINE
LIQUID PHASE OF p-AZOXYANISOLES IN THE FREQUENCY RANGE OF 10-50 MH,
Z Naturforsch (A) v21 n8 p1316-7 ('66)

Williams, R.,
DOMAINS IN LIQUID CRYSTALS,
J Chem Phys v39 n2 p384-8 (15 Jly '63)

Williams, R.,
LIQUID CRYSTALS IN AN ELECTRIC FIELD,
Nature v199 p273-4 (20 Jly '63)

Williams, R., Heilmeier, G.H.,
POSSIBLE FERROELECTRIC EFFECTS IN LIQUID CRYSTALS AND RELATED LIQUIDS,
J Chem Phys v44 n2 p638-43 (15 Jan '66)

Williams, R.,
INTERFACES IN NEMATIC LIQUIDS,
Adv Chem Ser #63 p61-7 ('67)

Williams, R.,
OPTICAL ROTATORY EFFECT IN THE NEMATIC LIQUID PHASE OF p-AZOXYANISOLE,
Phys Rev Letters v21 p342 ('68)

Williams, R.,
OPTICAL-ROTATORY POWER AND LINEAR ELECTRO-OPTIC EFFECT IN NEMATIC
LIQUID CRYSTALS OF p-AZOXYANISOLE,
J Chem Phys v50 n3 p1324-32 (1 Feb '69)

Winsor, P.A.,
BINARY AND MULTICOMPONENT SOLUTIONS OF AMPHILIC COMPOUNDS - SOLUBILIZATION
AND THE FORMATION, STRUCTURE, AND THEORETICAL SIGNIFICANCE OF
LIQUID CRYSTALLINE SOLUTIONS,
Chem Rev v68 p1-40 ('68)

Woodman, C.M.,
EQUIVALENCE IN ANISOTROPIC NUCLEAR MAGNETIC RESONANCE SPECTRA. SPECTRUM
OF ETHYL IODIDE IN THE NEMATIC PHASE,
Mol Phys v13 n4 p365-72 ('67)

Woodmansee, W.E.,
CHOLESTERIC LIQUID CRYSTALS AND THEIR APPLICATIONS TO THERMAL
NONDESTRUCTIVE TESTING,
Mater Eval v24 p564-72 (Oct '66)

Woodmansee, W.E., Southworth, H.L.,
DETECTION OF MATERIAL DISCONTINUITIES WITH LIQUID CRYSTALS,
Mater Eval v26 n8 p149-54 (Aug '68)

Woodmansee, W.E.,
AEROSPACE THERMAL MAPPING APPLICATIONS OF LIQUID CRYSTALS,
Appl Opt v7 p1721-7 (Sep '68)

Wysocki, J., Adams, J., Haas, W.,
ELECTRIC-FIELD-INDUCED PHASE CHANGE IN CHOLESTERIC LIQUID CRYSTALS,
Phys Rev Letters v20 n19 p1024-5 (6 May '68)

Wysocki, J., Adams, J., Haas, W.,
ELECTRIC-FIELD INDUCED PHASE CHANGE IN CHOLESTERIC LIQUID CRYSTALS,
Mol Cryst Liq Cryst v8 p471-87 (Jne '69)

Wysocki, J., Adams, J.,
MECHANISM OF FIELD-INDUCED CHOLESTERIC-NEMATIC PHASE TRANSITION,
APS Summer Meeting, Rochester, Abstract FB 1, (Jne '69)

Wysocki, J., Adams, Haas, W.,
ELECTROVISCOSITY OF A CHOLESTERIC LIQUID-CRYSTAL MIXTURE,
J Appl Phys v40 n9 p3865-6 (Aug '69)

Wysocki, J., Adams, J.,
KINETIC STUDY OF THE FIELD-INDUCED CHOLESTERIC-NEMATIC TRANSITION
IN LIQUID CRYSTALS,
ACS Meeting, 158th Annual, New York, Abstract 50 (Sep '69)

Yannoni, C.S.,
ANISOTROPIC N.M.R. INTERACTIONS IN LIQUID CRYSTAL SOLUTION,
Dissertation, University Microfilms #67-12282   ('67)

Yannoni, C.S.,
ORIENTATION OF CH$_3$D IN A NEMATIC LIQUID CRYSTAL SOLVENT,
J Chem Phys v51 n4 p1682-3 (15 Aug '69)

Yim, C.T., Gilson, D.F.R.,
N.M.R. SPECTRA OF O-, M-, AND P-DI FLUORO BENZENES IN A
NEMATIC LIQUID CRYSTAL SOLVENT,
Can J Chem v47 n6 p1057-65 ('69)

Young, W.R., Haller, I., Williams, L.,
MESOMORPHIC PROPERTIES OF THE HETEROCYCLIC ANALOGS OF
BENZYLIDENE-4-AMINO-4'-METHOXYBIPHENYL,
ACS Meeting, 158th Annual, New York, Abstract 93 (Sep '69)

Yun, Ch.-K., Fredrickson, A.G.,
SELF-DIFFUSION IN NEMATIC MESOPHASES,
ACS Meeting, 158th Annual, New York, Abstract 60 (Sep '69)

Zhdanova, A.S., Morozova, L.F., Peregudov, G.V., Sushchinskii, M.M.,
A STUDY OF LIQUID CRYSTALS BY RAMAN SCATTERING,
Opt & Spectroscopy v26 n2 p112-4 (Feb '69)

Zlochover, I.A., Schulman, J.H.,
A STUDY OF MOLECULAR INTERACTIONS AND MOBILITY AT LIQUID/LIQUID
INTERFACES BY N.M.R. SPECTROSCOPY,
J Colloid Interface Sci v24 p115 ('67)

Zocher, H.,
SOME TOPICS OF LIQUID CRYSTALS YET TO BE DISCUSSED,
Mol Cryst Liq Cryst v7 p165-75 (Jne '69)

Zocher, H.,
NEMATIC AND SMECTIC PHASES OF HIGH ORDER,
Mol Cryst Liq Cryst v7 p177-80 (Jne '69)

Zvereva, G.E.,
ABSORBTION OF ULTRASOUND IN LIQUID CRYSTAL CHOLESTERYL CAPRINATE,
Akust Zh v11 n2 p251-2 (Apr/Jne '65)

" "

NOTE: To obtain articles write to publisher for reprint or back issue.

To obtain government reports contact CFSTI:
Clearinghouse for Federal Scientific and Technical Information,
U.S. Department of Commerce,
Springfield, Virginia 22151

The price of each document is $3.00 per copy, and $.65 per copy
for microfiche. Books of ten coupons $30.00 per book for paper
copy documents; books of 50 coupons $32.50 per book for micro-
fiche documents. Money Orders and checks to be made payable to
"The Clearinghouse."

PRESENT AND PROPOSED
LIQUID CRYSTAL APPLICATIONS

ACOUSTIC BEAMS, Visualization
ACOUSTICAL HOLOGRAPHY, Sensors and area detectors
ADVERTISING
AIRCRAFT LANDING GUIDANCE SYSTEMS
ARCHITECTURAL GLASS, Variably translucent
AVIONICS DISPLAYS
BABY DISH or BABY BOTTLE, Temperature indicating
BAR-GRAPH TYPE DISPLAYS
BEAM SPLITTERS, Variable
BONDED STRUCTURES (for ex. in aircraft & aerospace), Flaw detection
BUSINESS MACHINES (displaying alphanumerics and graphics)
CAMERA SHUTTER APERTURES, Electrically adjustable
CHARACTER RECOGNITION
CHART REPRESENTATIONS
CLINICAL THERMOMETERS, Fast recording, throwaway
CLOCKS, Digital
CODED KEY SYSTEMS, (credit cards, checks, price tags, etc.)
COLOR COMPOSITIONS, Apparatus for making
COMPUTER, Readouts
COUNTERS, Digital
COUPLING, Light (as between optical fibers, etc.)
CURRENT NODES AND LOOPS IN LECHER SYSTEMS, Device to indicate
CURRENT SENSORS
DASHBOARD DISPLAYS, Automobile
DATA MEMORIES, Computer
DETECTION & ANALYSIS OF MATTER (both quantitative and qualitative nature)
ELAPSED TIME INDICATORS
ELECTROPHOTOGRAPHY, B&W, line and half-tone, also colored images
FIELDS OF FORCE, Simulation
FOOD PREMIUM ITEMS, Temperature indicating
FRESHNESS INDICATORS (for perishable artcles)
FREQUENCY INDICATOR (for analysis of ultrasonic wave spectrum)
GAS CHROMATOGRAPHY
HIGH-POTENTIAL ELECTRICAL DISCHARGE PATHS, Observation and recording
HIGH-RESISTANCE CONNECTIONS IN CIRCUIT BOARDS, TRANSISTORS AND
    INTEGRATED CIRCUITS, Observation
HONEYCOMB SANDWICH MATERIALS, Adhesively bonded, flaw detection

ICE WARNING DEVICES

IMAGE AMPLIFIERS

INDUSTRIAL EQUIPMENT, High temperature indication

INFRARED INDICATING AND IMAGING DEVICES

INTEGRATED ELECTRONIC CIRCUITS, Reliability control

LASER BEAM PATTERNS, Observing and recording

LASER OUTPUT MEASUREMENTS

LEAK DETECTION

LENSES, Variable transparency

LIGHT BEAM SCANNING DEVICES AND DIGITAL DEFLECTORS

LIGHT DEPOLARIZING MEANS, Passive, tunable

LIGHT ENERGY MEASUREMENTS

LIGHT FILTER, Color, tunable

LIGHT FILTER, Neutral density, variable

LIGHT MODULATORS

LIGHT POLARIZATION CONTROL CELLS

LIGHT POLARIZATION ROTATORS

LIGHT POLARIZING FILMS AND SHEET MATERIALS

LIGHT POLARIZERS, Circularly polarizing

LIGHT SWITCHING MEANS

MAGNETIC FIELD PATTERNS, Mapping

MAGNETIC FIELD PROBES

MARINE DISPLAYS (for radar and navigation)

MEDICAL ELECTRONICS

METALLIC & NONMETALLIC MATERIALS, Surface and subsurface flaw detection

MICROCIRCUITS, Measuring operating temperatures

MICROWAVE SPECTRAL FREQUENCY DISTRIBUTION, Recording

MICROWAVE FIELD INTENSITY, Real-time displays

MICROWAVE FLUOROSCOPES

MIRRORS, Rear-view, automatically dimming

MONOCHROMATOR, Continuously tunable

NIGHTTIME VIEWERS (for police and battlefront applications)

"ON-OFF" INDICATORS (for operating parts)

OPTICAL ELEMENTS (with tunable degree of birefringence)

PARAMETRIC VISUAL SYSTEM INDICATORS

PENETRANT DETECTION

PHOTOCOMPOSITION AND RECORDING

PIEZO-ACOUSTIC STRESS PATTERNS, Detecting and measuring

PLOTTING BOARDS

PRESSURE SENSITIVE OPTICAL CELLS

Q-SWITCHING

R.F. HOLOGRAPHY, Sensors and area detectors

REFRACTIVE INDEX MONITORS

RESISTIVE DEFROST COATINGS ON COMMERCIAL AIRCRAFT, Study of the uniformity

SATELLITE OR MISSILE TRACKING

SCOREBOARDS

SECOND- and THIRD-HARMONIC GENERATION, Optical

SEMICONDUCTORS, High-resolution temperature patterns

SENSE OF COLOR, Training

SHELF-LIFE INDICATORS

SHIELDING ANALYSIS (A.C. Fields)

SHIFT REGISTERS (for computing apparatus)

SHOWER NOZZLES and BATHTUB LINERS, Temperature indicating

SHUTTERS, Electro- (magneto-) optical

SIGN DISPLAYS (signboards)
SIMULATION DISPLAYS (for pilot training in aircraft & spacecraft)
SKIN TEMPERATURE PATTERNS, Demonstration (cutaneous thermography)
SPACECRAFT ATTITUDE CONTROL SYSTEMS
STANDING WAVES ALONG A TRANSMISSION LINE (adjustment of load for proper match)
STERILIZATION INDICATORS
STOCK TICKERS
STOVES AND KITCHEN UTENSILS, High temperature indicating
SUBMARINE TRACKING SYSTEMS
TARGET ACQUISITION
TEMPERATURE CONTROL SYSTEMS, Automatic
TEXTILE PATTERNS, Means for designing
THERMAL CONDUCTIVITY TESTS
TOY PRODUCTS AND NOVELTY ITEMS
TV-SCREENS, Flat (home, TV studio and monitor equipment)
TUNING INDICATORS (for radio receivers)
ULTRASONIC WAVES, Visualization and recording
VACUUM SYSTEMS (indication of controlled atmosphere reactions)
VOLTAGE MEASURING DEVICES, Analog or digital
WAVE PLATES (or fractional wave plates), Optical
WELDINGS, Flaw detection
X-RAY PATTERNS (conversion into visible light patterns)

" "

ANNOUNCEMENTS

STATE OF THE ART REVIEW No. 2

LIQUID CRYSTALS AND THEIR APPLICATIONS

op